Behind the Door: the Real Story of Loretta Young

Edward J Funk

ISBN-10: 0-9971054-3-7

ISBN-13: 978-0-9971054-3-8

All photos from the Salvador Iglesias Collection

Permission to use from the Loretta Young Estate

PROLOGUE:

I received several forwarded articles in December, 2011, both print and electronic, including one from *The London Telegraph*. All informed me of Judy Lewis's death. The headings came down to this: "Hollywood's Secret Baby" dies. They detailed how Judy was the progeny of a married, thirty-four-year-old Clark Gable and his twenty-two-year-old co-star of CALL OF THE WILD, Loretta Young. In November, 1935, their daughter was born in secret, and, in time, adopted by her then single, biological mother. Judy was an adult before she knew that Loretta and Clark Gable were her biological parents. I had worked with Loretta Young on her biography throughout the last years of her life. I can attest that the above facts are true.

Several other items written in Judy's 1994 book, *Uncommon Knowledge* were of questionable accuracy. A prominent feature of Judy's book and her subsequent interviews was a two hour visit she had with her father at her home when she was fifteen. According to this account, Loretta had initially been in the room but soon faded away, leaving her and Gable alone. Judy didn't understand why Clark Gable was visiting with her and why he was treating her so tenderly. She recalls that as he was leaving, he cupped her chin and kissed her on the forehead. According to Loretta, this visit never occurred. Also challenged was Judy's quote in which Loretta allegedly said, "Clark offered to divorce his wife and marry me, and I said no. It was the biggest mistake in my life."

I read these articles and then called Judy's brother, Christopher Lewis. We talked for an hour and a half, and during that time we discussed Judy and her book. I mentioned to Chris that as I was leaving his mom's funeral, I approached Judy and said, "Let's have lunch. I think I can fill you in on some of your missing history." Her response was, "Maybe." Chris's take was that Judy didn't want any facts to get in the way of her narrative. As he put it, "Judy's always lived in Judy's world."

I hung up and thought, "The real story needs to be told." The story of Clark and Loretta having a beautiful love affair ending with Loretta's pregnancy is a gross simplification of what was, in fact, a complex, messy, confusing relationship that can only be understood in the context of its time and place.

Loretta could have told a very different story. She chose not to. I could, and with this book, intend to. Our original book was never published mainly because Loretta refused to discuss the Clark Gable/Judy saga. At one point, she did allow me to go to her sisters and get the story from them. Other times she would drop her guard and share insights from her perspective.

This is a story of many perspectives. Loretta not only encouraged her sisters and brother to talk with me but also her sons, Christopher and Peter Lewis. She also asked her two closest friends, Josie Wayne (first wife of John Wayne) and Jane Mullen Sharpe to add their voices. I interviewed her brother-in-law, Ricardo Montalban, as well as Susie Tracy, daughter of Spencer Tracy. I had access to her former husband Tom Lewis's unpublished autobiography. Actor Robert Mitchum and Greg Fischer, a man who worked for Loretta, were willing participants. But mainly, the reader will hear the voice of Loretta Young, and if this book reads like a story told over time, it was. I knew Loretta well for the last ten years of her life.

Loretta told me I was free to tell as much as I knew of the Clark Gable/Judy saga after she died. I have not because my life has gone in a different direction, and the notes, tapes, and earlier manuscripts regarding Loretta have been sitting in boxes in my garage for more than a decade. But there was another reason for my reluctance. When I participated in the 1998 A&E Biography, *Loretta Young: Hollywood's Heavenly Beauty*, I questioned how they were handling the Clark/Judy saga. A staff member replied, "Every child deserves to think they were conceived in love." I asked myself, "Even if it's not true?" Still it made me ponder, and I became hesitant to push a story that I knew would be very painful to Judy Lewis.

In the intervening years, I have reflected on Loretta's life and concluded a man other than Gable was much more influential. The slamming of a door when she was age four set the template for Loretta's relationship with men for the rest of her life. Her dad, John Earle Young, walked out, climbed onto his motor cycle and was never seen by his wife and children again. Loretta vaguely remembered seeing her dad ride off but didn't know if it was that particular day. It probably was. Why else would it have made an impression?

Loretta didn't like to think about her dad and particularly didn't like the idea that his leaving might have changed her life one way or another. But, it did. She would spend the rest of her life seeking the approval of others, women one way, men another. The male conquest came easily as she quickly grew into a beauty that was hard to resist. But, for reasons she chose not to contemplate, the men she invited into her life couldn't or wouldn't stay. Just like her dad. She didn't contemplate such issues because she viewed personal introspection as self-indulgent, and she had better things to do. Indeed, as a glamorous star of Hollywood's golden era and a pioneer of the early days of television, she did a great deal.

Loretta exhibited an interesting dichotomy. The fact she was heard saying late in her life, "I can't stand someone not liking me. It cuts me to the quick," didn't stop her from being a star who had struck fear in the hearts of studio-heads, producers, and directors. She was dubbed both a "Steel Magnolia" and "A Chocolate Covered Butterfly", the source of the latter, according to Loretta, was Bette Davis, hardly a shrinking violet herself. There's an explanation of how and why these two sides of Loretta came to be, actually how they melded together, but that also would be getting ahead of the story.

In just a few paragraphs, I've shared my psychological overview of Loretta. As I compiled this final manuscript and reread the words of the first hand participants, I realized that the story really tells itself. Consequently, I've eliminated much of my own voice so that the reader can draw their own conclusions.

Though Loretta's relationship with Clark Gable was not the pivotal point of her life, it did have lasting influence both personally and professionally. Let's begin with him.

Chapter 1: Clark Gable

Career-wise, Clark Gable was riding high. At age thirty-four, he would soon win an Academy Award (February 1935) for his role in the surprise hit, IT HAPPENED ONE NIGHT. In his personal life, Gable was stuck in an unhappy marriage. Ria Langham Gable, a wealthy divorcee from Texas, had met Clark Gable, seventeen years her junior, when he was performing on the New York stage.

Loretta pleaded not to do CALL OF THE WILD. The screenplay was based on the Jack London story set in Alaska and was about gold prospectors fighting off greedy villains. Loretta felt she wasn't suited for an outdoor action picture. Nevertheless, studio head Daryl Zanuck ordered her to do it, and Loretta reported to the train station for the trip to Mt. Baker, Washington for locations shooting. Frances Early, a friend of Loretta's older sister Sally (birth name Betty Jane), accompanied her as a companion. Loretta first met Gable on the train.

Clark Gable's pursuit of Loretta began immediately. She wasn't particularly surprised; leading ladies were used to getting that kind of attention from their leading men. However, Clark Gable wasn't the average leading man. Loretta recalled, "He wasn't called the King without reason. One facet of his enormous attraction was a pure male animal instinct over which he had complete control. He could turn it on or off at will. He had played a couple of villains at the beginning of his career, and he was extremely good at it. He looked a little dangerous and that added to his sexual attraction."

The CALL OF THE WILD cast and crew was billeted in the buildings of a summer resort. Loretta recalled, "We were on location for nine weeks, and we got about six day's work out of those nine weeks. The studio was very foolish to send the whole company up there knowing what the weather was like. Most of the time it hovered around 20 degrees above zero, but sometimes it dipped to 10 degrees below zero!

"The main lodge of this resort had burned down before we arrived, so we were living in the building that quartered the housekeeping staff during the summer months. The walls were paper thin because they were built only for summer use. Franny and I had a double room: with two beds, a dresser, a closet, and a tiny shower; that was it. To get to where we ate, which was in another temporary building about a half a block away; they strung a rope from one building to the other so that you had something to hold onto. It was snowing so hard that the path would get covered up, and you could have ended up anywhere. "

Despite the unbearable climatic conditions, it didn't take long for Loretta to fall for Gable's charm. Loretta remembered it as "A beautiful fantasy, his liking me, my liking him, just for those moments. It was all very romantic, and I didn't care if anyone thought I had a crush on him. I did. There is nothing wrong with having a crush on someone, particularly when he has one on you. You can't help what you feel. We had a lot of fun, and it was for everyone to see."

The subject of Clark's unhappy marriage never came up; nevertheless, it established the parameters. Loretta recalled, "What we normally would have talked about together, we weren't allowed. There were other ways of flirting. I always had a record player and records on the set. There was one song that Clark loved and he played it a lot. It's called *The Very Thought of You* and the lyrics begin with, 'The very thought of you, and I forget to do, the little ordinary things that everyone ought to do .....' I understood it to be his way of talking to me, and I was thrilled and, for the moment, happy." But Loretta added, "I don't know if I was really in love with Clark, and as the weeks went on, I realized that I was still in love with Spencer (Tracy). I was greatly relieved to hear the announcement that we were returning to Los Angeles."

That train trip home would change Loretta's life irrevocably. For the first time since meeting Gable, Loretta no longer had the protection of her companion, Frances Early. Gable arrived at Loretta's train compartment uninvited. She recalled, "I allowed him in as I would have any member of the crew, thinking he was there for a visit. He had other intentions. Very persistent intentions. He wasn't rough, but I kept saying no, and he wouldn't take no for an answer."

In 1998, when Loretta was eighty-five, she was watching television with Edward Funk. There was the mention of date-rape on the news, and she asked him what exactly did that mean. He explained to the best of his ability. The following day, Loretta called her daughter-in-law, Linda and said. "I know now that there was a word for what happened to me with Clark." Loretta came to this realization sixty-three-years after the fact. Had she had that perspective from the start, would she have branded herself as an adulteress for that single encounter and carry guilt for the rest of her life?

Later, Loretta asked Linda not to share the date-rape realization with the family. She was afraid it would only damage an already fragile relationship between her and Judy.

Back to February, 1935: Loretta and Clark chose to get off the train in Pasadena, and Loretta's mother Gladys arrived at the station to find the two breakfasting together. Loretta introduced them, and Gladys and Gable never saw each other again.

Loretta received a phone call from Ria Gable a few weeks later. Loretta recalled, "I was in Mama's room and I picked up the phone. Mrs. Gable said, 'This is very presumptuous of me, but you may or may not know that there are rumors flying around town about you and my husband.' I did know about the rumors. I don't think they were in any papers, but there were rumors because Clark had made no bones on the set of asking 'Where's my girl?' Apparently anything he said was worth quoting.

"Anyway, Mrs. Gable continued, 'I'm giving a cocktail party Friday night for the press, and since you're doing a picture with him, I thought it might put the rumors to rest if you'd come to the party?' I said, 'I'm sorry, I couldn't.' And I meant it. I couldn't carry it off. Also, I felt, 'There is no dignity in that at all. I can't help it if I had a crush on this man that I'm working with. I certainly don't suddenly put on a show for the press.' The minute I said, 'I'm sorry, I couldn't,' she said, 'Oh! You're sure?' I said, ' Yes, Mrs. Gable, I'm sure.' She didn't press the point. After I hung up, Mama asked, 'What's that all about?' When I told her, she said, 'How dare she put you in that position!' I said, 'I don't blame her. She's protecting her marriage, and she doesn't know what's true or not. '"

In a bizarre twist, it was Clark Gable who first suspected that Loretta might be pregnant. CALL OF THE WILD was still shooting on the studio's back lot, and about to shoot a water scene, Loretta was asked if she was on her period. She responded no, that her period was late. Gable overheard this and when he was able to get Loretta alone, asked, "You don't think you're pregnant, do you?" Loretta's periods were often late, and the thought hadn't crossed her mind.

It was very much on her mind a few weeks later. Her sister Sally recalled, "I was walking by Loretta's room one afternoon and heard her crying. I went in to see what the matter was, and Loretta told me she thought she might be pregnant. I couldn't believe it. I told her, 'Maybe you just have a cold.' There were many times that I'd be late if I had a cold, and if I had a massage, it seemed to put everything back on track. I recommended that she try that. She went and had the massage and nothing happened. A day or two later we went to Mama. I was so afraid for Loretta; not that Mom would be hurtful, you just didn't want to say or do anything that would hurt her. But Mom was very understanding. After we all had a good cry, she called and asked our family doctor, Dr. Holleran, to come over to the house. He examined Loretta and said, 'I have wonderful news for you, Loretta. You're going to have a baby.'

"From then on, Mom was cool; she knew what to do. She had always been the one adult whom kids could always go to. When we were in high school, Polly Ann (the oldest sister) and I had brought girls in trouble to Mama, and Mama would tell them how to dress and what to do, and they would have the baby and no one ever knew. Now that it was one of her own, Mom was just as cool-headed.

"From that day on, Mom didn't want us to make too much of it. She wanted all of us to just go about our lives. And then, of course, Mom handled it all. Loretta just put everything on her shoulders, and Mom could do anything. Mom never doted on us like a lot of mothers. She never checked to see if you brushed your teeth or had done your homework. But something important, we always knew we were safe once Mom was handling things. We trusted her for everything."

Polly Ann recalled, "I remember when Mom first told me about Loretta, I said, 'Well, she is and that's it.' We would proceed from day to day. At that time, I could wear the same size clothes that Loretta wore so I would go down to Bullocks Wilshire, pick out some things and take them home. If Loretta liked them, she'd keep them; if not, they'd go back. She dressed herself very well, I thought, considering."

Sally had her thoughts regarding the circumstances of Loretta's pregnancy. "Loretta flirted with every leading man she ever had, and I guess that most leading ladies do. I can remember that I did, even with Randolph Scott whom I found so dull. But, up in Washington, all these men were after Loretta. Everybody watched her and Gable on the set. Little Jack Oakie (actor), and the director, that awful Bill Wellman, everybody was after her, and they were mad that he was making headway. With all the other men there, I guess Gable was embarrassed to come on too strong. He didn't knock her down. He didn't. But once they left there, he made his move. Any representation saying that it was a love affair as though it had existed all during the picture and after the picture, and until the birth of the child is a total, total lie. Loretta was never in love with Clark Gable. She was fascinated by what she saw in the movies. A star. He was a man. Very aggressive. No love at all. Love didn't come into it."

Loretta did not share Dr. Holleran's proclamation, though well intended, that her pregnancy was wonderful news. Rather than a love child, it was a child she didn't want. She saw no way out. She reflected, "Working in the picture business, I knew girls who had had abortions. It would not have been hard to find a doctor to perform one, but my religion taught me that it would be taking a human life. I remember thinking if only I had a miscarriage but again, I wouldn't have done anything to provoke one."

Meanwhile, Loretta continued to work nonstop. Her next picture was SHANGHAI co-starring Charles Boyer. That was followed by Cecil B. DeMille's THE CRUSADES.

Clark Gable arrived on the set of THE CRUSADES one night. Loretta recalled, "Most people who work in movies are blasé about stars on the set, but with Clark you could feel the stir in the air. He definitely got their attention. He waited until I was through and then offered to take me home. We went for a drive up in the Hollywood Hills. He didn't say much, but it was apparent that he was agitated. With the long silences, I felt very uncomfortable and finally felt the pressure to say something. I blurted out, 'Would it make any difference if I told you that I wasn't pregnant?' He turned and looked at me and then asked, 'Well, are you or aren't you?' I felt like such a fool. I didn't know why I had said that except that I had tried to think of something to say he wanted to hear, my inherent need to please taken to an illogical length. I had to tell him that I was pregnant. His look toward me was one of total exasperation, and very little was said as he drove me home." There would be some phone calls in the interim, but it would be more than a year before Loretta would see Clark Gable again.

Meanwhile, 20th Century-Fox had purchased the rights to RAMONA from the novel by Helen Hunt Jackson. The studio saw it as a star vehicle for Loretta, but by the time she finished THE CRUSADES, she was nearing her fifth month of pregnancy. Loretta insisted that she was exhausted and needed to get away, a claim quite credible in light of seven films she had done back to back since she had joined forces with Daryl Zanuck. She and her mother, Gladys Belzer, sailed for Europe on the ILE DE FRANCE.

The rumors about Loretta and Gable now expanded to the possibility that the trip to Europe was a cover up for a secret pregnancy. In 1935, United States society had very strong notions of what was moral and immoral. Much was at stake. Celebrities who, by their actions, challenged those notions were almost sure to fall into disgrace. All the studios had what was referred to as a morals clause in their contracts, which stated that the contract could be broken by "any act or thing that would tend to bring the undersigned into public hatred, contempt, scorn or ridicule, or tend to shock, insult or offend the community." In 1935, having a child out of wedlock would evoke most of these negative responses from the public.

The rumors were countered by the very visual and active social life in which Loretta and her mother participated while in Europe. In England, they were hosted by Irving Asher, a nephew of studio head Jack Warner. They met Jules Basch (of Basch Brokerage House) at a dinner party in London, and he made it his business to host them during their stay in Paris. Charles Boyer was their sight-seeing guide. They stayed with Countess Dorothy DeFrasso in Rome. Later, the Countess would have the dubious distinction of having an affair with gangster Bugsy Siegel. Through it all, Loretta and Gladys were seen nightly at black tie events.

Loretta and Gladys returned to the United States after two and a half months abroad, and Polly Ann and Sally met them at the train station in Pasadena. At first sight, Sally thought Loretta had lost the baby and then realized that she was holding her body so tight as not to show. This realization made Sally feel increased compassion for her younger sister. Once home, Dr. Holleran issued a statement explaining that Loretta continued to suffer from exhaustion, and that bed rest would be needed if she was to recover her full energy.

Today it's hard to appreciate that the scandal of Loretta's having a child out of wedlock could have had repercussions felt by her entire family. It even threatened Polly Ann's engagement to businessman, Carter Hermann, a member of a socially prominent Pasadena family. Polly Ann explained, "Carter had kept asking me why I hadn't set a date for our wedding. His parents wanted to know. I finally decided to tell him about Loretta's situation, and then if he didn't want to go through with it, he was free to go. It didn't sway him. I was still reluctant and added, 'I don't want your parents hurt by any scandal. So if you wait until after the birth of this child, and if everything goes right, then I'll set a date'. He understood."

Loretta's activities out of the house during these final two months were strictly nocturnal. Sally recalled, "We'd wait until late at night and we'd drive the car to an unfamiliar neighborhood, and Loretta would get out and walk. It was important to make sure she was getting enough exercise for herself and the baby." Polly Ann recalled that she and Carter took Loretta to outdoor movies.

Sally, too, had become engaged, and it wasn't her nature to be concerned about the repercussions of scandal. The prospective groom was Norman Foster, an actor who had worked with Loretta in earlier films. He had changed his focus to directing and had worked himself into the good graces of Sol Wertzel, a producer at Fox.

Gladys was not enthusiastic about Norman. Sally hypothesized, "Since I had so many beaux who had a lot of money and some of them, titles, I think Mama expected me to marry wealth. She had married someone who wasn't wealthy and found out that it brought her a lot of difficult days."

Norman wasn't Catholic, so they were married in the living room of their home located on Sunset Boulevard. A Catholic priest officiated. The date was October 8, 1935. Sally recalled a conversation with Loretta just before the ceremony. "Loretta was in her room, and I went in to give her a kiss. What she said surprised me; 'Honey, if you really don't want to get married, back out now. You don't have to, you know.' She felt that Norman was immature, and that older men made better husbands. I just thought that it was so sweet of her, that she cared so much about me, and that she had the courage to suggest something like that considering all the guests were already downstairs. And just the fact that she was upstairs and couldn't come down, it made me cry. I came out in the hall, and my brother was there to walk me down the steps and with his big old hands, he kept patting me on the way down the stairs. I cried all the way through the wedding, and nobody knew why. I remember Dorothy Parker kept asking, 'Sally, for God's sake, what made you cry?' I said, 'I haven't any idea.' Then I said, 'I had a fight with Mama this morning,' I did, too."

Loretta had few visitors. Fan magazine writer, Dorothy Manners, and her husband, Walter Ramsey, were two who did see her. Dorothy Manners remembered, "*Motion Picture Magazine* had scheduled Loretta for the cover, and I needed an interview for the feature article. Here was this poor dear. I had heard the rumors that the trip to Europe was concocted to conceal a pregnancy, but decided to give Loretta the benefit of the doubt."

One day Spencer Tracy telephoned. Loretta remembered the conversation. "He said, 'I understand that you're not feeling too well. I would like to come over and say hello.' I froze; just the sound of his voice made my heart jump. I said, 'Spence, I don't think so.' He said, 'Just for old times' sake. I just want to see that you're all right and bring you a box of candy, that's all.' "

Spencer came over that afternoon. They were both reticent and exchanged pleasantries. Nothing personal was discussed until he started to leave. He said gently, "I love you." She said, "I know; I love you, too." Sixty years later, Loretta was still convinced that by bundling up under comforters during that visit, Spencer never suspected that she was pregnant.

Loretta was convinced that a lot of people around her didn't know her situation when, in fact, they did. One day Josie Wayne walked in the back door while Loretta was sitting in a kitchen chair. She threw her arms around Loretta's middle to give her a hug. Once again, Loretta froze and nothing was said. In fact, the two women would remain best friends their entire lives and the subject of Judy and Clark never surfaced. Loretta also believed that her sister Georgiana, at age twelve, was too young to realize what was going on during Loretta's pregnancy. Georgiana did know, but again, the subject would never be discussed between the two.

The house that Gladys selected as the location for Loretta to give birth was in Venice, California, a Los Angeles beach community just south of Santa Monica. Polly Ann recalled, "It was two stories, and it was the only house on that block except for one directly across the street. But that house was on another level, so it didn't seem that close."

Gladys had made the necessary preparations including borrowing Sally's massage table and having it set up in an upstairs bedroom that would serve as the delivery room. Polly Ann described how all the plans went into action on November 21, 1935. "Carter and I took Loretta down the night before, and the next day, Carter drove Dr. Holleran; he had left his own car at the Sunset house. When Carter would drive in, he would drive right into the garage which was hidden from the street; it was under the house, and since you went down, no one could really see who was coming or going.

"On the day that the baby was born (November 22, 1935), here's who was in the house: Loretta, the doctor, a nurse whom we called Frenchy, Carter and I. No one else. We had put blankets on the windows of the bedroom where Loretta was to muffle any sounds she might make during labor. The only people we were concerned about were the people across the street.

"The doctor had arrived around noon, and shortly after that I remember looking out the living room window and seeing a convertible parked on the street. There was a man in the driver's seat and a woman sitting on the other side, and they didn't seem to get out or do anything. I mentioned it to the doctor and he said, 'That's all right, Polly. That's another doctor, just in case. He won't come in. I'll just go and nod to him when he can leave.' Suppose something had gone wrong. Suppose both Loretta and the baby needed the attention of a doctor at the same time. Dr. Holleran had thought that through.

"I was waiting downstairs until the doctor asked me to come up. He needed a little help; he wanted me to help support Loretta's feet while the baby was being born. I remember feeling queasy and Doctor Holleran telling me, 'Just look down.' I wondered how my sister could have taken it all; she had only some chloroform for an anesthetic. I wouldn't say it was a difficult birth, but all births are not easy, particularly so for this mother who tried so hard to contain her pain. I don't remember that it took too long. I was still close to fainting, so the doctor said that I could leave. I think the baby was born between 2:00 and 3:00 in the afternoon. Loretta had selected the name of Judy, in honor of St. Jude, the patron saint for impossible situations.

"I didn't see the baby right after she was born. I realized that the doctor and the nurse had a lot of work to do. The baby was being cleaned and dressed, and they were taking care of Loretta, and I would have just been in the way. He didn't want some woman on the floor passed out. He didn't need that. The doctor left instructions for the nurse, and Carter took him back to his car around 5:00 p.m. Carter and I went up to see the baby about 8 or 9 p.m. She was a normal sweet baby girl. Later that evening, we took my mother down to see the baby. She loved holding her."

Sally recalled those days and stated, "Judy was Loretta's daughter, period, and she never thought about putting Judy up for adoption. I don't think any of us gave it a thought. We had a big family to welcome Judy, and Loretta knew that everyone would love Judy and we did. She was a darling little child."

Loretta contradicted Sally's assertion regarding adoption. She said, "Adoption wasn't an option because Clark's and my legal name would have had to appear on the papers. Otherwise, Mama and I would have stayed in Europe and had the baby there. Of course, those thoughts all changed once Judy was born. She was adorable and I wanted her."

Additional memories from Polly Ann, "For a few weeks, Loretta, the nurse, and Judy all stayed in the house in Venice. I would bring things during the day, groceries and such, and Carter would bring whatever they needed in the evenings. One afternoon, I was coming home alone. There was no one else on the street; Venice Avenue was a quiet two lane road in those days. But then I stopped at a light and recognized a reporter. I don't remember his name, but I can still remember seeing him that day. He had a pale complexion and there was another man in the car with him. I think maybe he worked for *The Hollywood Reporter*. I thought, 'Oh my word! What's he doing down here?' That's the only time I actually saw him, but I figured from that that they must have tried other ways of following us, either Mom or one of us, so I kept my visits to a minimum."

In a preemptive move to foil any curious reporters closing in on the Venice house, Gladys had already rented a little home in Westwood. The nurse was dismissed and Parsaita, the maid from the Sunset House, moved in to care for Judy. Polly Ann recalled, "I can picture that little house being on an incline, and I can remember seeing Parsaita holding the baby. She was so loving and caring, and she was wonderful with Judy. Loretta went to see Judy every day. Even after she went back to work, Herman, her driver, would take her to that little house on the way to the studio and again on the way home so that she could spend time with the baby. I know that Loretta was concerned about what the neighbors were thinking, but she went ahead anyway. That's one reason why I didn't stop too often. I didn't want too many of us seen in that neighborhood. Remember at this time, this was still news and scandalous. I did not want to lead any newsmen to Judy."

Sally first saw Judy in the Westwood house. Sally recalled, "I remember taking an odd route to get there; my mother didn't approve that I was going at all because of all the secrecy, but I was dying to see the baby. She was very big by the time I did. I just loved her looks and kept saying, 'Oh Loretta, I hope I have a baby that looks just like this.' In response to my enthusiasm about Judy, Loretta referred to Gable's visit earlier in the week, the first time he had seen his daughter, and said, 'Yes, and do you know after all that has gone on, all that we've gone through, instead of having any interest in his daughter, he tried to knock me down on the bed! Can you imagine, Sally? That bastard! Who the hell does he think he is?' And I thought, 'With all that's happened, she thinks he's a bastard. How awful all this must have been for her.' Made it twice as bad as far as I'm concerned. He really was insensitive; he didn't understand that Loretta was a human being that had suffered very much."

Gable did not contribute to Judy's care. Polly Ann explained, "Loretta didn't need Clark Gable's money to take care of Judy. Matter of fact, she told him not to get involved in that way. Mom thought she was making a mistake. Loretta said, 'No, it's finished and there's nothing more. I don't want to have anything to do with him, Mom.' Mom said, 'I'm just thinking of the child's sake in case anything happens to you.' Loretta was right as it turned out."

From all appearances, there wasn't a baby in Loretta's life, and the rumor mill ground down for the time being. RAMONA was on hold when she reported back to the studio in January 1936. While Loretta had been away, it was decided that RAMONA would be the studio's first feature length Technicolor production. THE CALL OF THE WILD proved to be a bonanza at the box office, and Zanuck wasn't going to waste any precious time. Loretta would squeeze in two films while the studio finished preparations for RAMONA.

The first one, THE UNGUARDED HOUR, was a loan out to MGM. The film's trailer began with "Loretta Young, back on the screen – more glamourous – and stunningly beautiful than ever." (Metro Goldwyn-Mayer, 1936). The story offered British courtroom intrigue, but perhaps Loretta's best performance on that set came while the cameras weren't rolling. Clark Gable and Spencer Tracy were working on a nearby soundstage filming SAN FRANCISCO, and they surprised Loretta by arriving on her set together. Loretta acted like she couldn't have been more flattered that MGM's two biggest male stars would come to see her. Under her smile she thought differently. She reflected, "I thought how different these two men were. Clark who was still married to Ria was in a hot romance with Carole Lombard. He was like a child, totally unaware of all the difficulty I'd been through. As for Spencer, I was afraid to look him in the eyes. Would they show love? Would they show hurt? I didn't have to look to know that they'd show both. All I could do was go home that night and block it out of my mind."

PRIVATE NUMBER was the story of the maid in a household who falls in love with the young man of the household. Robert Taylor played the male lead. There is a scene in the movie that eerily reflected Loretta's reality. Two thirds into the picture, Loretta's character is hiding out at a farm-house with her secret baby, along with her girlfriend, played by Pasty Kelly. She had covertly married the rich son of the household. Two gruff-looking men come to the door to serve Loretta a legal paper. Loretta opens the envelope, looks at its content and silently falls back on a chair. Patsy Kelly takes the letter, reads it, and exclaims, "Ellen, if they annul your marriage on account of fraud, do you know what that makes your baby?" Loretta responds, "Gracie, they couldn't do that! They wouldn't!" (20th Century-Fox, 1936)

In 1936, the word "bastard" was too harsh to be spoken on the screen, but audiences would have had no problem understanding the horrible dilemma the young mother was facing. Most likely, the day that Loretta was shooting that scene at 20th Century-Fox, on her way to the studio that morning, she had stopped by to see her own hidden baby, ensconced in a bungalow less than a mile away. A baby the world would mark as a bastard if her origins were known.

Polly Ann and Carter married in February, 1936. She continued to work, grinding out low budget pictures. Carter's parents had been charter members of the exclusive Los Angeles Country Club, but now Carter was asked to resign because of his marriage to an actress.

Loretta continued her schedule of spending early morning and early evenings with Judy, making movies during the day, and being seen in the right places at night to affirm her status as young actress with a busy social life. She could carry this off because she was surrounded by people absolutely loyal to her. Sally had been so closed-mouth that she hadn't even told her new husband and wouldn't for several years.

A turncoat threatened to crack that wall wide open. Polly Ann recalled, "The nurse Frenchy had gone to Parsaita, saying that the two of them could blackmail Loretta for a great deal of money. Parsaita absolutely refused and came to Mom and told her. Apparently, the nurse felt that she needed someone to collaborate and had also approached Dr. Holleran. Imagine Frenchy going to him with such a proposition! He worked at Queen of Angels Hospital, and she was on the staff there. His response to her was, 'As long as I work here, I don't ever want you on any of my cases.'"

The situation now was getting too hot for Gladys and Loretta to manage in a town full of reporters. Gladys decided to relocate Judy out of town for several months and place her under the care of the Daughters of Charity that ran St. Elizabeth's orphanage In San Francisco.

This chapter has raised so many questions. When twenty-two-year-old Loretta stepped on the train heading for location shooting of CALL OF THE WILD, she had already starred in more than fifty films. How did she get there, and how did she get there so fast? What had been Polly Ann's and Sally's routes to leading lady status? Who was this mother, apparently capable of solving the most challenging of problems? Had Spencer Tracy been the love of Loretta's life? To answer these questions and so much more necessitates circling back to Salt Lake City, the time, a few weeks after Loretta's brother Jack was born.

Papa John Earle Young holding Betty Jane (Sally) and Gladys
resting her hand on Polly Ann's shoulder.

Young Gladys....but was she ever young?

Five-year old Polly Ann holds eighteen month old Gretchen (Loretta) with three year old Betty Jane (Sally) at her side.

Chapter 2: Abandoned

Loretta reflected, "What I knew about Papa, I didn't like. I only have one clear memory of him, and this is what happened. It was Christmas time, a few weeks before my fourth birthday, and we were still in Utah. There was a swinging door from the dining room into the kitchen, and as I opened it, I saw my Grandmother Young at the sink washing jars, and my mother turned toward the cupboard holding my brother Jack in her arms. Papa was standing next to her. He was facing toward me; Mama wasn't. As I came in, I saw him hit her and she fell back onto a stool that was behind her. I flew at him screaming, 'Don't you hit my mother! Don't you hit my mother!' and I beat on him as hard as I could. I was incensed but the grownups started to laugh. Mama said, 'Oh Honey, oh Honey,' and Grandma finally put her arms around me and started to say, 'Oh Honey, your daddy was ..... ,'. But by this time I was crying, and she picked me up and carried me out of the room without me understanding what had happened."

Loretta would be a grandmother herself before she understood what had really transpired in her only clear memory of her father. Instead of him hitting her mother as she perceived, he had plopped his hand on her shoulder to let her know he'd reach for a jar, and she could remain sitting on the stool. How damaging was this misperception in terms of Loretta's future relationships with men? There's no way of knowing.

To have a better understanding of Papa and Mama, one needs to go back farther. Little is known about the early days of "Papa" or John Earle Young. He was born in the town of Chaffee, Boyd County, Kentucky, in1890. His mother, Laura Victroy Young, was married twice; her second husband was a Mr. Young by which she had a daughter, Grace. John was born during her first marriage, but his mother confided to her grown granddaughters many years later that he had been a love child, his father's surname, Mendell.

At age five, a life-threatening illness necessitated that John's right leg be amputated. Maybe because of his handicap, maybe because he represented a lost love, Laura Young spoiled her only son excessively. In return, he charmed her shamelessly, and in the process, honed skills that would eventually characterize him.

John left Kentucky while still in his teens and found his way to Denver, Colorado. At some point he landed work as an auditor for the Rio Grande and Western Railroad. He was a big man, tall, with dark eyes, dark hair, and a soft spoken voice. Apparently, John's wooden leg did not deter him from being quite the ladies' man. He was so skilled with his prosthesis that he enjoyed a reputation as a beautiful dancer.

"Mama" was Gladys Royal Young. Her parents had grown up in the South as well, her mother, Fanny Watkins, in Tennessee, her father in Mississippi. Robert Royal was a practicing dentist, but soon after his marriage, was attracted west by the lure of land speculation. The Transcontinental Railroad had only been completed twenty years when Gladys was born in Los Angeles, California in 1888 (The 1890 census reported a population of 50,395 for the township of Los Angeles).

Shortly thereafter, the boom went bust and the family returned to Tennessee. They stayed at the plantation belonging to Fanny's brother Al, and that's where Gladys's younger sisters Collie and Cherrie were born. Their mother died when Cherrie was an infant; cause of death was dysentery.

Dr. Royal placed his young daughters in a Catholic convent school near Bardstown, Kentucky. Neither he nor his wife had been Catholic, but he had a great aunt, a nun, living at the convent. Under her watchful eyes, they would get the kind of education their mother would have wanted for them. The curriculum emphasized beautiful manners, floral arrangement, and an appreciation of the arts, everything to prepare their young charges to be wives of substantial husbands. Dr. Royal proceeded to Denver, Colorado, to pursue his business interests. He would visit his young daughters from time to time, but in many ways, Gladys became the parent of her younger sisters, a relationship that would remain in place throughout their lives.

It was to Denver society that Gladys Royal was introduced as a debutante. Gladys had a habit of lowering her head and covering her mouth when she laughed, but her shy manner did not diminish her striking beauty. Her chestnut brown hair was silky and thick, her cheekbones high, her skin milky fair, and her intelligent blue eyes suggested gentleness. Although medium in height and large busted, she managed to convey a willowy demureness.

Gladys soon met a young gentleman and became engaged. She saw him as a wonderful man for all the right reasons. The kind of man for whom she had been raised to marry, have his children, and manage his home. But then, the paths of John Earle Young and Gladys Royal crossed somewhere, somehow, in Denver. Possibly it was at a dance; Gladys loved to dance. Young was so handsome, and his very presence could set a sparkle to a dull room. He now called himself Earle, and how he could dance; the convent-bred Gladys was literally and totally swept off her feet.

Gladys ignored a signal that her fiancé was an experienced ladies' man. Loretta recalled a story her mother told her, "The day before they were married, one of Papa's old girlfriends said, 'Gladys, you know that Earle has an artificial leg.' Mama responded, 'He has not.' 'Well, you'll find out,' the young woman replied. And, indeed, Mama did."

The year of their marriage was 1907; both the bride and the groom were
still teenagers. The following year Polly Ann was born in Denver. The baby's arrival necessitated a moment of reckoning for Gladys. She had to decide in what faith Polly Ann would be baptized. Gladys's convent school education tipped the decision toward Catholicism, and not only was Polly Ann baptized Catholic, but so were Gladys and Earle, and their marriage blessed by the Church.

The growing family moved along with Earle's job. In July, 1910, enroute to their new home in Salt Lake City, Utah, the imminent arrival of a new baby forced them to get off the train in Salida, Colorado. Betty Jane was born in an old hotel near the tracks.

By 1912, Gladys was pregnant again. Gretchen Young was born on January 6, 1913 in Salt Lake, City. As a teenager, she would become known as Loretta Young. John came along twenty months later. The family would always call him Jack.

Earle was at his best when the babies arrived. Gladys later told Betty Jane that for the following two weeks, he brought her a breakfast tray with a flower and waited on her hand and foot. But, generally speaking, Earle's strength was charm rather than consideration. His passions were apparent and could be contagiously thrilling for those around him. Betty Jane remembered Earle's passion for Italian opera divas. "Papa had this gramophone that he wound up. Then he would bring home posters of these women in bodices displaying their small waists and big hips, and we'd listen to their records. We knew them by heart. Papa was always saying, 'Just listen to that!'"

Gladys and Earle were a study in opposites. Her reserve prohibited any overt demonstrations of affection. Even with her children it was a soft smile rather than a spontaneous hug or a kiss. Earle was earthy. He was a hugger a kisser, a toucher. He said and did what he felt. Unfortunately for his marriage, this freewheeling spirit included womanizing.

Gladys wasn't one for confrontation, but this didn't mean that she would tolerate a demeaning situation. Whether it was meant as a permanent separation is unclear, but Gladys packed up and took the children to Los Angeles where her sister Carlene ("Collie") and her husband, Ernest Traxler, and their daughters were living. Dr. Royal had provided the financial means for the trip. Los Angeles had grown ten-fold since Gladys had been born and now had a population of a half million people.

Polly Ann recalled: "We arrived in Los Angeles in the afternoon, and we took a red streetcar that stopped at Hollywood Boulevard and Highland Avenue; that's where that particular line ended. What impressed me as we came into Hollywood were the eucalyptus and orange trees. The eucalyptus trees lined the streets and orange trees seemed to appear in most peoples' yards. The smell, the combination, was wonderful. Meeting us were Uncle "Trax" and Aunt "Collie," and we walked to their house on Selma Avenue which was just down the street from Famous Players-Lasky Company (Studio). They had two daughters, Colleen who was Gretch's (Gretchen) age, and Valerie who was the same age as Jack."

Actor Sessue Hayakawa, who worked at Famous Players-Lasky Company (Studio), lived next door to the Traxlers. Betty Jane recalled, "We knew that he was someone famous, so we would climb up in an orange tree and then onto the fence to get a good look. He would turn around and go 'RRRRRR!' He was Japanese, funny looking to us, you know. But he was sweet. I had the feeling that he liked us."

One day Earle reappeared into their lives. He had moved to nearby Altadena and was working as an accountant at the Midwick Country Club. His mother was also living in Los Angeles, and it was probably through her that he traced Gladys and his family. Most likely, it was at this time that Gladys moved from the Traxlers' into a little rented house on the same street a block and a half away. It was a reconciliation of sorts. Earle did not actually live there, but he stayed over from time to time. Also, they re-established a joint bank account. There was enough money for Gladys to hire a maid.

Betty Jane was the most happy when her father reappeared. She recalled his putting them to bed one night, "'All right, come on kids,' he said, 'I'll give a nickel to the first one who falls asleep.' Then I would say, 'Well, I'll go to sleep if you just sleep with us.' And he'd say, 'Yes I will,' as he would remove his limb. Since he was our father and we never knew him without it, it seemed perfectly natural. And unless I saw that artificial thing over there against the wall, I wouldn't go asleep. When he was real tired, I would think, 'Oh, isn't this heaven, he's going to sleep with us all night.'"

Per usual, Earle's presence brought a joyous air, particularly on the evenings when the Traxlers and other friends were in the house. These were pre-radio days, but there was music aplenty. Earle could play the accordion and mandolin, and Uncle Trax was a very good piano player. The carpets were rolled up, and the grownups danced while the Young children and the Traxler girls crept from their beds and sat at the top of the stairs to listen. But for Gladys the excitement was hollow. She had been married to Earle for nine years and she knew him. Gladys suspected that the focus of his affections extended beyond her, and the old pattern of suspicion and tears was back.

It was a summer day and Earle was going to take Betty Jane with him to the country club. Part of the day's thrill would be getting to ride on the back of Papa's motorcycle. As they were getting ready to leave, Betty Jane felt tension. She recalled, "Kids know when there is something wrong in the family, and I asked Aunt Collie, 'Why is Mama so mad at Papa? She won't kiss him good-bye.' She said, 'You're too young now. When you get older, your Mom can explain.'"

Earle had been sleeping with the young maid, and Gladys knew it. By the time Earle and Betty Jane returned that afternoon, it appeared that both he and Gladys realized that the time had come for him to leave. Betty Jane recalled, "I was standing in this little tiny hall in front of the cloak closet, and Papa came up to me. He brought a grocery bag full of hard Christmas candy, and he said, 'I won't see you for a long, long time'. He kissed me good-bye and I cried.

"Mama was standing by the door. As she looked directly at him, she said, 'Earle, I don't wish you any misfortune, but I wish to heaven, I'll never have to see you again so long as I live. 'He replied, 'Don't worry; Gladys, you never will' and then turned and walked out of the door."

Gladys never did. Nor did she have any idea where he went. But she was to quickly discover that he had stopped at the bank and cleared out their account.

Gladys Royal Young was a clear-thinker. John Earle Young's venue was the emotions; once he had you on that side of the line, everything was his call. Early in their marriage Gladys had stepped back on her side and basically stayed there. With Gladys, Earle could no longer transcend his shortcomings by turning on the charm full-throttle. He must have resented her for it.

What Loretta thought the facts were about her father and his disappearances contributed to her development more so than what the facts had really been. It would be another twenty-five years before she understood that Gladys, in her gentle way, had basically thrown her father out. It would be seventy-four years later before Loretta found out that Mama had left Papa when she packed up and brought her young children to Los Angeles; Loretta had always thought that Papa had left the family high and dry in Utah. Nor did she understand that Papa had never really lived with them in the house on Selma Avenue. Throughout the childhood years that strategically shaped Loretta, she had certain perceptions ingrained in her mind, that Papa was a philanderer, but that Mama had strived to keep the family intact, that one day Papa just disappeared, clearing out the bank account on his way. That this man, of whom her clearest memory was seeing him hit her beloved Mama, had willfully and callously abandoned her.

CHAPTER 3: ON THEIR OWN

Now, everything rested on Gladys's twenty-nine-year-old shoulders. Loretta explained her mother's course of action, "She went to see the Catholic Bishop of Los Angeles, Bishop Cantwell. They had never met, but after conferring, he suggested to Mama, 'Why don't you open a boarding house?' The Bishop then offered her a loan from his own personal finances. He was from a well-off San Francisco family.

"So shortly after Papa left, we moved to a larger house on Green Street, and Mama started an account with Barker Brothers, a large furniture store in Downtown Los Angeles. It was so much her nature to make things beautiful. Not everything was new, but little touches made a big difference. Five tired-looking chairs exuded remarkable style after Mama recovered them with black-and-white-striped canvas. She had good taste, and her boarding house was way above the competition. The boarders, too, were a cut above. They were mostly families, substantial people. Usually, they were referred by a friend who would say, 'I hear that Mrs. Young will soon have an opening. '"

Gladys and children settled into the routine of the boarding house. Apartments weren't abundant in Los Angeles in 1917; if you didn't rent or buy a house, boarding houses were considered a respectable alternative. They offered several advantages: your meals were prepared, beds made, and your clothes laundered. Gladys hired a cook, a houseman and two maids to assist her.

The children played with other children living in the boarding house and in the neighborhood. But they also learned that work was to be part of life's rhythm; they knew that the staff wasn't there to wait on them. Mama and the help had their hands full with washing and ironing, cooking and cleaning. The girls learned early to make beds, fold napkins, set tables and to perform whatever tasks Mama asked. Loretta recalled, "Nothing was considered menial; anything worth doing was worth doing well. If I were to wash the porch, Mama would say, 'Now, I don't care how long it takes you to do it, but just see how sparkling clean you can make that porch out there.'"

Months earlier, Uncle Trax had presented a different avenue of work, one that would be prophetic for Loretta. Ernest Traxler was a production manager for George Milford, a big director at Famous Players-Lasky Company (Studio). Loretta remembered the day he came into the back yard on Selma Avenue. "He asked, 'Who wants to go to the studio and work today and make three and a half dollars in the bargain?' I yelled, 'I do! I do!' just copying Pol, and Bet, and all the older kids who were there. Anyway, he picked me, Colleen, Valerie, and Jack because we were the littlest, and we went over to the studio. He took us into the costume department, and they put a little tulle with a big bow around our naked little middles and put on funny little wings. We went onto the set where they attached wires to us and told us to fly around like fairies. The other kids got scared, but when I flew around, I thought it was wonderful. From the very first day, I thought that being on the set was magical."

The year was 1917, the picture was THE PRIMROSE RING starring Mae Murray and directed by her husband, Robert Leonard. What made the experience all the more special for Gretchen was the pleasure of bringing home three dollars and fifty cents to Mama.

A couple of months after Gretchen and Jack had worked in THE PRIMROSE PATH, Universal Pictures were casting SIRENS OF THE SEA. It would be shot on location on Santa Cruz Island and star Jack Mulhaul and Louise Lovely. Again they needed little nymphs but, this time, they were the non-flying type. Betty Jane recalled the experience, "We were over there for a couple of weeks. After we were on the island for a few days, they ran out of food and all that they were serving were hard boiled eggs and tea.

"Jack Mulhaul was doing a scene one day, when he unexpectedly saw something bobbing in the water. He said, 'I think there's a kid out there.' He immediately jumped into the water and went out and grabbed two-year-old Jack and brought him back. He had wandered into the surf and was going out to sea with the tide."

If little Gretchen stood on the porch and looked toward the top of the hill, she could see the Botiller mansion, home of one of Los Angeles's first families. Dionysio Botiller had become the County Assessor and parlayed his small inheritance into a fortune built upon Los Angeles real estate. There was a Botiller Building, a Botiller Hotel and so on. By the time that the Youngs were residing down the street, the occupants of the Botiller mansion were Dionysio's widow, one son, two daughters and a son-in-law, Mr. Lindley, a lawyer. Mr. and Mrs. Lindley would soon encounter curly-haired, two-year-old Jack and fall in love with him. It started when Jack had walked down the alley and struck up a conversation with the chauffeur who was working in their garage. He sent Jack to the back door to ask for donuts, so that the cook would see the cute little guy, and she in turn drew everyone to the window.

Jack missed his father even though he had no memory of him. He recalled, "I was always going down on the corner of 9th and

Green to look for my father. I just stationed myself near where the streetcar stopped. One day, this fine looking man got off and I said, 'That's my father!' And I ran out to him and threw my arms around him. It was Mr. Lindley, the lawyer who was married to Ida Botiller. Mrs. Lindley was watching from the window, and she came down and whispered to him, 'Don't tell him you're not his father; it might break his little heart.' This was probably a month or so after I had been to the kitchen door asking for the donuts."

Jack became a regular visitor to the Botillers throughout the following year. They customarily had afternoon tea in the grape arbor, and Jack had found a little opening in the fence where he could slip through. They all doted on him, and they would phone or send a note asking if he could stay for dinner.

Gladys found a better property to operate her boarding house business nine blocks further up Green Street. When Ida Lindley heard of the impending move, she almost had a nervous breakdown. She was unable to bear children and vicariously, she had been living with the idea that Jack was her own child. Mr. Lindley asked Gladys if they could adopt Jack. According to Loretta, her mother's response was, "'No, I couldn't let you do that. He can be with you as much as he likes, but I can't give him up." But as Gladys and the girls moved to the new house, four-year-old Jack moved into the Botiller home. It was understood that he could return permanently anytime to live with his family, but from then on, he would only visit his mother's home. Thus began a casual arrangement by which, eventually, he would be known as Jack Lindley. Jack stated, "I had no qualms about the arrangement because I'd go back to my mother's house all the time to visit. The Botillers knew that I missed my sisters and my mother, so they'd send me over every week or two."

Gretchen and Colleen had also fulfilled a childless woman's vicarious need for children, only this woman was the movie star, Mae Murray. Mae's stardom was in ascension in 1917. She had appeared in the Ziegfeld Follies at age fifteen, and then became a particularly bright luminary of Hollywood's glamorous Roaring Twenties. She nurtured her reputation as a clothes horse, and her gowns were the envy of all the women who saw them. Her biggest success would be in 1925 with MGM's THE MERRY WIDOW, co-starring John Gilbert.

Mae spotted Gretchen and Colleen while they were on the set of THE PRIMROSE RING. She asked Gladys and Aunt Collie if they could "loan" their girls to her. Recognizing that this was a unique opportunity for the girls and understanding that they would come home on weekends or whenever they wished, the mothers complied. Loretta recalled the experience: "We went to stay at one of these great-big-movie star houses, lots of stairs leading up to it. It was like a party all the time; like a movie, only we were living with the movie's star."

Gretchen had already drawn her conclusions observing Mae Murray on the set. "I didn't want to be an actress particularly, but I did want to be a 'Mae Murray' because everybody liked her. She was like a queen; you knew that all the activity revolved around her. They'd get everything in place and then they'd say, 'We're ready for you, Miss Murray.'

"When Mae was home, I don't remember her doing anything. She didn't make beds or cook like Mama. Every day, we always dressed in what I call Sunday dresses: little organdy dresses with fancy aprons on top of them, and black Mary Janes and white socks. We called her Maestie. When Maestie was home, she'd bring us dolls and we'd play in the garden.

"Finally after six or nine months, we were home for the weekend, and we were getting ready to go back, I said, 'Colleen, do you want to go back?' She said, 'No, I don't.' Mom overheard us and said, 'Well, I think you better go back and tell her.' We did and we were home in a couple of days. I had missed Mama and the kids. At Maestie's we got what little rich kids got: a governess, good food, nice clothes and dancing lessons, but we didn't care. We wanted to be home with our family where we belonged."

But the seed had been planted. Polly Ann observed, "From the time that Mae Murray took Gretch and Colleen to live with her, from that time on, the ambition to become an actress grew. Oh yes."

Gretchen's next film project was THE ONLY WAY with Fanny Ward and Theodore Roberts. Loretta identified this film as the real beginning of her acting career, "The director asked me; 'Can you cry?' I said, 'Oh, yes, I can cry.' He said, 'Now, in the next scene you come in, and you look at that lady and you just cry. Your heart is broken. Think that your favorite doll is all dead and broken, and you're never going to see that beautiful doll again, and then you cry.' I thought, 'That's a silly thing to say; I don't have any favorite doll.' I didn't know what he was trying to do. He said, 'Roll the camera; she's ready now,' and then he said, 'Now cry.' And, of course, I just looked at him. I thought, 'Here goes my chance to work in movies.' I couldn't have been more than five, but I knew that if I didn't do what the director told me, I couldn't go to the studio anymore. Finally, he said, 'Cut!'

"Uncle Trax was right there and he said, 'Just a minute.' Then he said, 'C'mon Gretchen,' and he took me by the hand. He ran me around the lot; my feet were just barely touching the ground. I was flying in the air, but he had a good hold of me. Then he brought me back and stood me in front of the camera and said, 'Cry.' He clapped his hands very forcefully in front of my face, and it scared me. I was out of breath anyway and excited, and I started to cry, and started to cry real tears, and my instincts told me this was what the director wanted."

Gladys had a casual attitude about her daughters' educations. They lived next door to the Cathedral School, and it took a nun's inquiry before Gladys enrolled Polly Ann at age eight. She went straight into the third grade, and Betty Jane was enrolled simultaneously into the first.

As a mother, a case could be built that Gladys's priorities were not typical: allowing Jack to drift into the Lindley household, "lending" Gretchen to Mae Murray, not enrolling the girls in school at the appropriate time. And observing her easy manner and hearing her soft voice, one might conclude that her fragility permitted her to be overwhelmed by events. More likely, the opposite was true. Although she would always treasure graciousness and good manners, her inner strength was such that her decisions were not dictated by convention. Rather, it was whatever she thought was right. As she explained years later to Polly Ann about the older girls not being in school, "I was so accustomed to having you at home, I thought, 'It was fine with me.'"

Betty Jane offered her own theory on Gladys's lackadaisical attitude concerning school. "Every time we were late, and we were going to be embarrassed in front of the whole classroom, we'd turn around and come home and say, 'Oh Mom, please, let us stay home. We'll do all the housework and all the cooking,' and she'd say, 'Oh no, you don't have to do anything, just stay.' Mom really loved being family and being with us. Her mother wasn't with them. It had just been the three girls."

Gladys's attitude toward school served as a great relief to Gretchen who entered Cathedral School at age five. It didn't take Gretchen long to feel a sense of inadequacy. Being a whiz at math didn't seem to compensate for her great difficulty with reading and spelling. She soon learned that if she claimed to have headaches, Mama didn't make her go.

Gretchen was sent home from school one morning. Loretta recalled why: "We were supposed to look after our own things; Mama wasn't there to dress us. The first one out of the house was the best dressed and the most completely dressed. One day I had gotten to school without any socks on. Sister said, 'You go home during recess and get some socks.' When I got outside, I saw Mama watering the front lawn, and I started to cry and ran up to her and threw my arms around her legs. I had been embarrassed. Apparently, even then, I couldn't take too much disapproval. It cut me to the quick. Mama said, 'Come on, we'll find you a pair of socks.' I can still see her. She had an apron on, and she had it turned up and tied around because she wanted to keep even the apron clean. Her hair was very soft. She was smiling and she kept patting my head, asking me not to cry. The reason I recall this incident is because of the warmth I felt in her just being there. I knew she'd solve my problems, and I wouldn't be scared anymore."

By the summer of 1920, Famous Players-Lasky Company (Studio) had assumed the name of it distribution arm, Paramount Pictures, and Uncle Trax's boss was directing THE SHEIK. To simulate the Sahara Desert, location shooting was being done near Oxnard, California, 30 miles north of Los Angeles. It would be the signature film for its twenty-six-year-old star, Rudolph Valentino. Background shots called for numerous little Arab children to be running around the village, and the call went out for child extras. Uncle Trax arranged for all four of the Young children and both his daughters to be hired.

Gladys stayed home. She was pleased with the opportunities that the movies were providing her daughters and grateful for the income that their work as extras generated, but she was not personally enamored with the movie industry or the people in it.

Aunt Collie went along to supervise the children. There was one huge circus-like tent where all of the families lived for the five week duration. Screens were put around each family area affording a semblance of privacy.

Polly Ann has vivid memories of location life when the cameras weren't rolling. "Most of the adults working on the picture would go into town at night. In silent films they had musicians who played off to the side of the camera to help create a mood, and some of these musicians would come over after work to play for us children. Sometimes Valentino would come over to the tent and play his guitar for us kids. He played beautifully. He didn't go into town most of the time because he was so uncomfortable. He had boils all over his body, mainly on his buttocks, and he had to ride that horse every day. Some evenings he would bring his horse over, and he would let us take turns going for a little ride. We knew he was 'Valentino,' a star, like everyone else did. But he was a nice man, and that's what counted with us kids."

Loretta didn't remember much about that summer on location. As a small child running around in the background, she was oblivious to whether the cameras were rolling or not. Little Gretchen was often oblivious, living in a world all of her own. Betty Jane, on the other hand, was ready to take on the world. She didn't back off when it came to confrontation, and that included confronting emotions as well. Betty Jane would display enough emotion to make up for the reticence of the rest of the family. Polly Ann was a little Gladys in the making with a solid disposition. She too had a mission, Mama's champion.

The boarding house residents provided the girls with a captive audience for their own productions. Loretta remembered, "I wouldn't be in the play unless I could play the lead part. Betty Jane took the tickets; we charged five cents apiece. Polly Ann was always the man because she had long hair and could tie a rubber band around it and bring it around as a beard. The other kids in the boarding house would play extras.

"I lived in a dream world, but they were beautiful dreams. I wanted to be the Fairy Princess of everybody. I used to love to dance in front of the boarders, and do anything to amuse them and just show off. I wasn't embarrassed. Bet and Pol would say, 'Well, I haven't got the right dress, or I don't know what to say,' all that kind of stuff. Well, it didn't make any difference to me. I always assumed that all the boarders loved me. At least they all treated me as if they did. So, the more they loved me, the more pleasant and adorable I wanted to be to them."

This need for approval was a constant. A rewarding smile could literally transform her. Betty Jane remembered, "Gretch would not be doing much of anything until there was an audience, an adult, someone who thought she was pretty. I've never seen anyone come alive like that. She just always was like that. If you ever saw her shine as a little girl, she was absolutely fantastic. It was wonderful to watch, even for me, although sometimes she annoyed the daylights out of me by not sharing the responsibility of the housework. She was as capable as we were, but she wouldn't most of the time. If an adult was watching, that was different. Then she'd work her little fanny off."

Gretchen was also willing to work at ballet. Studying at the Ernest Belcher's Dancing School was one such effort. At age eight she took the streetcar to Mr. Belcher's by herself.

Gretchen had made up her mind that she'd either be an actress or a dancer. Being a star was not only glamorous, but it would solve a lot of problems. Loretta recalled, "I was in the second grade at Cathedral Chapel and one day, Sister Marina said to me, 'You just have to learn to spell.' I said, 'I don't have to spell; I'm going to be an actress.' Sister said, 'But you'll have to write letters.' I replied, 'No, an actress has a secretary, and she spells.' I knew all about this because Mae Murray had a secretary. She also had a cook, a butler, and a maid, and a personal maid. She just sat around looking beautiful. I didn't realize that she had to work and pay for everything."

Gladys kept moving into better neighborhoods. Moving from one house to the next didn't faze the girls. Loretta explained, "We didn't care where 'home' was as long as Mama was there. Mama was 'home' as far as we were concerned." Gladys was, indeed, the core of their lives. Loretta described how masterfully she met the challenge, "To me Mama was all understanding and all compassion but all firmness. She was not jelly. She had standards that you lived up to; you did as she did. We wanted to be like Mama. She was attractive. She was beautiful and spoke with a Southern accent which she claimed she didn't have. She was always saying, 'Oh yes, Dee-a.' She told us what was right and wrong, but she never made an issue of it. If we did do something wrong, I must say, usually she was the first person we went to."

At one time Gladys maintained two boarding horses next door to each other. One house had a large-sized dining room where all the boarders ate, as many as thirty at one time. It meant a lot of hard work, and even someone as strong as Gladys had her breaking point. Loretta had an early Christmas morning memory. "I had asked for a new dress for my doll. It was now three in the morning and, half asleep, I needed to go to the bathroom. I had to go through the room in which Mama was sewing to get there. She was sewing my doll's dress. I remember that she was in her slip, and her hair was down, and she looked beautiful. I hesitated, but I had to go to the bathroom, so I started in anyway. She lamented, 'Oh honey! Why did you have to come in here?' I replied, 'I'm not looking, I'm not looking,' and then ran back again. But when I left I saw her put her face in her hands, and she was crying."

One day the doorbell rang, and Betty Jane answered it. It was a man looking for a room. Betty Jane recalled that afternoon. "He was so clean, clean, clean. His shirt was starched, and the tie was right, and the hair was cut the right length, and it was very straight, and he had the bluest eyes. After showing him the room, I ran to my mother and said, 'The handsomest man I've ever seen came to the front door, and I showed him the room, and he loves it.' And Mama said, 'Are you sure he just doesn't love you?' I said, 'No. Hurry and comb your hair and put on some rouge.' To me that's when she was dressed up."

That man's name was George Belzer.

CHAPTER 4: THE WORLD EXPANDS

Gladys quietly began procedures to divorce Earle and started dating again. Mr. Belzer wasn't the first in line to escort her for an evening out. Another boarder, Mr. Roake, had that honor. Then there was a Mr. Cruz who had possibilities until he shared his dream of being a rancher. Gladys did not envision herself or her daughters as cowgirls out on the range.

The girls, too, were making new acquaintances. Polly Ann and Sally became good friends with a neighbor girl their age by the name of Josephine Saenz. Her mother was of French origin and her father of Spanish. He had been a physician-surgeon and then joined the United States Diplomatic Corps as a Consul to Cuba and eventually to Panama. Josephine was called Josie by friends and family. She had sparkling brown eyes, smooth dark hair and flawless skin. John Wayne loomed in her future.

Looking toward her daughters' futures, Gladys enrolled them in the Sacred Heart Academy, a boarding school in nearby Alhambra, operated by Dominican Sisters. Gretchen was eight. The mostly German nuns had a penchant for modesty and made the girls take a bath in three inches of lukewarm water under a sheet. They were also big on cleaning and kitchen duties. Summer didn't come quick enough for the Young girls.

It was that summer that Loretta recalled, "I was walking to the movie theater at 2nd Street and Western Avenue. While I was waiting on the curb, I spotted *him*: Ronald Colman! He was sitting in a roadster, waiting for the old-fashioned wooden "Stop and Go" signal to change. He was just a few feet away from me; I must have stared so hard that he felt it. Just as the signal changed, and just before the car drove off, he turned, looked at me, and gave me a warm smile. At that moment I knew that I loved him and that he loved me, too. Also at that moment I renewed my vow to become a movie star."

The Young girls did not return to Sacred Heart, and at midterm the following school year, enrolled at Ramona Convent School, another Catholic girls' boarding school, also located in Alhambra. Operated by French nuns, it offered more of what Gladys wanted for her daughters. Betty Jane remembered, "At Ramona you learned how to sew and embroider and how to model fruit. You learned table manners. You were waited upon."

Gretchen made a new best friend, Jane Frances Mullen. Jane's mother was from old Los Angeles money, and her father was the Mullen of the department store, Mullen and Bluitt. Jane Mullen Sharpe described Ramona Convent School, "It was the best girls' school in Southern California; the students were mostly from 'good families.' Boarding school was the in-thing to do in those days. Your family didn't send you off to get rid of you like they do nowadays. It wasn't the policy to take students on credit as it were, but for Gretch's mother, that was the case. The Archbishop, or someone who knew her to be a very good woman, must have said, 'Take these girls and I guarantee you, you will be paid off.' When Gretch and I met, we were both nine, but we soon celebrated our tenth birthday just weeks apart. Since we only went home once a month, our whole world was Ramona and your best friends were such best friends."

Gretchen enjoyed Ramona but it was still school, and she hated that part of it. "If I could have spelled, I would have enjoyed school. But if you can't do something and you keep pushing on it, you're butting your head on a stone wall. I just thought that I was dumb, but it didn't make any difference since I was going to be a 'movie star.' And I didn't think that I was dumb in anything except in the schoolroom. I knew that I was always a pleasing child, very pliable and wanting to please."

The Ramona experience lasted just one year, from January to January, interspersed with the summer break. Shortly after coming home, they were in for a big surprise. Gladys and George Belzer had been married in Santa Ana, California, by a Justice of the Peace. Someone told the girls that afternoon about the marriage. Loretta recalled, "We kids decorated Mama's bed by draping flowers all over it so we knew that marriage had something to do with the bed."

Gladys had moved again, this time to a house at Harvard and Washington. With each move, they progressed to a better neighborhood, and Gladys continued taking in boarders. As luck would have it, it was right across the street from where the Mullens lived, so Gretchen was able to see Jane when she came home from Ramona once a month. Still pre-adolescent, they spent much of their time playing on the gym bars in the Mullen garden.

Ernest Traxler, like Earle eight years previously, left his family. As Gladys had turned to Aunt Collie in Los Angeles when she left Earle in Salt Lake City, it was now Gladys's turn to rescue. Gladys helped Aunt Collie set up a boarding house operation next door to her own. It was natural for Gladys to take responsibility. The pattern had been established with the three Royal girls long ago in the convent school. Gladys would be strong enough for all of them.

A new baby arrived and was named Georgiana after her father. The only one of the girls to have blue eyes, she seemed quite exotic, and her sisters played with her like an adorable doll.

When Polly Ann was 17 and Betty Jane 15, they started attending the Saturday Afternoon Tea Dance at the Coconut Grove which was located in the Ambassador Hotel. Betty Jane recalled those afternoons. "We each paid $2.50 for which we got a tall drink of tea and a pastry. We'd all come single, and there would be twelve girls at a huge round table. We'd be wearing dresses or blouses and skirts, always looking clean but not chic. Mom made most of our clothes. And, of course, the guys would be there. Some looking for the prettiest girl, but others were trying to figure out who was the best dancer because they wanted to win the cup which was given away every Saturday."

The guys were flocking around Betty Jane, not only because she was pretty, but because she was, indeed, a good dancer and won quite often. Betty Jane remembered, "I expected to win and when I did, I would sell the cup back to the hotel for $15.00. Then I'd take my share of the money, go buy fabric, and Mom would make a new dress."

Jack and Bill Hearst, sons of William Randolph Hearst, were smitten by the older Young sisters. Bill set his sights on Polly Ann and Jack was in love with Betty Jane. Jack Hearst had a motorcycle and Betty Jane loved cruising around Los Angeles with her hands around his waist. In their youthful exuberance, they became secretly engaged for a brief time.

An opportunity arose to work in movies through dancing at The Coconut Grove. Betty Jane explained, "Milton Bren, he eventually married Claire Trevor, was a darling boy who also came to the Saturday afternoon dances. He was a second assistant director on a picture at MGM called BROWN CULVER starring William Haines and directed by Clarence Brown. Clarence Brown was watching a dance sequence in rehearsal and complained, 'These kids, these extras, they're not like school children. They are too damn dull; there's nothing going on.' Milton Bren was listening and he said, 'I'll get a whole gang.' Milton called us. We all went to the studio and each of us got $7.50 a day. We danced before the cameras rolled, after the camera shut-off, anytime."

Betty Jane had struck up a friendship with a girl from Texas, two years older than she, who was an up and coming actress at MGM. Her name was Joan Crawford; she was already a leading lady but not yet a star. Betty Jane described the relationship. "I was Joan's lackey. I just was. I'd go to her apartment to do her hair all the time because she had a permanent and it frizzed and I would unfrizz it. In return she'd give me all kinds of dresses and stuff to make up."

Through Joan, Betty Jane got work in Universal's Collegiate pictures and was able to bring Polly Ann along as well. They worked at Universal for a year before Betty Jane was rediscovered again. She explained. "I was at the Coconut Grove with my boyfriend, Tommy Lee, and Felix Young heard me laughing. He passed a note asking if I would come to Paramount for a test. Tommy just wanted to cut Felix's throat he was so jealous. But I did go, did the test, and got a contract."

Betty Jane recalled her first meeting with Bud Shulberg who ran Paramount Studios. "He had been out of town when the studio signed me. When he came back, someone told him, 'We signed the cutest little girl, and her name is Betty Jane Young.' He said, 'Good, good, good.' So I went to his office and he said, 'Good God! That doesn't suit you at all.' I didn't know what he was talking about. It was my name. They gave me the name *Sally Blane*, and I didn't answer to it for, I guess, two months."

Sally was making $50 per week as a Paramount stock girl at age fifteen, considerably more than her step-father, George Belzer, was earning as a bookkeeper. She assumed the debt still owed Romona Convent and would go to the school to make the payments. Sally remembered, "The nuns were absolutely shocked when I went out there wearing the make-up from the studio."

Sally's career looked very promising that first year at Paramount. At age 16 she was already a leading lady in CASEY AT THE BAT, SWISS MISS and DEAD MAN'S CURVES, the latter with Douglas Fairbanks, Jr. These films were in the twilight of the silent movie era.

Sally's career may have been in full gear, but she managed to maintain a very active social life. The family had moved to a home they purchased at 6507 W. 5th Street, and with Gladys's encouragement, it was the in-place to be. In addition to the Young girls, Josephine Saenz and Jane Mullen helped attract the waves of young men.

Gretchen, too, got her share of attention, much to the chagrin of Joan Crawford. Dorothy Manners, another girl from Texas, who attended the Saturday Afternoon Tea Dances at the Coconut Grove, and who would become a major Hollywood columnist, recalled, "I got a phone call from Joan Crawford one evening. 'Dorothy, this is Joan. Guess what happened? We have to take Gretch to the Tea Dance on Saturday!' I asked, 'Who's going to pay for her?' Joan replied, 'Mrs. Belzer's going to pay for her.' Joan was dating Mike Cudahy of the meat-packing-family and had borrowed his car for the day. When we picked the Young girls up, Gretchen was such a beauty; it was embarrassing. She was wearing a floppy hat with a rose on it. When we got to the Ambassador Hotel, all the stags made a rush for Gretch, and Joan was furious. The usual pattern was that Joan held forth at our table, and all of us other girls were like ladies-in-waiting. After we let the Young girls off at their home, Joan said, 'Well, that's the last time Gretchen is ever going to go with us. I don't care if it breaks up my friendship with Pol and Bet.' "

It was a different story at school. Loretta recalled, "I didn't talk because I knew I wasn't a good student and I didn't want to draw attention to myself." One day at St. Thomas, when Gretchen was in the eighth grade, this exemplary behavior backfired. Loretta further recalled, "A lady lay teacher said, 'This class is rowdy and I don't want any more of it. We're going to have spelling in about twenty minutes, and whoever in the room has behaved the best will be allowed to give out the spelling words.' Twenty minutes went by and I heard her say, 'All right, Gretchen, you may come up and give out the spelling words.' I went cold because I couldn't read them. I just looked at her, and she repeated my name again. I had to get up, and everybody was looking at me as I went up. I thought, 'Well, I can't just stand here, so I said softly to her, 'I can't read them.' She said, 'Sit down right next to me, Gretchen because I don't want to have to hurt my neck.' She moved over her chair, and she whispered each word to me. From that moment on I adored the ground that woman walked on."

Polly Ann was already dating college men. One day while working on location at Southern California University as Dolores Costello's stand-in for THE COLLEGE WIDOW, she met a football player named Marion Morrison who eventually would change his name to John Wayne. Shortly thereafter, she was his first date at a fraternity function after he pledged Sigma Chi. Later on he asked out Carmen Saenz, sister of Polly Ann's childhood friend, Josie. When they returned to the Saenz residence, Josie was home. A week later, he was dating Josie.

Polly Ann also did stand-in work for Joan Crawford. Being made up like Joan and wearing her clothes, she often posed for the billboard art that promoted Joan Crawford movies. The casting director thought of Polly Ann when Clarence Brown was preparing to shoot an MGM picture in Colorado. The leading lady would either be Dolores Costello or Joan Crawford; it was still undecided, so in the interim, Polly Ann was hired to go to Denver to do the long-shots. At the same time, Mervyn LeRoy, a gag-writer for Colleen Moore at First National Studios and also serving as a casting director, called Polly Ann at home. There was a bit part as one of five girls in a boarding school in the Colleen Moore comedy, NAUGHTY BUT NICE. Polly Ann recalled, "Mervyn LeRoy had given me a lot of work, and I didn't want to say no, but this picture in Colorado was coming up in about two weeks. I said, 'Oh, Mom, what will I do?' She said, 'Call Mervyn back and ask him if he can use Gretchen instead.' So I did, and then I went on to Colorado to do the picture for Metro."

Mervyn did call back for Gretchen. Loretta recalled, "He asked if I wanted to come to First National Studios for an interview and added, 'Just ask for Mervyn LeRoy who's working with Colleen Moore.' I said, 'Fine.' I went and told Mama all about it, and she said, 'Well Honey, if you want to go, I'll give you the money for the fare, but you'll have to go alone. I'm not going to transfer on the bus three times to go out to First National Studios. '"

Thirteen-year-old Gretchen did go, and although she did have to transfer three times that day to get to Burbank, she had no idea what a fast trip she was taking.

Chapter 5: LEADING LADY

Mervyn LeRoy thought that Gretchen would do nicely for a bit part in NAUGHTY BUT NICE. She would have two words to say, and since it was a silent picture, it wouldn't make any difference what her voice sounded like. But mouthing those two words made it a bit part which was a step higher than a walk-on. The next day, Gretchen again transferred three times on the bus, and started work.

Gretchen continued to get bit parts in First National Studios films and a few months later was assigned to HER WILD OAT, again starring Coleen Moore. Miss Moore wrote in her 1968 autobiography, *Silent Star*, "One day I saw among the extras the most beautiful little girl I had ever seen. I suggested that we make a test of her. When I saw the test the next day with the studio brass, I was elated. She was even better than her promise. Convinced now that they had another Corrine Griffith on their hands, the bosses wanted to change her name to something more romantic than her own name of Gretchen Young. So I named her after the most beautiful doll I ever had: Loretta."

Loretta recalled her mother reading the paper one day and saying, "'Well, you've got a new name I see.' I really didn't like the name Loretta. There was a girl who sat right in front of me in the second grade with beautiful, long, dark braids. I was so jealous of those braids that I couldn't see straight, and her name had been Loretta."

As for salary, Loretta held out for the same amount Sally got at Paramount. Polly Ann recalled, "The first time Gretch came home with her weekly contract check, she handed it to Mom and said, 'Mom, look!' Mom said, 'What is this! A child making fifty dollars a week!' Mom just couldn't get over it; she was so happy. That became the regular pattern. Loretta gave whatever money she earned to Mom to handle, unquestioningly."

Loretta would go to the portrait gallery and pose for pictures on the days she wasn't working on the set. She emulated Corrine Griffith, First National Studios's resident beauty and heroine, and would ask the hairdresser to do her hair like Miss Griffith. She also learned to pose like her by keeping her lips slightly parted. After pretending to be Corrine Griffith for six months, Loretta recalled a meeting with Studio Head, Al Rockett, "I went into his office, and he had a bunch of my pictures on his desk. He said to me, 'I had these sent over because I don't want to see one more picture of you trying to look like Corinne Griffith. We already have a Corrine Griffith here; you can't be a second anything.' I didn't quite believe it, but I didn't pose like Corrine Griffith anymore because I knew that he'd see the pictures and would bawl me out again. That was my first lesson on *originality*. That's the name of the movie star game: Be one's self at all costs."

Colleen Moore left First National Studios, and Loretta decided to move her things into the vacant star dressing-room. Her logic was that by moving into the star dressing room, she would be a star. After a few days, she was, once again, summoned by Mr. Rockett. Loretta recalled, "In a very understanding voice, he said, 'Gretchen, I'm fully confident that someday you are going to be a very important star. But you're not there yet and for the time being, I'm going to have to ask you to take your things back to the dressing room that you were sharing with the other stock players. '"

Loretta went on location to San Juan Capistrano for THE ROSE OF MONTEREY starring Mary Astor and Gilbert Roland. It was another bit part and Loretta was accompanied by Gladys and Mrs. Holiday, the tutor assigned to Loretta. These were still silent movie days, and Loretta remembered the process as pretty simple. "You didn't have a script. You didn't know anything. The director would say, 'Now you walk in the room and you go over there and stand by that chair, and that man will come into the door, and you look at him, and you like him a lot, and then he'll come over to you, and probably put his arm around you, and you will be shy, and then you'll pull away from him. Do you think you can do all that?' 'Well, yes.' The mood music added to the ease of the experience. They always had a little organ and a violin or maybe a guitar and they played music all day long. "

Loretta played star Estelle Taylor's daughter in THE WHIP WOMAN. The role wasn't much, but it caught the attention of Herbert Brenon, the temperamental director of such hits as PETER PAN and THE PASSION FLOWER. Brenon was casting LAUGH, CLOWN, LAUGH at MGM, a Lon Chaney vehicle about a sad clown who falls in love with a young girl only to lose her to a younger man. Brenon considered forty-seven young actresses and then chose Loretta. She recalled him telling her, "'Your legs can be padded, likewise your body. It's your eyes that are getting you the part.'" Loretta was just fourteen-years-old when she was selected to play the leading lady role at a prestigious studio like MGM. It was a leapfrog jump to her objective of becoming a movie star, but there was a price to pay. Herbert Brenon.

Loretta recalled, "He had had a nervous breakdown and been in a sanitarium, but since he had just done PETER PAN, and it was a big hit, that made him a hot shot, no matter whether he was crazy or not. He made my life miserable. He would tell the entire company to sit down, and then he would stand me up and go on a tirade. Every day, after lunch, I'd get this bawling out for no reason at all. His assistant director had said to me, 'Now, he doesn't like crybabies, so don't cry.' So no matter what he said to me, I wouldn't cry; I'd just gulp it down. The worst part was that when he would tell me how terrible I was, I believed him."

Polly Ann was under a six month stock contract to MGM at the time. She remembered, "It was late in the day, and I went over to the set where Gretch was working, and she saw me and came running up, 'Oh, I'm so glad to see you. Pol; the director is so mean to me.' Loretta then quoted Brenon , 'You can't do anything right. I should have had your sister Polly Ann instead of you.' That was cruel. So I would go over there as often as I could just to give her support. She would just shake before she would go on the set to work."

Loretta expanded on why her fears of Brenon were well founded. "One day, apparently I wasn't moving quickly enough, and he threw one of those canvas director's chairs at me. If he had hit me he could have killed me. Everyone else was horrified, but they were also scared to death of him. He would pick on one person mercilessly, and they were all afraid that he'd switch from me to them. Another day, we were filming on location in some botanical gardens in Pasadena, and I was supposed to climb over this fence that was covered with greenery. It had barbed wire under the greenery; he couldn't see it, but I could. I kept saying, 'This barbed wire hurts.' He said, 'No, no, no, just keep climbing, just keep going up.' My legs were a mess, they were bleeding, but I kept climbing because I was really frightened of him.

"Another day we were in a theater on the back lot of Metro, and it held about 1,000 people, all extras. The scene centered on me walking a tightrope across the stage. What everyone is afraid about walking a tightrope, besides falling off, is that when the wire rolls, if you don't roll with it, it will roll against you and cut your feet. The camera was way in the back of the theatre, and Brenon came up to the stage and said, 'Now Loretta, all you have to do is walk onto the stage, take a bow and go up and stand with the parasol, and I will cut to the double going across the line.' Finally I get up there and I stop, and he yells, 'You're spoiling my shot. Walk across the wire.' I looked down. 'Oh, all right,' I said to myself. So I'm walking across the wire, and I was doing fine until I looked down on the first rows, and there were a couple of extras that I had worked with before, and this one woman had this horrified look on her face. That scared me, and I lost my balance and fell. The stage was wood, and as I slid across it, the splinters dug into my legs. The whole audience was appalled. Brenon came tearfully down the aisle. 'Oh my little star. Oh, what have I done! I've injured my little star.' I remember thinking, 'Oh, shut up! You're a mean, nasty man; you really don't care at all. '"

Brenon's torment of Loretta ended the day that Lon Chaney returned to the set unexpectedly and witnessed the cruelty. Loretta recalled, "From then on, Lon Chaney would not leave the set when I was working, and Brenon pulled back. Lon Chaney was wonderful to me. If I couldn't get it on the first or second take, he'd come up behind me and say, 'Try this, or try that.'" Chaney, the renowned genius at body makeup, personally designed the padding to convert Loretta from a skinny teenager to a shapely leading lady.

LAUGH, CLOWN, LAUGH did well at the box office. As far as the leading lady's contribution, *Variety* pronounced, "Loretta Young was a rather pale personality for the principal feminine role." Nevertheless, LAUGH, CLOWN, LAUGH established Loretta as a leading lady. Loretta reflected, "From then on I stayed in leads. It wasn't because I was a better actress than some of the other girls that were under contract, but I looked like a leading lady. I was delicate looking, and that's what they thought women should look like in those days, slender, soft and vulnerable."

Loretta's next picture was a First National Studios comedy, THE HEAD MAN, directed by Eddie Cline. Cline had played one of the

Keystone Cops for Max Sennett, providing him an excellent background for comedy.

A loan-out to Paramount followed. THE MAGNIFICENT FLIRT was a period drama directed by Harry D'Arrast. One day, he said to Loretta, "'In this scene you cry. You can cry?' I said, 'Oh yes', but when the scene came along, I couldn't. The director asked, 'Is there anything I can do to help you?' I said, 'Mr. Cline used to put his arm around me and just say, 'Oh, Honey, Oh, Honey.' He said, 'What?' Anyway, he thought I was crazy, and he didn't attempt it. The assistant director came over to me and asked, 'Loretta, do you think if we could get Eddie Cline over here?' I said, 'I just finished a picture and I cried all the time.' So they called Eddie Cline at First National Studios. He came over to Paramount and walked me around the block about five minutes, and I came back crying big tears." Loretta theorized, "I could never cry for Harry D'Arrast because I had had a big crush on him, and I was embarrassed." Crushes would practically become standard procedure for Loretta with each ensuing movie.

Both Loretta and Sally were leading ladies, but their priorities weighed differently. For Sally, it was just another facet of her very full, very fun-filled life. Loretta recalled, "For every suitor that Polly Ann or I had, Sally had three." Jane Mullen Sharpe recalled, "By far, Sally was the most beautiful when they were young. She was dazzling."

For Loretta, being a leading lady was deadly serious. Her zeal to progress as an actress was noticed when, still at age fifteen, she played the captain's daughter in First National Studios's SCARLETT SEAS, starring Richard Barthelmess. Barthelmess had been D.W. Griffith's favorite male actor and was considered quite the romantic hero and a big star. One day Loretta was doing her studies on the side of the set with her tutor, Mrs. Holiday. Loretta recalled, "We were sitting right near the door. The producer came in and said, 'Hey Dick, I just saw the rushes; this little lady is a scene stealer.' I got red as a beet. Dick Barthelmess looked at me. I tried to get deep into my books and study. He walked over to me and said, 'Gretchen, when you get to be a big star, and I think you're going to be one, remember, always get the very best actors around that you can. The better they are, the better you look, and, if it's a Loretta Young picture, you get the credit for it; they don't.'"

SCARLETT SEAS was released in December, 1928 and was billed to have sound. It wasn't a "talkie" but had sound effects. Hardly revolutionary at this point since Warner Brothers had released THE JAZZ SINGER ("Al Jolson sings!") in October, 1927. The Warner brothers, who originated from Youngstown, Ohio, scored such a coup that they could afford to buy the First National Studios and move their operations from Sunset Boulevard to First National Studios's expansive Burbank lot.

SCARLETT SEAS did represent an important first for Loretta. It was the first time that she saw her name on the marquee. She remembered, "I just stood and looked at it for quite a while. I was thrilled."

To see her name on many more marquees, Loretta would have to prove herself as a talking actress. Her first trial came with THE SQUALL directed by Alexander Korda. Set in Hungary, the story dealt with evils brought upon a household when a gypsy girl, played by Myrna Loy, descended upon them. Loretta's first words ever heard on screen were, "Look, it's the gypsies!"

Promoted as "All Dialogue" the ponderous script vocalized every thought. Sound stages had yet to be developed, and the company shot the whole picture at night. Loretta recalled, "Many times we stopped in the middle of the scene, and the director would say, 'Sorry, we got a truck. All right, start all over again.' The camera was in a booth, so you didn't hear the click, click, click sound. The microphone was the god on the set. If you turned away for a second, they would stop and say, 'I'm sorry; I didn't get it on the microphone. '"

Reviewing Loretta's performance in THE SQUALL, *Variety* stated, "Loretta Young as the innocent Irma is a beautiful screen subject. Her voice, however, is identical with commencement exercises in a grammar school."

Loretta played the title role of a movie theatre ticket seller in THE GIRL IN THE GLASS CAGE. A fight over her character, resulting in murder, culminated in a courtroom finale. In real life, Loretta was the one who won a reprieve. THE GIRL IN THE GLASS CAGE was originally slated to be all dialogue, but it ended up "dumb," and the verdict on Loretta's speaking voice would have to be weighed in Loretta's next film, FAST LIFE.

Loretta was sixteen when she made FAST LIFE, the first of six movies that she would co-star with Douglas Fairbanks, Jr. Released before GIRL IN THE GLASS CAGE, *The New York Times* gave this review of Loretta's performance, "Loretta Young shows more promise with each production. One of Hollywood's prettiest ingénues, she is also gifted with an excellent speaking voice." Loretta had triumphantly navigated the hurdle of Talking Pictures. Huge stars of the silent screen such as Colleen Moore, Mae Murray and Corrine Griffith would all fall by the wayside within the next few years.

Hollywood was in transition. When Warner Brothers took over First National Studios, their publicity man, Hal Wallis, became the Studio Manager. Daryl Zanuck also arrived from Sunset Boulevard to the Burbank lot. Loretta remembered that he was "one of the little writers."

Polly Ann, Sally, and Loretta were all working in films; Loretta and Sally as leading ladies, and Polly Ann as a contract player. However, Polly Ann's and Sally's careers were about to hit snags. MGM did not pick up Polly Ann's option after she appeared in MGM's FLESH AND THE DEVIL as John Gilbert's scorned lover, and jobs became more sporadic. Sally's troubles began when a top studio executive wanted Sally to be his mistress. Sally remembered, "He even had the studio attorneys come and tell what they would give me, and how they would write it into the contract." Sally, still a teen, had a very adult problem and no one to come to her rescue. The only way that she could extract herself from the mire was to walk away from a contract with Paramount, one of the premier studios in the industry.

Gladys wanted the girls to know and stay close to their faith and invited a priest to dinner on Thursday nights, usually Father Ward. He was a Jesuit who taught at Loyola High School. Loretta remembered, "After dinner, everyone did the dishes, including the guest, and it was like a group therapy session. We had a marvelous time, and Father Ward handled it very well."

Gladys's concerns about her daughters' development went beyond spiritual considerations. She would invite an English teacher friend a couple of nights a week to help the girls polish their diction as well as discuss topics such as Opera and Art. Polly Ann reflected back on these sessions, "I knew that this was all good for me, hut I often wished that lady just wasn't there. I probably had to endure more of it because Gretch and Sally were working more regularly."

Loretta lived more autonomously than Polly Ann and Sally. She recalled those days, "Pol and Sally shared a bedroom. Either I got the pull-down bed in the alcove off the living room, or if visitors came, I had the maid's room downstairs, and the maid slept on the back porch. The point is that I had my privacy quite early." Loretta also recalled, "I thought I was a big, hot-shot, movie actress at this time, which indeed, I was. But at home I was Gretchen fitting in where I could."

Her career continued in high gear. She starred opposite Douglas Fairbanks, Jr. in THE CARELESS AGE, a musical comedy set in England. It was advertised as "All Dialogue" and this distinction would soon become an assumption. Loretta would never backtrack again to the silent movie days.

Loretta was cast in another musical, THE FORWARD PASS, and again, paired with Douglas Fairbanks, Jr.. *Variety* reviewed it as: "Football backed by a quartet of tunes, one of which Loretta Young warbles. A contralto, she's not hard on the ear."

LOOSE ANKLES with Douglas Fairbanks, Jr., followed. Loretta had every reason to feel that her career was progressing nicely. The studio provided the ultimate affirmation by picking up her option every six months and raising her salary by $50 per week. They got their money's worth. At one time she was actually making three pictures simultaneously. Loretta remembered, "There was one in the morning, one in the afternoon, and one at night. Mrs. Holiday never knew about the one at night because they would say to me, 'We're going to dismiss you and you go to the dressing room, but don't take your make-up off. Then Mrs. Holiday will go home, and when she's gone, then you come back on the set, and we'll work tonight.' It never bothered me; I loved working."

However, the studio didn't play fair. Loretta was sixteen when she was hospitalized for complications of a painful ovulation and the studio took her off salary while she was ill. Loretta recalled a young visitor who came to see her. "The nurse came in and said, 'There's a little boy outside. He said his name is Mickey Rooney (at age nine).' The nurse didn't seem to know who he was. She said, 'He's got a bunch of flowers, and he wants to give them to you.' I said, 'Ask him to come in.' He gave me the flowers and I asked him, 'How did you get down here?' He was just a little kid. He said, 'My car and driver brought me.'

"He asked me, 'How much do you work?' I told him that I worked a lot, sometimes doing three pictures at the same time. He asked, 'Do you work Saturdays?' I said, 'Yes,' and it bothered me because I used to love going to the Coconut Grove Tea Dances. He said, 'Well, you're a minor. You don't have to work Saturdays or Sundays. You can work only five days a week, and you have an hour and a half for lunch, and you work from nine until six, and that's it. You have to have four hours of schooling and four hours of acting.' I said, 'Oh,' and the whole thing began to open up. They would work me so hard, and then if I'd get sick, they'd take me off salary. I wouldn't have minded it if they hadn't taken me off salary. I knew that was wrong.

"When I returned to work, I went to see Hal Wallis. I waited a couple of hours to see him and finally the secretary said, 'All right, Gretchen, you can go in.' I said, 'Mr. Wallis, I've been in the hospital.' He said, 'Yes, I know.' Then I said, 'I've been told that since I'm a minor, I have certain rights.' He said, 'You're absolutely right; that's true.' So, I said, 'From now on, I'll just work from nine until six, and I'll have an hour and a half for lunch and a rest period.' He said, 'Fine.' And, those were the hours that I put into my contracts for the rest of my career."

Even though Loretta was, at age 16, an established leading lady, she was still travelling back and forth to the studio on a streetcar, or a bus, or with friends. Loretta remembered missing a bus and feeling panicky. "I knew I was going to be late, and I was scared to death. I had been bawled out by Herbert Brenon for being late on the set of LAUGH, CLOWN, LAUGH, and I never wanted to be late again. I called a friend, Bill Geotz, who was Daryl Zanuck's assistant. I was crying, and I said, 'Bill, I'm at the corner of Sunset and Cahuenga Boulevard. I missed the bus.' 'All right, all right, Gretch, calm down. I'll come and get you.' He got in his little car and picked me up. I did just get on the set on time."

Loretta was determined to get her own car. She recalled, "I went into Jack Warner's office. I don't think I even saw him, but I told the secretary that I wanted to see if Mr. Warner would loan me the money and then take it out of my salary." A few weeks later Loretta recalled participating in a Motion Picture Rally at the Los Angeles Coliseum. "All the starlets from different studios rode around in open cars. I was sitting on the back of a convertible touring car. Jack Warner jumped on the running board and said, 'Hey Kid,' and patted me on the head. 'You're going to get the car; I'm going to give you the loan.' It made my day."

Loretta was seated next to a curly haired, ruggedly handsome, Warner Brothers leading man, Grant Withers. At 6'3, 185 pounds, Withers was a big guy. The hunk and the fragile beauty. They looked like a perfect Hollywood couple.

CHAPTER 6: LEADING MAN

In 1931 and 1932, Loretta Young was featured as leading lady in fifteen pictures; each film was in production for a period lasting ten weeks to three months. Loretta remembered, "When you worked as hard as we did, and in as many different pictures, you really didn't depend on your social life for your recreation because there was so much of it while you were working. If you were fortunate enough to fall a little bit in love with every leading man, it substituted for any sort of serious romance that you might have. Then you went home and slept so that you could come back onto the set the next morning."

Loretta played opposite John Barrymore in THE MAN FROM BLANKLEYS. This would be Barrymore's last picture playing the romantic lead. Loretta recalled the experience, "I had an enormous crush on him. On the set he looked absolutely marvelous. The story centered on a dinner party and he was wearing dinner clothes. We shot it at the old Warner Brothers studio on Sunset, and you had to go up a flight of stairs to get to the dressing rooms. I was just leaving my dressing room for the set one morning when this wild apparition flew up the steps wearing pajamas and an overcoat flowing back, and what hair there was, flying in the wind. He flew past me and said, 'Good morning, Loretta.' I didn't realize who it was until he walked on the set. He said, 'Now, 1 wasn't very long, was I?' 1 had seen him before he got all his make-up on, and his corsets, and everything he was wearing at the time. The crush was crushed, I'm sorry to say."

Grant Withers was a twenty-four-year-old leading man when he and Loretta were paired in SECOND FLOOR MYSTERY. Grant must have been a refreshing change for sixteen-year-old Loretta compared to the forty-six-year-old Barrymore. Grant was from a Pueblo, Colorado newspaper family and had held several adventure jobs before crashing through Warner Brothers' studio gate. He had been a fire warden, a fireman, and a driver for one of Los Angeles's police riot cars. Withers had appeared in over a dozen pictures before SECOND FLOOR MYSTERY. Per usual, Loretta developed her leading man crush.

Loretta saw Grant as "more of a nice fellow than a masculine lead" and her family saw him as just another beau. Loretta recalled, "I had kissed him, but never in what I would call a passionate way. I don't think I knew much about that at sixteen years of age." But she was feeling some kind of pressure. Sally remembered that Loretta had said to Gladys, "'No matter what I say, don't give your approval to marry Grant. '"

Loretta recalled when Grant did ask her to marry him. I said,
"'Oh, I don't think so.' Then he told me, 'I'll die if you don't. I'll
kill myself.' Like an idiot, I believed him. It was very difficult for
me to say no to anybody about anything. I just wanted to please
people." She was now faced with Grant's life in her hands.
Masking the ominous nature of this responsibility were her
romantic fantasies. She would be the leading lady who runs off
with the leading man, and they would live happily ever after.

Grant had been a teenager at the time of his first marriage. He
was not Catholic but his first wife was, and they had been
married in the Catholic Church. They had a son, Robert Granville
Withers. The previous marriage prevented Grant and Loretta
from marrying in the Catholic Church, so he made arrangements
for an elopement. Loretta didn't share her secret elopement
plans with her sisters or friends. Polly Ann and Sally shared
everything with each other, but it was Loretta's reflex to keep
her thoughts to herself. It was also her lifelong reflex to avoid
confrontation which surely would have ensued if her plans
became known.

Sunday morning, January 26, 1930: it was not quite three weeks
past her 17th birthday when Loretta slipped out of the house
while Gladys was at Mass. She remembered her thoughts as they
flew a chartered plane to Yuma, Arizona. "I told myself that I

really wasn't getting married anyway because the ceremony was going to be performed by a Justice of the Peace, and that it wouldn't be recognized as legitimate by the Church." Upon arriving in Yuma, Loretta recalled, "We went to an office; it wasn't a house. It was very hot and I remember thinking, 'This is no way to get married.' We didn't know anybody and I thought, 'Oh, it smells, and it's dirty, and it's hot.' The Justice of the Peace was in his shirt sleeves, and the only other person there was his equally untidy wife."

The *Los Angeles Herald* would report the next day, "They were married by Justice of the Peace Freeman while the idle motor of their plane whirled in impatience."

Meanwhile, Gladys began to suspect something was wrong. She would tell Loretta later that the fact that Loretta had washed all of her nightgowns and had packed them in a neat little pile was a clue because ordinarily, she would have just washed one thing at a time. Polly Ann remembered, "I was so mad at Grant. I was madder at him than I was with Loretta because right as they were running off to get married, he had sent Mama a telegram which I think was so rude. It was like an old cheap dime novel: "By the time you read this, we will be married ..... "

Loretta recalled the newlyweds' plane landing back in Los Angeles. "As I looked down at the field from the plane, the place was filled with cameramen and newsreels. We were both under contract to Warner Brothers, and they were making a screaming circus out of this. I could see Mutt (George Belzer's nickname) standing down there waiting for me. We got out of the plane and he looked furious. He said, 'Your mother wants you to come right home! Right home!' I said, 'All right.'

"When we got home, Mom said, 'What would make you do a thing like this? You know it is a mortal sin for you to be married outside of your own religion.' I said, 'Grant's been married before; we couldn't be married in the church.' She said, 'That's no excuse.' I said, 'Mama, you're the best woman I know and you were married out of the Church.' She just looked at me. Tears popped into her eyes, and she left the room. I think she cried for two days."

Gladys wanted the marriage annulled. First she explored the grounds that Loretta was too young to marry. However, sixteen was old enough for a girl to marry without parental consent in the state of Arizona. They had a family meeting with a lawyer in attendance; even Grant's mother was called in for the conference. The best case was made for the young couple to agree to an annulment, and it looked like they would comply. Loretta continued to live at home, and, two days after the wedding, Grant, speaking for him and Loretta, issued the following statement from the Warner lot on Sunset where they both were working: "We're sorry we eloped and we will abide by Mrs. Belzer's wishes."

Loretta recalled, "Both of us agreed that we would not consummate the marriage. But Grant was feeling a lot of pressure. I think that it was his ego more than anything else because the press was in on the act, and sometimes the press pressures people into doing things that they really don't want to do. They had romanticized this whole thing, and he felt, he never said this to me, but I think he probably felt, 'Ah hell, if we call this whole thing off now, I'll look like a bigger jerk than I am.' So, he talked me into running away to the apartment we had rented at the El Royale to live as husband and wife. Of course, the press loved that."

Loretta's next film was ROAD TO PARADISE. She was playing a dual role as twins, and Polly Ann was working as her double. Loretta recalled, "She was sitting just inches from me, and she didn't speak to me for the whole picture. Mama wasn't speaking to me either. I'd call Mama every day, and she would not come to the phone. One of the girls would say, 'Gretch, I'm sorry, Mom's lying down,' or something. I was so family-oriented, and when my family didn't speak to me, I was isolated and felt like I had done something terrible. I kept calling Mama for two months. Finally, I guess she decided that not speaking to me was no way to handle the situation, so one day she came to the phone and said, 'Yes, Dear.' I said, 'Well, yes Mama, uh, umm, hmm, I just wanted to know, Mama if I can come over to see you?' She said, 'Well, as a matter of fact, I have to go downtown on some errands and if you would like to drive me, you can pick me up.' I was back in good graces. And the minute Mama said it was all right, everybody else loosened up. And, I already knew by that time that I wanted to get out of the marriage."

If Loretta didn't have the fortitude to say no to Grant when he asked her to marry him, it was that much harder to tell him that she wanted out. Loretta entered a state of suspension. She remembered, "I wasn't unhappy with him, and I wasn't happy with him.' They went about the business of living together. Loretta recalled, "He slept in his room and I slept in my room. The honeymoon, of course, we slept in the same bed. But it wasn't anything I wanted to run back to. I knew nothing, absolutely nothing at 17-years-old, and I frankly was a little surprised, quite surprised, and not too enchanted. It wasn't that he was forceful or anything; he wasn't. I must say that he was very patient, but, either I was too dumb or he wasn't very confident. I'm sure I did a lot of play-acting then."

Old friend, Father Ward admonished Loretta a few months after her marriage. She recalled his reproach, "'You cannot be a movie star and go around behaving as if you are little Jane Doe and have nobody paying any attention to you. Everything you do is going to be noted and judged. So better a stone be tied around your neck and dropped into the bottom of the ocean than if you give a bad example. And you have already done it. Two sixteen-year-old Catholic girls have been married out of the Church. Each of them pointed to your example as an excuse. Those sins are on your soul. So decide now whether you want to be an actress and take a chance of losing your soul, or be an actress and behave yourself. It can be done. Other people have done it. '" Loretta's initial inclination was to dismiss Father Ward's reprimand, but as the years passed, his words would ring louder.

She continued to work non-stop. She did KISMET and THE TRUTH ABOUT YOUTH for First National Studios and then was loaned out to MGM for THE DEVIL TO PAY. It had only been eight years earlier when nine-year-old Gretchen had spotted her heartthrob, Ronald Colman, at the intersection of 2nd Street and Western. She was now his leading lady. Loretta recalled, "The first couple of days, I was so crazy about Ronald Colman that I was tongue-tied around him. Director George Fitzmaurice discovered the source of my problem, and he must have said something to Ronald Colman because from then on, Ronnie was just warm enough to make me feel a little bit more at ease around him and still not mislead me in any way." Recounting her crush on Ronald Coleman during THE DEVIL TO PAY, Loretta had forgotten the context of her situation, that she was Mrs. Grant Withers at the time.

BEAU IDEAL, a loan out for RKO, was followed by THE RIGHT OF WAY filmed on her home lot. THREE GIRLS LOST was another loan out, this time to Fox, and it cast her opposite Josie Saenz's boyfriend, who by now called himself John Wayne. In retrospect, Loretta recognized that by this time, both her and John Wayne's screen personas, at least at their core, were already in place.

Grant's screen career was slipping. He was working but not as constantly as Loretta, nor were his films as substantial. Grant used to go hunting with other men from the studio including writer Daryl Zanuck. Loretta remembered, "Grant must have gotten in some sort of argument with Zanuck on one of these outings because a remark got back to me in which Zanuck said, 'He's a half-assed actor anyway. Who cares?' Grant never said anything to me about it, and I didn't want to embarrass him by asking."

The First National Studios brass decided to capitalize on teen-star Loretta's marriage to Grant by pairing them in a film based on the stage play BROKEN DISHES. The studio, not so subtly, retitled it as TOO YOUNG TO MARRY. Grant had received top billing a year earlier with SECOND FLOOR MYSTERY. This time, reflecting the direction their careers were heading, Loretta's name came first.

Grant's need to be a man's man cast further shadow on their fragile marriage. He wanted to be the kind of guy who could drink with the best of them, tease the women, and keep raising the ante at a game of poker. His young bride had initially only a hazy notion of this side of her husband's personality. Once this became more apparent, she missed her mother and sisters all the more.

Loretta's family was aware that Withers' marriage had serious problems. Polly Ann remembered Loretta confiding, that in spite of their combined generous salaries, they only had twenty- five dollars in the bank. And Georgiana, who was seven at the time, recalled, "I had gone over to spend the night with Gretch, and the two of us were sleeping in her bed. I remember being awakened out of a sound sleep. Gretch had gotten up. Grant had come home drunk, and I remember they had a terrible fight. Screaming and yelling, pounding and everything! I remember that I became very afraid. When I got home I told Mama, 'I don't want to go back to Gretch's. '"

Loretta's next two films were for First National Studios. BIG BUSINESS GIRL was followed by I LIKE YOUR NERVE which she co- starred with Douglas Fairbanks, Jr. in their fifth picture together.

Grant was "between pictures" and a few weeks after Loretta's eighteenth birthday, he accepted an offer to go on a personal appearance tour on the vaudeville circuit.

Loretta recalled, "The minute Grant got out of town, I called Mom and said, 'I'm coming home,' and I moved back to 6507 W. 5th Street. Grant wrote letters, but I didn't answer them. I was leaving him; I didn't want to write him any love letters, but I was too much of a chicken to write him and say that I wanted a divorce. One day, Mama said to me, 'Grant's going to call you, and you have to talk to him. You have to be honest with him.' I was too embarrassed to say, 'I don't love you anymore.' That wasn't romantic enough for my ideas in those days. In fact, I didn't know how you were supposed to get out of difficulties in my fantasy world. But I did finally get up the nerve to tell him on the phone."

"When Grant came home, Mama said, 'You two talk it out alone.' Grant kept asking, 'Why?' I said, 'I'm just not in love with you anymore, Grant.' I didn't dare tell him that I never was in love with him. I may have been a lot of things at eighteen years old, but I don't think that I was vicious or cruel. Finally, Mama joined us. She said, 'Grant, she's just too young to be married. And, if she doesn't want to be married, you don't want someone who doesn't want to be married to you.' Poor man. I felt so sorry for him but not sorry enough to stay with him."

On July 2, 1931, Loretta sued for divorce. A hearing was held in Judge Henry M. Ellis' court on September 15, 1931. "No support" was entered as grounds. There was ample evidence that Grant had been a lousy money manager. Although he was still under contract to Warner Brothers at $750 a week and had earned $1,500 a week on the vaudeville tour, he was unable to keep up with his child support payments. Loretta's salary had been attached to pay an account at a drug store. Sally summed it up bluntly, "Grant took Loretta for everything she had. He was in a lot of debt. Apparently, he gambled."

Loretta was seldom conscious of her father and never realized how much Grant had been like him. He was a good-looking man, nice but weak. She had expected him to take care of her but, in the end, he had left the bank account drained.

If Grant was like Earle, Loretta was like her mother, capable of taking care of herself. Her career in high gear, Loretta was now viewed, not only as a leading lady, but as a budding star.

Chapter 7. CONSEQUENCES

Sally's career was in descent. After she walked away from her lucrative Paramount contract, she signed with FBO (Film Booking Office) Studios shortly before the studio was renamed RKO (Radio-Keith-Orpheum). It was Sally Blane who switched the FBO sign for the new RKO. The event was captured by studio photographers and released to wire services. Even at Paramount, she was one of those actresses better known for publicity shots than her movie roles. Photographer John Engstead later told Sally, "You were the Marilyn Monroe of the studio. Whenever they wanted to sell anything, they called you into the portrait gallery."

Sally described the roles she was playing at this time: "The typical leading lady or second-lead love interest. I always played someone full of vim and vigor." William LeBaron, head of RKO, saw a lot of promise in Sally and provided her with various coaches. Mr. LeBaron cast Sally in his pet project, THE VERY IDEA. Not only did Mr. LeBaron adapt the screenplay from a play he had written, but he also cast Hugh Trevor, his nephew, to play the male lead. Unfortunately for all concerned, THE VERY IDEA was a major flop. It hastened Mr. LeBaron's exit from the studio as well as Sally's.

Loretta shared a memory about this time, "Sally and I had the biggest fight we ever had. In Pol and Sally's room, they had a chaise lounge. It was supposed to be what ladies reclined on, but it wasn't very comfortable, so it was just in the room for looks. Sally and Pol used to keep a Spanish shawl draped over it. The shawl had a lot of fringe, and Sally liked to keep it just perfect. I came into the room and flopped down on this lounge, and the fringe went every which way. Sally grabbed me by the hand. She yelled, ' Oh, I just finished straightening that fringe!' Well, I was so surprised, and she was so mad, and then I got mad. The situation escalated, and we literally started slapping each other. Mama came in and said, 'All right, that's enough you two!' And she separated us. That couldn't have been what made her so mad; I don't know what was really behind it."

Everything had come so easily for Sally. She was the one who had been "discovered" and then rediscovered time after time. She was the one considered the family's great beauty. Now she was working freelance. Simultaneously, Warner Brothers determined that the name *Loretta Young* could carry a movie, and that she was worth a lot of money as a loan out.

Loretta was loaned to Columbia to play the title character in GALLAGER with Frank Capra as director. Jean Harlow was cast as the second female lead. Loretta recalled, "Jean looked so voluptuous, so ready to pluck, that when she walked on the set, all the fellahs would go 'UHHHHHHHH' as she walked by. She really didn't walk; she kind of undulated, and she didn't even know she was doing it. I think that's just the way her body moved because she could laugh quicker than anybody else could, and you'd have to take yourself very seriously to pull her sensuality off and not be natural. Frank Capra and Bob Briskin would sit right there on the set and rewrite and add scenes for her just because she was so appealing. I was sitting on the set watching them do it and thinking, 'Gee, I wish they wouldn't do that, but I sure know why they are.' If Jean and I walked into the room together, you weren't going to be looking at me. Then they changed the name of the film from GALLAGER, my character, to THE PLATINUM BLONDE."

However, it was that film in which Loretta learned from Frank Capra the most important lesson that would shape her as an actress. She explained, "We were rehearsing a scene and Robert Williams, the male lead, said, 'Let's try doing it this way.' Being from the New York stage, he was used to improvising. Then Frank said, 'I don't think I like that idea. Where did that come from?' They were talking and, in the middle of it, Frank said, 'What do you think, Loretta?' I said, 'It doesn't make any difference what I think, Mr. Capra. Just tell me what to do; I'll try to do it.' Very gently, he said, 'Oh no, Loretta. THAT'S ALL

ACTING IS: THINKING.' It made sense to me, and Frank Capra was considered the best director in the business. I liked the idea that an actress could think.

"What Frank meant was that I was to put myself into my character's shoes, and that I would listen and react according to what the character would think. You learn to know your character. That character has to have good qualities, bad qualities, irritating qualities; she has to have all the qualities that every human being has. Some of them, if you run out of them, you borrow from yourself; either you exaggerate them or pull them down.

"Frank had a wonderful talent for wooing a performance out of actors. He would say, 'Well, that's charming. Oh do that; I like that.' Of course, that opens you up for the next idea that comes along. If he didn't like something, he'd say, 'You know, if I were you, I think when you come into the room the first time, don't accept him that easily. You'll find your way to do it, but just don't accept him so quickly.' That's what I call direction."

Gladys, too, was about to make a professional leap. Loretta commented, "Decorating had always been in Mama's blood; she had pushed the furniture around with every residence that she called home." But now she was serious and enrolled at the

Chaunnard and Parsons School of Design at the Otis Art Institute in Los Angeles.

Gladys's marriage was floundering as her decorating career was ascending. Like Earle Young, George Belzer had a wandering eye that led him astray. Again, Gladys was unwilling to look the other way. Georgiana recalled how painful her parents' problems were to her, "My mother and father and I shared a bedroom, and we had a long sleeping porch. And I remember Dad's bed was out on the sleeping porch. They were like brother and sister, and I just hated that."

The Belzers and the Young sisters made a major move from 5th Street to Sunset Boulevard in Bel Aire. The white brick home, with gracious columns, was a Southern Colonial built to Gladys's specifications. Polly Ann and Sally now shared a suite instead of a mere room. Everyone contributed, but it was Loretta's salary that primarily made this transition possible.

David Niven, a friend of a friend of Sally's and fresh from England, made his entrance into their lives. He managed to parlay an invitation to stay in their pool house for a couple of days into over a year. Georgiana was acutely aware of his presence as Niven eventually was given her room while she was relegated to the sun porch.

Loretta was too busy working to notice. THE RULING VOICE dealt with a macabre story involving rival gangsters threatening to kidnap each other's children. TAXI, with James Cagney, followed. Cagney had his first major screen success the previous year with PUBLIC ENEMY, but it is dialogue from TAXI that Cagney's imitators have used ever since: "You dirty rat, you." Loretta recalled, "I loved TAXI. I had a big crush on Jimmy, but it was the sweetest, nicest and purest kind of crush. He never knew it. He wasn't one bit interested in me, romantically. He was very happily married. I remember one particular scene set in a nightclub. He's sitting there, and I'm right next to him. He's got his arm around me, and I've got my head on his shoulder, perfectly relaxed. I think our two characters had just been married, and that's the way she felt about him. She was thinking, 'He'll take care of me, this tough little fellow. '"

"I admired the way Jimmy worked. He was all business and still polite at all times. He didn't even particularly talk fast off screen. But the minute the camera rolled, he was that tough character, no getting around it. And I think for a woman to have a man who is violent that way, but she's the only one he's sensitive with, his caring is doubly important to her. Even though I was only playing a part in a picture, I felt a part of that."

TAXI was one of a growing list of Loretta's films that had a strong social message.

She was Warner Brother's perfect victim for the harsh realities of the times. Even when she played characters with a tough edge, her big eyes could retract from a look of defiance and flood the screen with tears.

Writer Daryl Zanuck was instrumental in Warner Brothers' successful thrust of grabbing their storylines out of the newspaper headlines. Loretta never liked Zanuck. She remembered thinking, "He was a pugnacious little man, yelling and screaming all over the place. Daryl always scared me, even then. I found him so ill-mannered; one never knew what to expect."

Loretta also didn't like Howard Hughes, at least as a boyfriend. Loretta recalled, "I just went out with him a few times. He had thrown a party for my nineteenth birthday, but I barely remember it because I wasn't particularly interested in him. He was too bossy, too possessive, too self-oriented."

Loretta did love her increasing financial freedom. She remembered, "I used to get all dressed up. I'd put on my beautiful Russian broadtail coat, gloves, alligator bag, and the right hat, and I'd go to Irene's shop located in Bullocks Wilshire. I would walk in and say, 'Evening clothes.' Someone would say, 'Oh yes, Miss Young,' and they'd parade these evening clothes out and I'd sit and choose one or two. Then I would go and buy shoes. I just loved doing that. It was my idea of being a successful movie star."

Loretta always pre-checked with Gladys to see how much she could spend. Gladys handled all the finances, and Loretta, the major breadwinner, never questioned how the money was used or the amount she was allotted.

Loretta co-starred with Edward G. Robinson in THE HATCHET MAN, her first picture directed by William Wellman. She played a young Chinese girl who, yearning for more excitement, leaves her older husband, and runs off with a younger man. Loretta recalled the elaborate make-up required for the role. "I thought that make-up was just beautiful. Perc Westmore did it. He cut a little hole in some pigskin, and then placed it on the outside of each eye, gluing it down with spirit gum. There was string attached to the pigskin, and they'd pull the two strings in back and tie it behind my head. Of course, it pulled everything back creating a very flat effect. It was marvelous, and the first day on the set, oh, I had the best time. I knew that I looked gorgeous.

"On the third day, when they took the make-up off, there were little chunks of flesh sticking to the pigskin. I started to bleed and we had a terrible time. They sent for the doctor right away, and I didn't work for two days. When they did place new pigskin on again, it burned like mad. It got so that I could work one day, and I had to be off three days, and that's how I did the picture."

The Depression was hurting the movie business; 5,000 of the country's 16,000 movie theaters were closed. In 1932 Fox Studios lost 17 million dollars and Warner Brothers ran an additional deficit of 14 million. In August of that year, the brass decided to cut salaries. Loretta's $1,000 weekly salary was reduced to $800.

Warner Brother's PLAY GIRL was Loretta's last film Loretta released in 1932. Her co-star was Norman Foster who had made a name for himself on the New York stage.

Loretta and Norman were paired immediately again in WEEKEND MARRIAGE. Norman's relationship with Claudette Colbert was cooling, and he was falling under Loretta's spell. He knew that Loretta loved to dance, and asked Sally to show him the latest steps. He didn't see that Sally was falling for him. Georgiana recalled, "Sally was crazy about him. One night Sally and I were watching Loretta leave with Norman, and I remember

Sally running to her room, crying." The fact that Loretta had little interest in Norman aggravated the situation. George Brent, the second male lead in the picture, had caught her attention.

Meanwhile, Polly Ann was playing John Wayne's or Buck Jones' leading lady in a series of Westerns. Polly Ann barely remembered these days, "I couldn't tell you what any of them were about. You could make them in ten days or two weeks; you just said your lines and that was it. Alan Mulbray, an actor who was a good friend of mine, dubbed me *Queen of Poverty Row* because I was the leading lady in so many of these cheap pictures. They weren't all Westerns; some of them were whodunits."

Loretta said of Polly Ann, "She was a beautiful girl, just beautiful, so naturally they would use her in these parts, but Polly Ann really wasn't that hell-bent for a career. I can't imagine her arguing with the director about what she did or did not want to do. I think, for Polly Ann, making movies was just something to do."

Loretta related a revealing story about herself and Polly Ann and how they viewed their perspective careers, "We were both going to the Academy Awards, and both of us were having dresses made by Irene (Irene Sharaff, costume designer, who also had a shop at Bullocks Wilshire) who was a wonderful designer. We went together for the fittings. I kept telling Irene how I wanted my dress to look, whereas Polly Ann just stood there and let the designer design. The night of the Academy Awards she was dressed before I was, and she came into my room. I said, 'Oh Pol, that dress looks great!' Then I put my dress on, and she said, 'Gretch, it's awful!' I looked in the mirror and said, 'Oh, it isn't as bad as I think it is, is it?' She said, 'Yes, it is.' She said, 'Now Gretch, it doesn't make any difference what I look like, but it does make a difference what you look like. So, I'll wear that and you wear this.' And she did, and I did. Pol thought it was important because they were going to photograph me more than they would her."

Loretta and actor Eric Linden were husband and wife in LIFE BEGINS. The film was considered controversial because the subject of pregnancy had been considered too delicate of a topic to be discussed openly. Loretta had gone to a local maternity ward to prepare for her role prior to the filming. Frank Capra's message, that acting required more than what the director told you to do, was penetrating.

George Brent co-starred in THEY CALL IT SIN, and shortly thereafter, they went on a personal appearance tour together. Loretta explained, "We would appear in movie theaters before the feature and play a little skit where we were supposed to be a honeymoon couple. We put this skit on five times a day for a two week period, and I loved every moment of it."

Loretta recalled a particular moment with George Brent while they were on tour, "Isn't it funny the images you have of people? Mama had gone out with some friends of hers, and we were having supper served in my suite. They had brought in a table all set with everything. He was sitting in the chair; he had his legs crossed, and he looked so comfortable and so easy. He was a good looking man. As the waiter came in to take the table away, he was just sitting there with a cigarette, and he looked just like a painting. It was the best looking thing I ever saw, just sitting there quietly, a soft smile on his face.

"I was crazy about him and he was crazy about me. We decided that we were very much in love with each other. In those days I don't know whether I was interested in marriage or not, but I was certainly interested in being in love. George had made a picture with Ruth Chatterton prior to our going on tour, and there was publicity in the papers about the two of them being engaged. He never mentioned Ruth except to say that it was over with her. He must have told me a hundred times how much he loved me.

"We finished the tour in Washington, D.C., and Mom, George, and I, took a train to Chicago. There, Mom and I were to board a train for the coast, and George was going to New York to tell Ruth about the two of us. We were about to go to one train and he to another, and I remember him saying to me, 'No matter what happens, no matter what happens, I love you.' I responded, 'I love you, too!'

"I gave his parting comment one slight, little thought, and that was all. Mama came into my compartment and woke me up the next day. She was carrying a newspaper in her hands, and she said, 'Gretch, I didn't want you to see this in the dining car.' It said in great big print, "George Brent and Ruth Chatterton Marry." He had gone to New York to meet her the night before; she was coming in from Europe, and they went right to a Justice of the Peace and got married. 'So that's what he was talking about,' I thought. I said, 'Oh Mom, I don't believe it.' I made myself sick about him. This went on more or less for about a year. My stomach would jump if I saw his car go by."

If Loretta was suffering in real life, so was the character she was playing in EMPLOYEE'S ENTRANCE. Loretta played a model in a department store who, although married, sleeps with the big, bad, boss, played by Warren William. Plagued with guilt, she takes poison only to be rescued by her husband.

Meanwhile Sally was busy freelancing. She recalled, "I did five or six Zane Grey Westerns with Randolph Scott. I remember Randy telling me, 'Sally, whenever they have a Western that's coming up, and they need a girl that everybody can all stand to live with on location, they always say, 'Well, let's get Sally Blane. She's pretty, she's clean, and she looks like she's a good girl.'"

Loretta and Sally were clearly on different career tracks, and Sally remembered that the preferential treatment that Loretta had at the studio continued at home. "When Loretta would go to Warner Brothers, she had a wardrobe woman, a hairdresser, and a make-up girl. They all ran errands for her, bringing her tea, coffee, anything she wanted. She never lifted her little finger, and she'd come home, and she'd just say to Mom, 'Oh, I'm tired.' So my mother would go in and get hot cloths and put them on her eyes and then put on cold cloths, and she would rub her feet. Mom was just always very, very close to Loretta. Now, I would go out and do a five-day picture. I didn't have the hairdresser, any make-up woman, any of this. I did the same thing. I'd come home and say, 'Oh, I'm tired.' Mom would reply, 'Go to bed, Dear.' So, that was the difference."

In Loretta's days of movie making, no matter how torrid a screen kiss might appear, there was never any tongue contact, just closed lips kissing. The one exception occurred during the filming of GRAND SLAM. Loretta played the wife of Paul Lucas who, at age thirty-eight, was twice as old as his leading lady. Loretta recalled, "Paul dived down my throat in a kiss, and I was so horrified, I backed up. Sidney Hickocks was the cameraman and saw what happened. He said to Paul, 'You son of a bitch; if you ever do that again, I'll blast you!' He didn't do it again."

Loretta had another kissing problem on the set of ZOO IN BUDAPEST. She related, "I didn't like kissing this little monkey; she was smelly and she scared me to death. She would get a hold of my blonde wig and keep pulling on the braids. Putting it politely, she used my wig as her litter box, and I spent a great deal of time changing wigs. We finally had four wigs in all, two in the wash, two ready to wear." ZOO IN BUDAPEST, despite these problems, won raves from the critics and was Loretta's first picture to appear at the Radio City Music Hall in New York.

THE LIFE OF JIMMY DOLAN was Loretta's sixth and final picture opposite Douglas Fairbanks, Jr. The film was successful, and Loretta was good in her role, but she was getting tired of playing leading ladies in movies where the story was constructed around the leading man's character. This became a growing complaint.

Loretta remembered, "One night at the dinner table, I was crying about some part that I was scheduled to do, and I didn't think it was good enough. Sally was there and finally she said, 'Oh, you just make me sick. I'd give my eyetooth for that part, and here you are crabbing about it."

Gladys, meanwhile, was focused on her new career. She was absorbing everything that she could at design school and then practicing at home. Loretta recalled, "One year, Mama redid the Sunset house twice, including rugs, drapes, even the wallpaper. Everything. It was an expensive process, but I was working, Sally was working, Pol was working."

Leslie Howard, though married, was reputed to be a ladies' man. His and Loretta's paths crossed when they were both staying at the La Quinta Inn near Palm Springs. Howard and his wife were staying in a room right next to Loretta's, and he was bold enough to call Loretta and suggest a tryst. Loretta laughed him off, but he had enchanted her. Loretta consequently pestered her Warner Brother's bosses to play opposite Howard in the upcoming BARCLAY SQUARE. She didn't get it, and as punishment for her willfulness, Warner Brothers loaned her out to MGM for MIDNIGHT MARY. Loretta remembered, "I was sick because I thought it was such a little nothing picture. Warner Brothers sent Bill Wellman over to MGM as well; he was also being punished for something."

Loretta played the sweetheart of gangster, Ricardo Cortez. In one scene, Cortez slapped Loretta around convincingly when his character believed she was two-timing him. Loretta recalled, "Ricardo Cortez was perfectly cast. He was mean. You know, there are some actors, when they are relaxed, they're mean. He was!"

Something must have seemed convincing to the audiences. Loretta recalled,
"MIDNIGHT MARY was one of the best pictures of the year. It ran three weeks at the Roxy Theater in New York, which was just unheard of because that was MGM' s *big house*."

Loretta was next reunited with Richard Barthlemess in HEROES FOR SALE, directed by William Wellman. Franklin Roosevelt had only been in office for four months when this picture was released, and the country was still entrenched in the Depression. The story revolved around Bartheless's characters whose travails travel from his drug addiction consequent to his World War I injuries, through a series of financial and legal inequities. Loretta's character didn't fare any better. Loretta said, "All I remember about HEROES FOR SALE are the horses' hooves." As well she might, since her character was trampled to death by a horse while authorities quelled a labor protest.

Loretta stated, "That magical thing called chemistry was missing with Victor Jory in THE DEVIL'S IN LOVE. We were standing, and he leaned over to kiss me. His breath kept blowing my hair as he was talking, and it annoyed me to no end. It was very warm on the set, and as he leaned in for the kiss, I just shivered. I didn't mean to, but I did, and William Dieterle, the director, said, 'Cut.' Dieterle came up to me and asked, 'What's the matter?' I said, 'I don't know, but I can't kiss him.' He said, 'You have to. It's a love scene.' I said, 'I don't care. He blows on my hair.' Dieterle said, 'I can't tell him not to blow on your hair.' I don't remember whether I kissed him or not."

The chemistry was much better between Josephine Saenz and John Wayne. They married on June 24, 1933 at Loretta's Sunset House. Josie recalled, "Loretta was my maid of honor. She looked gorgeous in a pale, pink chiffon dress. We walked down the steps and into the garden, and there were about 400 people there." The Waynes moved shortly thereafter into their honeymoon apartment in the Circle District of Los Angeles. Gladys decorated; the Waynes were her first clients outside of her family.

The honeymoon between George Brent and Ruth Chatterton was short-lived. When it was announced that they were getting divorced, Loretta recalled, "I was thrilled to death. He called me immediately and made plans to have dinner at the Tracedero. All during dinner I kept looking at him, expecting ... something. He said, 'Would you like to go someplace else?' I said, 'Yes.' I couldn't figure out what was wrong. About four or five days later we had dinner at his little house in Toluca Lake. I remember we were sitting on the couch and talking, and I went sound to sleep. He seemed perfectly happy; he put my head in his lap and he was smoothing my hair. I had a good hour's sleep, and when I woke up, he kissed me a couple of times, and I kissed him, and I said, 'I think I'd better go home now,' and he took me home.

"It just wasn't the same. You can kill love very easily by not nurturing it. It's so sad because I remember thinking, 'Now that I can have him, I don't want him.' He was Catholic, but he hadn't married Ruth Chatterton in the Church, so that wouldn't have been a problem. He told me what had happened when he met Ruth in New York. She said, 'I know you're not in love with me, and I can see why you might be in love with Loretta. But, it's too embarrassing for me, a woman of my age, especially after all the publicity announcing our engagement. We can get married, and if you don't like it, you can leave.' He agreed. Hearing all this killed it for me. Not that he had done anything malicious, but what he did was out of weakness, and I'd pictured my lover always as a strong man."

George Belzer was feeling lost and emasculated. He had left his auditing job at the bank years earlier, shortly after Loretta went under contract. Loretta remembered him telling her aunt, "'It takes the wind out of your sails when a thirteen-year-old girl comes home with a paycheck once a week that you don't get for the month, and there are three of them in the house, all bringing home paychecks.' He gave up."

Loretta's next film was SHE HAD TO SAY YES. An attempted loan out to MGM for THE GAY BRIDE followed. The female lead's character would be a "bad girl" and Loretta felt that the audience wouldn't like her. She went straight to Louis B. Mayer, head of MGM, and in a teary plea, extricated herself from the project. Her next loan out would present a different kind of problem. His name was Spencer Tracy.

Chapter 8: COLLISION

Spencer Tracy was thirty-three, and Loretta twenty, when they met on the set of A MAN'S CASTLE. Loretta described Spencer as having, "gray-blue eyes, reddish blonde hair and a stocky build." She recalled, "I quickly fell in love with Spencer Tracy; I think the first day or two. Anybody would if you were around him. When he showed you attention, it was just like he played it on the screen. It was like a little pearl given to you on a silver platter."

A MAN'S CASTLE was another Depression story, this time about a group of unfortunates living in a shanty Hooverville along New York City's East River. Amidst all the indignity of poverty, Spencer's and Loretta's characters fall in love. She is certain that she has found her happiness, but he, having always felt trapped by life, is unwilling to make any kind of commitment. The sound of a train whistle always suggests freedom for him.

Loretta related what it was like to work with Spencer: "He was an absolute pleasure. You never knew when he was rehearsing, or when the camera was going. He didn't seem to have any nerves. You didn't sense any surge of adrenaline, but he knew exactly where he was going at all times, and if you were lucky, he carried you along with him."

They were several weeks into production, and Loretta recalled, "We finished early, and I invited him home to lunch. He said, 'I'd love to meet your family.' Anyway, I called Mama, 'Mama, I'm coming home for lunch, and I'm going to bring Spencer with me.' She said, 'Fine,' I had talked a lot about him. She had a quick and nice lunch thrown together, and he was charming; everybody was crazy about him. When he left, she said, 'Gretch, don't get serious about this boy; he's separated from his wife. He's married and as far as you're concerned, he will always be married because he is married in the Church.' She asked him all these questions while I was out of the room, and he had been completely honest. 'Oh, Mom, I'm not serious about him. He's just very nice to work with.' I thought, 'He's a charming friend, that's all.' Little did I know how love can wind you around its little finger."

Spencer Tracy had met Louise Treadwell ten years earlier. She was an actress, but immediately gave up her acting career when they married. Their son, John Tracy, was born in 1924 and their daughter, Susie, in 1932. When Spencer met Loretta on the set of A MAN'S CASTLE, the Tracys had been separated for a month and Spencer was living in a town-house.

Loretta observed that their real feelings toward each other came through on the screen, "The closer the part is to home the easier it is to do because you call on all those emotions that you feel anyway. As I recall, some of those scenes were so casual, that if we hadn't been falling in love with each other, we would have done much more with the scenes. But because we were, all I had to do was just lean up and whisper something in his ear, and he'd say, 'Now go on home.' When you feel something, it does register on the screen."

What did Loretta find so attractive about Spencer? She recalled, "Part of Spencer's allure to me was that he played it very cool. Just like in the picture, he kind of brushes her off softly, but she knows deep down that he's wild about her. He played it the same way. Never, for instance, was he demonstrative: no holding hands, or kissing in public, or anything like that. He was always just kind of amused at everything that I did. He used to call me, 'Little Ol' Who's It'. He took it right out of the movie. It was his way of saying, 'Little Ol' Nothing .....but I love you anyway.'

"I felt that he was always perfectly at ease with himself. He seemed to roll with everything. Unlike so many of us actors, he didn't demand the center stage. What I remember mostly about him was his delightful sense of humor. We laughed a lot. He didn't take himself too seriously. He was not devoted to his job, yet I don't think that he could have ever thought of being anything but an actor. He really did love it. He used to say, 'Oh, there's nothing to it. You just know your lines and be on time and just say the words.' But, indeed, there was much more to it than that, and he knew there was."

Most seductive of all to Loretta was how Spencer felt about her. She recalled, "He said he couldn't imagine anyone as beautiful as me being in love with him. I knew that it was love talk, but it was love talk that my romantic nature longed to hear from him. He treated me like I was the only one who mattered in the world."

Warner Brothers offered to renew Loretta's contract but without the $100 per week raise she had expected. She remembered Dave Thompson, the former manager of First National Studios, saying, "'Loretta, if you ever need an agent, call me. '" She did, but even with his intervention, Warner Brother's balked.

At that same time, former writer, turned producer, Daryl Zanuck was forming a new studio, 20th Century. He would be Head of Production and through her agent, Zanuck offered Loretta a seven year contract starting out at $1,731 per week. Loretta accepted. She was not yet twenty-one, so Gladys was required to sign the new contract. Gladys found these interchanges with the studio brass distasteful. After returning home she said, "'Dear, I don't know how you take it. Daryl Zanuck doesn't even know enough to stand up when a lady enters the room. By the time this seven year period rolls around, you'll be old enough to sign your own contract, and I'll never have to go near a studio again.'" But it wasn't merely a matter of manners. Loretta summarized her mother's distrust of Zanuck. "Mama saw his display of bad manners as his way of manipulating the situation, his way of showing that he was in charge and how little you mattered to him."

Nor had Loretta forgotten her distaste toward Zanuck stemming from his negative comments about Grant while they were married, as well as his braggadocio in the Executive Dining Room at Warner Brothers. But, she thought, "You don't have to like a man to work for him as long as you get the parts you want."

Agent Dave Thompson's concerns about Loretta went beyond negotiating her contract. He also wanted to protect her in her personal life. Loretta recalled, "One day Dave called Mama and said, 'I think Loretta ought to know that Spencer Tracy has a drinking problem.' She told me this, and I said, 'Oh no, Mama, he means Lee Tracy.' I just didn't believe him. When we went out, he seldom drank anything, and when he did, it was only one drink. I didn't drink anything but tea or soda. What I didn't know was that Spencer was a periodic drinker; he would go and hide and drink for several days at a time."

A favorite get-away for the couple was a little restaurant on San Vincente Boulevard called The Thistle Inn. Loretta recalled, "We used to go there when we were first going out together because it was private. We would walk back through a little arbor into this restaurant, and they had private booths. I guess we chose this place because we knew we shouldn't be seeing each other. But we must have gotten over the need to be hiding because I wound up every Sunday afternoon at the Will Roger's Polo Field. Spence played with Zanuck and that group, and the thing to do was to go out and watch them play."

Loretta only met Spencer's son, John, once, and that was at the Polo Field. She recalled, "Spencer brought him over to me, and he was charming. He was stone deaf. The boy turned around to do something, and to get his attention, Spence just tapped the ground twice with his foot, and the boy turned around and looked at him. I remember thinking, 'How marvelous, they know each other so well; they can communicate with the vibrations of the ground.'

"Spencer talked tenderly about his daughter, Susie, but I do think that Johnny was the most important person in his life. He certainly talked about him the most: how bright he was, how responsible he felt for him, how he wanted to make him secure for life. I don't think Spencer would have done anything to make Johnny's life more difficult such as divorcing his mother and marrying someone else. I don't know why I say that, but the last person in the world that Spencer would hurt would have been Johnny; I mean any more than he already had by not living at home with his family."

Loretta knew that Spencer had had something going with both Joan Bennett and Bette Davis and suspected that might have precipitated the separation from his wife. A story that Spencer told Loretta about a visit he had made to Joan Bennett when she was in the hospital reveals his idealistic view of woman. Joan's foot had been sticking out from under the covers and he exclaimed, 'She had nail polish on her toenails!' He looked so horrified. The influence of Jansenism in Spencer's Irish Catholic background was showing; the part of him that was looking for purity and innocence. That's probably why he was so tolerant of Loretta's desire to not cross certain boundaries in their love making; it was okay if he brought himself to an orgasm, but there would be no intercourse. Loretta defended the limitations of their love making, "I thought that was perfectly normal in those days. I remember him saying something about another woman, 'Oh, sure she's had all of them, but none of them are ever going to marry her.'"

Georgiana reflected, "Spencer was just the love of Gretch's life,
I'm sure of it. He used to come to our house every night, and if
Gretch was working, the two of them used to have dinner on
trays by the fireplace. I would sit on the floor by Spencer. He was
darling, and I remember he would put his arm around me, and
I'd just be rubbing his hand. Spence was very fatherly, and I just
loved him so much. Everybody loved Spencer. And he was madly,
madly in love with Gretch. You felt it; even I, as a child, felt that,
and it felt so good to be in the room with the two of them
because there was so much love there."

Loretta visited Spencer's town-house on only one occasion. His
mother happened to be there and behaved in a very cold manner
to Loretta. Loretta recalled talking about it later to Spencer. "I
asked him, 'Does she think that I'm your mistress?' He replied, 'I
think she does.' I said, 'Then you better straighten her out.'
Loretta and Spencer didn't see their relationship as a married
man with a mistress. They just saw themselves as deeply in love,
but in a hopeless situation. Loretta reflected, "When you're in
love, you can close your mind to an awful lot no matter how
dangerous a situation it may be.

"I don't think he ever would have gotten a divorce, even if I'd
asked him, and there was no point in my asking him because I

couldn't marry him in the Church. I had already gone that route with Grant, and I knew that didn't work."

Chumming with the Waynes offered Loretta and Spencer a situation of propriety. Loretta explained, "They'd rent a house in the desert for a couple of months and they were the perfect chaperons. Josie and Duke took their babies, their nurse, and their cook and we all had a ball."

Loretta had two stipulations when she signed with Zanuck: she wanted an annual paid vacation, and she did not want to work with the older, English actor, George Arliss. She knew she'd end up playing Arliss' daughter, yet another ingénue bland part. Zanuck complied but said, "I can't put it into your contract because then everyone else will demand a vacation and special considerations." His duplicity was soon evident. Loretta first picture for 20th Century was THE HOUSE OF ROTHSCHILD starring George Arliss. She was cast as his daughter.

Following the wrap of THE HOUSE OF ROTHSCHILD, Loretta and Gladys set sail for Hawaii for the first of her paid vacations. Loretta recalled, "We were only there for a few days when I got a telegram from Zanuck's office to return immediately. That took a few days because we had to go by ship, but the script was waiting for me when I got home. I read this thing titled BORN TO

BE BAD. I made an appointment to see Zanuck and walked into his office and said, 'Daryl, I can't play this.' He said 'You're going to play it. Jean Harlow was set for it, but she's no longer available. You're an actress and you're going to play it.' I said, 'But this says she walks into the room and she's so sexy, the men drop over dead. If I have appeal, it's not that, and I know it. I've done a picture with Jean, and I know what that's all about.' Zanuck wouldn't listen.

"There was one scene where my character is on the telephone. She's wearing a pair of step-ins and a bra, and my figure wasn't anything to speak of. We made the test, and they said, 'Well, can't you make them skimpier?' I said, 'Sure, but it still won't make me sexy;' I weighed 110 pounds dripping wet. I've watched this film in the last few years, and I noticed in that scene, I came out in these brief little things, and I had a bathrobe over one shoulder, still trying to hide. I don't know if it was modesty as much as being ashamed of my shape."

As the male lead, Loretta remembered, "Cary (Cary Grant) had such a nice tan that he didn't wear any makeup. He told me that after his shower, he spent four minutes under his sunlamp. He had a little tiny sunlamp on the set, so in case he missed it in the morning, he got some time during the day."

Loretta's next picture was CARAVAN for Fox. CARAVAN was a musical set in nineteenth century Hungary and introduced French heartthrob Charles Boyer to the American screen. Loretta loathed CARAVAN. She said, "It's the only preview of one of my own pictures that I walked out on. Daryl Zanuck called me into his office the next day and said, 'You walked out of the preview last night. Don't you ever do that again.' I said, 'I'm sorry, I couldn't stand it.' The picture was just awful."

There was time for a brief California holiday. Loretta remembered, "Spencer had finished a picture at Fox, and I had finished mine. Mama would meet us in San Francisco, and Duke would also join us the days he wasn't working. It was Spence's idea that he, Josie, and I would go to Santa Barbara, have dinner and spend the night at the Biltmore. Then, we'd 'drive up the next day. He had a driver, and he also had his stand-in who was kind of his right hand man, so there was this big limo, big enough for five of us, plus luggage.

"We got as far as Santa Barbara. I wasn't conscious that Spencer had been drinking. The three of us were having dinner and, all of a sudden, he was absolutely stoned. Finally, I looked at Josie, then excused myself and called his stand-in who was in his room. I said, 'I think something's wrong with Spencer. I think he's drunk.' He said, 'Oh no!' Just the way he said it; I thought, 'What's going on?' He came down. Spencer said 'Now, now, we're all going to have a nice nightcap before we go to bed.' He wouldn't eat any dinner.

"I was sitting there looking at Josie and looking at this fellah, and I heard a train whistle, and it dawned on me that the train goes right through. I don't know how we got on it that night; I think I called the desk clerk, and he told me the train stopped in Santa Barbara. I asked Spencer's double to get our luggage out of the car. He did because he knew the routine: once Spencer started to drink, he was on it for ten days to a couple of weeks. This was all new to me; I could hardly believe it.

"Josie and I got on the train and went up to San Francisco, and we were all staying at the Mark Hopkins Hotel. On the third night of our stay, Mama had accepted, for all of us, a dinner invitation from her friends the Zellenbachs, hoping that Spencer would have arrived by then. At the very last moment, they had to be notified that 'Mr. Tracy was detained and would not be joining us.' Right in the middle of this elegant dinner party, held in the main dining room of the Mark Hopkins, I suddenly saw Spence slipping into the room, walking very carefully, indeed, and I knew he was still drinking. It was soon obvious he was looking for me. He went from table to table scrutinizing each lady. Begging their pardon, he'd go on to the next table. As

embarrassed as I was for him, I knew I would be more embarrassed for myself had he found me. I excused myself and asked Josie to alert me in the ladies' room when he'd given up and left the dining room. It was three days later he called my room, sober and apologetic. He charmed his way back in. When you love someone, it
colors everything."

After the Santa Barbara/San Francisco incidents, six months went by before Loretta suspected that Spencer was battling the bottle again. She recalled, "Josie, Duke, Spencer and I were going to the Academy Awards. I was dressed and waiting, and he just never showed. I called Josie and said, 'Josie, Spencer hasn't shown up. He may never come, so you and Duke go ahead.' She said 'No. We'll come and pick you up, and you leave him a message to meet us down there.' Spence never did show up, and it was a whole evening fighting tears.

"I didn't hear from him for two weeks, and it was after midnight when Mama came in and woke me up. She said, 'Gretch, Carroll (Carroll Tracy was Spencer Tracy's older brother and business manager) is on the phone; he wants to talk to you. I think you'd better.' I said, 'All right.' Carroll said, 'I hate to do this to you, but I'm here in the Beverly Wilshire Hotel with Spence. He won't eat, and he's been drinking for two weeks now, and he says that if you're not mad at him, and you'll come over here and ask him, he'll stop drinking.'

"I asked, 'Do you believe that?' He said, 'Well, it's a chance. Would you come if I sent a car and a driver?' I said, 'Carroll, I'm not about to walk through that Beverly Wilshire Hotel lobby at 1:00 in the morning, alone, asking for Mr. Tracy's room.' He said, 'Well, here's what you do. The limo will bring you into the basement; I'll meet you at the elevator in the basement, and we'll take you upstairs through the back elevator.' I agreed to go. Spencer was sitting in the corner of the sitting room, just leaning against the corner, and he was drunk as a coot, and still in his pajamas. Carroll said, 'He's been this way for two weeks.' I put my arms around him, and he just hung on and started to cry. He said, 'I'm sure I wouldn't be this way if you and I were able to get married.' The only response I could give was to hold him in my arms.

"I asked, 'Has he had anything to eat?' Carroll said, 'He won't eat; that's the problem.' I ordered some soup, but when it arrived, and I tried to give it to him, he wouldn't open his mouth. I went into the bathroom to see if there was a funnel to use; there usually is a little medicine kit, and sure enough, there was a tiny funnel. I said, 'Open your mouth, Spence.' He opened his mouth and I put the funnel in, then Carroll held the funnel while I poured the soup down. Spencer was shaking his head back and forth, but he was so drunk he didn't know enough to open his mouth and let the funnel fall. Anyway, the funnel slipped a bit and some soup spilled on my hand, and I said, 'Oh God, Carroll, it's too hot! It's burning him!' Every time I think about this it makes me sick to my stomach. Needless to say, he didn't drink any more liquor; he couldn't; his throat was so burned. Carroll called the doctor who eased my guilt by telling me it was not serious. Spence finally fell asleep, and Carroll led me back to the waiting limousine in the basement.

"Three days later, he came over and started to talk about it and I said, 'Let's not. Just promise me you won't ... ' He said, 'Oh, never ... I promise .... ' At age twenty-one, I didn't know anything, and I didn't want to talk about it. You think it will go away. It won't. After that, I got used to his disappearing for ten days at a time, knowing that he was on a binge."

Loretta's next two films were with childhood heartthrob, Ronald Colman. BULLDOG DRUMMOND STRIKES BACK was a mystery followed by the historical epic, CLIVE OF INDIA. Loretta recalled, "It was a big picture: lots of sets, lots of costumes. I remember one scene when Ronnie was coming home from India, and in a burst of enthusiasm, was supposed to sweep his wife up in his arms and carry her up the staircase. I was wearing a hoop skirt that was eight feet across. Hoop skirts were four feet across normally, but I wanted mine eight feet. The bigger the skirt looked, the smaller your waist looked, too. But also, the bigger the hoop, the heavier. At rehearsal, Ronnie started to pick me up, and I said, "Oh Ronnie, don't, not in rehearsal.' He said, 'No, it's fine; you're not heavy.' With that he gathered me up and sailed up the staircase. When we reached the top, he laughed a little and put me down to catch his breath. By the time we finally got the take, I thought the poor man was going to have a heart attack."

Loretta was in the hospital for some minor operation when she was exposed to another of Spencer's drinking episodes. Josie was visiting and spotted him, saying, 'Oh my God! Look! There's Spencer coming down the hall. He's been drinking!' I responded, 'Hide me, quickly,' and she put me into the bathroom of my room and locked the door. It took her a half hour to talk him into going back downstairs where his driver was waiting for him."

It was the reality that their union could not be sanctioned by the Catholic Church more than Spencer's drinking that ebbed away at the happiness of their relationship. And, even though their love making never reached physical consummation, with the Church's strict guidelines, there were things to discuss in the confessional. Loretta recalled the priest telling her, "This is a married man no matter what you think; I can't give you absolution unless you promise me you're not going to see him again.' I said, 'He's right outside the church waiting for me, so I know I'm going to see him again. Please Father, I can't break it off this quickly; I'm in love with the man.' Anyway, he wouldn't give me absolution.

"So, I walked right across the aisle to Father Degman; he was known as a very tough confessor. I told him that Father Sheppard had just refused my absolution, and why. I told him the whole story. Finally, he said, 'If you promise me you'll be back here in this confessional every week until I tell you that you don't have to come anymore,
I'll give you absolution.' I went outside and explained the whole thing to Spencer. Being a Catholic, he understood the situation perfectly. He said, 'Thank God for Father Degman. At least it gives us some breathing room. '

"But the poor man was so frustrated because our romance was in no way a fulfilling life for him. It was not an affair; it was two people in love trying not to have an affair. I was a bundle of romance, and religion, and ambition to be a movie star. All these things were all wrapped up in me. I think, at that time, religion, to me, was mainly rules and regulations; I didn't understand much more. But I knew that when I deviated from those rules, I didn't find much satisfaction in my life. It always ended with me being very unhappy. I think if I had not been married out of the Church when I was 17, I might have been tempted to marry him. I'm not saying that Spencer would have; he never did. But I knew what a disaster the situation with Grant had been, and I hadn't even been in love with that man. Imagine the pain it would have been with Spencer? I knew better.

"We both knew better, and we talked about it an awful lot. When Spencer was serious, he was deadly serious, and it was usually about our situation. It was times like this when I would see the dark side of his Irish nature. In an unguarded moment, there was a sense of doom, something simply dark. We'd decide not to see each other. Then three or four days would go by; he'd call, and I'd say, 'Well, let's go for a little ride or something.' It took six months to make the wrench. Falling out of love with someone is kind of a little death in itself. I don't think I ever quite fell out of love with Spence."

Loretta and Spencer weren't the only couple in dissolution. The March 23, 1934 issue of *The Los Angeles Herald* announced that George and Gladys Belzer had separated. Looking back, Loretta theorized, "I don't think that it was too happy of a marriage for either one of them. I think Mama was probably too strong for him, too. I know she was too strong for my father."

Gladys was busy investing Loretta's money and perfecting her decorating skills simultaneously. She started buying homes in the flats section of Beverly Hills, decorating them and then renting them out furnished. Loretta recalled, "She'd charge $200 or $300 rent, just enough to payoff everything, including the taxes and whatever else came along. The houses would pay for themselves. Mama was very talented in many ways."

Loretta's work provided a source of distraction from her pain of breaking off with Spencer. Again, she was loaned out to Fox, this time playing a student nurse in THE WHITE PARADE, about a nurses' training school in the Midwest. Polly Ann also played one of the students. Jesse Lansky asked Loretta to come to his office while WHITE PARADE was in production. She recalled," He was going to produce a picture at Fox for which Spencer was already set, and he wanted me to play opposite. But, before he'd ask Daryl for the loan out, he was asking me. I told him that it would just start the whole thing over again, and it had taken so much for both of us to break it off. I'll always appreciate his sensitivity of not putting me in a spot of having to refuse a picture."

CHAPTER 9: STEEL BUTTERFLY

If Loretta thought breaking up with Spencer was tough, it was child's play compared to the Clark Gable/Judy saga which soon followed. She navigated the minefield of her secret pregnancy by turning it all over to Gladys to work out the details. After Judy was born, she returned to work soon as possible, first UNGUARDED HOUR followed by PRIVATE NUMBER

PRIVATE NUMBER had been her first film after the merger of 20th Century and Fox Studios. Daryl Zanuck, in charge of the new company, moved his major production work from Sam Goldwyn's Studio to the Fox Studio lot on Pico Avenue in West Los Angeles. Shirley Temple was the studio's biggest moneymaker, and was awarded her own bungalow. Loretta, the reigning queen as far as adult stars, was assigned the Number One Dressing Room. She recalled, "The new dressing room had an office, a kitchen, a large living room with an alcove off that, and a bath. Then there was the portable dressing room I used on the set.

"You surrounded yourself with as many niceties as you could because, at that time, we all thought: the more you felt like a star, the more you acted like a star, and the better actress you were. I must say, I enjoyed all that part of my career; you get spoiled very easily. There was a wardrobe woman to dress you, a make-up person to put your face on, a hairdresser and a stand-in, and they all liked you or they wouldn't be working for you. Then there was Pat Palimountion, my studio driver (Loretta had just bought a Cadillac town car.) That's all Pat did was take care of me. I also hired a cook who came on at 8:00 in the morning. She prepared coffee and doughnuts for the entire company, and Pat brought it to the set. She'd stay and cook lunch for me and whomever else I invited into my dressing room." Except for the cook, the studio picked up the tab for Loretta's entire entourage.

RAMONA finally got off the ground and it was just the kind of project that met her expectations. It was big budgeted, romantic, and the story revolved around her character. However, it was a disappointment at the box office.

LADIES IN LOVE starred three of the Thirties top leading ladies: Loretta, Janet Gaynor, and Constance Bennett. Playing opposite Loretta was a newcomer named Tyrone Power. Recalled Loretta, "I think the crush started the moment I saw him. He was unbelievably good to look at and with a great smile and a great laugh."

Zanuck decided to give Tyrone Power his big chance by casting him in LLOYDS OF LONDON and wanted Loretta to play opposite him. She was crazy about Tyrone, but unwilling to accept a role she considered window dressing. She explained, "I was looking for women roles, and Zanuck was using me as the leading lady. When I went to Zanuck and told him that I wouldn't do it, it became a shouting match that ended with me slamming the door on the way out. Anyway, I walked out of the picture and he took me off salary.

"I was going out with Eddie Sutherland at the time, a producer from Paramount. He said, 'You know, Zanuck could keep you out of the business forever. Dave Thompson can't handle this; you need Myron Selznick.' I called Dave Thompson on the phone, and I told him what Eddie said. He agreed. Eddie arranged for Myron to come to my house the following morning.

"Myron arrived in his big limousine. I told him what had happened, how unhappy I was that Zanuck was using me as a stock girl. He said, 'All right. What's your goal? What do you want?' I said, 'I want to finish my contract and leave the studio. I don't want to work for Zanuck anymore. He arranged a meeting with Zanuck that afternoon.

"Myron did all the talking. I think he did get me more money, but that wasn't my concern. I wanted better parts. Whatever the problems were, they were straightened out. What Myron did for me was take the whole burden of even thinking about Daryl Zanuck off my shoulders. Myron Selznick was the industry's first super-agent."

Audiences liked the chemistry between Loretta and Tyrone in LADIES IN LOVE, and Zanuck was happy to give them more. Ever since the success of Frank Capra's IT HAPPENED ONE NIGHT, all the studios were dishing out comedies to Depression weary audiences which detailed the chase between flip, spoiled heiresses and the equally flip, somewhat unscrupulous, but always handsome everyday guys. Loretta recalled her mindset during the filming LOVE IS NEWS, "As far as I was concerned, I was Barbara Hutton (heiress to the Woolworth fortune) but with more humor and a sense of fun."

Loretta and Tyrone were both twenty-three; it was the first time since her teen years that she had a serious crush on someone her own age. Loretta recalled, "I dated him as often as I could. In those days the women had to wait until the man asked them out, but believe me, if I wouldn't have been so embarrassed, I wouldn't have given him one moment's peace."

LLOYDS OF LONDON had made Tyrone Power an overnight sensation, and he received top billing in LOVE IS NEWS. Loretta's character in LOVE IS NEWS allowed her to push her performance beyond the usual leading lady part. Loretta commented, "That character was a lot more daring, more sophisticated; she was just more .... " It had only been ten years since she received that pivotal call from Mervyn Le Roy at First National Studios, and her screen persona in LOVE IS NEWS was so worldly compared to the little girl of her silent pictures. The transition deftly reflected the evolution of the real life Loretta. Living and working in the movie world for those ten years, exposure to all of the glamour and attention had made Loretta a very sophisticated twenty-three-year-old.

Although Tyrone was the third generation of an acting family, he was fairly new to the status of celebrity life for himself. Loretta recalled, "He wasn't quite as sure of himself as he wanted to appear because a lot of the time he would have his stand-in, who was a friend of his, call me and say, 'Tyrone wants to know if you've got a date for tonight.' If I had, I'd say, 'Well, yes I have ... ' If I hadn't, he'd say, 'Good, he wants to know if you want to go down to the Village theatre and see ..... ' I'd say, 'He's there; put him on.' Then he'd get on the phone, and I'd say, 'Well, yeah, I'd love to go. What's playing?' You see, that way if I did have plans, Tyrone wouldn't get rejected, the stand-in would.

"I found Tyrone very romantic. He loved spouting poetry, and he sent me sweet notes on and off the set. He always sent flowers, before and after a date, and nice little things like a bag of candy. I told him once how I loved English toffee, and he kept me supplied. We played together a lot on the set."

Loretta recalled the first time that she looked at proofs George Hurrell had shot of her and Tyrone. "I said to myself, 'Why, he's prettier than I am.' He was, too. Those eyelashes, his skin, the bone structure, even his eyelids, I thought were just beautiful. His skin was always squeaky clean. He didn't wear make-up sitting for stills, but he used to wear it on the set, and I'd say, 'Take the make-up off; you look so much better without it.' But at that time, he was still over awed by the rules and regulations of the studio."

LOVE IS NEWS was a huge success. It would be Loretta's biggest money making film of the Thirties. Zanuck wasted no time in pairing Loretta and Tyrone in CAFE METROPOLE. Said Loretta, "Same story, just a different cast; I made so many of these pictures that I used to get even the same cast some of the time."

She was then cast in two comedies which were released in the summer of 1937, LOVE UNDER FIRE and WIFE, DOCTOR, NURSE. In the latter, Virginia Bruce played the second female lead. Loretta reminisced about Virginia. "She was scared to death of me; she told me she was. I said, 'There's nothing to be scared of.

Just go along with me; I can't help it if I talk faster than you do. Just take your time, and then you'll stand out.' She said, 'Well, you're so sure of yourself. '"

Contrast this Loretta to young Gretchen who tried to fade back into her seat so that the nun wouldn't call on her to read. It was only now in her mid-twenties that she learned about dyslexia. Loretta commented, "I finally understood why I hadn't been able to spell or read because I was seeing some letters backwards." Ironically, Loretta's deficiency in reading and spelling had added to her determination to be an actress, and it was her recognized success as an actress that contributed to Loretta's self-assurance as an adult.

News of Papa came to the house through an intermediary. Polly Ann told the story. "When Carter and I were married, our picture was in *The Examiner* with an accompanying article. About two months later, the priest who married us called and said that he had received a letter from my father needing money for a new prosthesis. It would be $250.00. What right did he have to come and ask for that when he hadn't made any effort over the years to support his family? Maybe he couldn't have supported us the way we would have liked, but he could have sent something every month to my mother.

"The priest said, 'Of course, you can buy it for him, Mrs. Belzer.' Mom replied, 'I'll ask Loretta. After all, she's the money maker here.' We were all working but nothing like she was. Mama said, 'If she says yes, I'll call you and let you know.' So she asked Gretchen in front of all of us. Gretch said, 'Oh sure, Mom, if it's all right with you.' So Mom gave Father a check, and I guess he gave that to Papa. Of course, $250.00 was more than it is today but even at that time it wasn't outlandish."

Years earlier, Gladys had initiated a plan where they sent a monthly check to help support their Grandmother Young. Gladys felt strongly that families had a moral obligation to take care of each other. Soon after John Earle Young had reemerged, Gladys decided that they should send money to him on a continuous basis and called the girls together to discuss the matter. Loretta recalled the spirited interchange. "I said, 'Well, I don't want to see him, and I'm not going to give him any money.' Mama said, 'You don't have to see him, but he needs the money.' I kept refusing but Mama said, 'You have to honor your father and mother, and that means you won't see him go hungry.' I said, 'Well, I won't give it to him directly. Just up Grandma's monthly check. Whatever you think is necessary, give that much more to Grandma, and she can give it to him.' That's what Mama did."

While Gladys was looking after the welfare of her first husband, her divorce from George Belzer had already been finalized. She would remain an independent woman for the rest of her life.

It was decided that the rumors had died down enough by June, 1937, to attempt the daring coup of bringing Judy into Loretta's home as her adopted daughter. Polly Ann recalled, "I know that when Loretta and Mom were trying to figure out the publicity to adopt a child, they came up with the idea to adopt two children. They asked Dr. Holleran if he thought it was a good idea. Mom didn't think that actually adopting another child was a good idea, but maybe they'd borrow a child for a couple of months. Dr. Holleran said, 'You can borrow my youngest,' which was so sweet of him. But then he went home, and his wife vetoed the idea."

Plan B went into effect. Louella Parsons reported that Loretta had adopted two children, one child was June, age 3, and the other, Judy, age 23 1/2 months. Another source reported Loretta had adopted a 3 year old boy and a 23 1/2 month old girl named Judy. 20th Century-Fox's publicity department issued a release that appeared to clarify the situation. It stated that Loretta had attempted to adopt two little girls, June, age 3, and Judy, age 23 1/2 months. But, then, it went on to explain that an aunt of the girl's natural family decided to adopt June. Judy, in actuality, was

19 months old, but the stated 23 1/2 months tag was to throw anyone off who was counting the months since CALL OF THE WILD began shooting.

That didn't stop the old rumors from resurfacing: that Loretta was Judy's biological mother and Clark Gable the father. Another identified Spencer Tracy as the father. Reportedly Spencer Tracy got into a fight at the Tracedero Club with director William Wellman because Wellman was perpetuating rumors about Loretta. As for Loretta, she had nothing to say in public or in private, a stance she'd adhere to for sixty years.

Lifelong friend Jane Mullen Sharpe shared her thoughts on the matter, "What kind of life would it have meant for Judy? Even with two famous parents, a child born out of wedlock in the Thirties would still have been considered a bastard. Loretta would have wanted Judy to feel wanted. She would have wanted to give Judy a complete life, not lacking in anything, including, eventually, a father."

Judy's welcome into the Sunset house was both gracious and enthusiastic. She and her new nurse occupied the luxurious suite that Polly Ann and Sally had shared. Georgiana recalled, "I was 12 at the time, and I just adored Judy. She was the baby sister I always wanted." Polly Ann reflected on Judy's early life,

"Judy's young years were happy for us and Judy. She got a lot of attention from the family; we thought she was adorable. There were a lot of friends for Judy. My son Jim and Sally's daughter, Gretchen, and lots of other children were around her." Sally echoes Polly Ann's sentiments about Judy's early years, "Judy really had five mothers because we were all crazy about her. She was a good child and a happy little girl."

Loretta and Tyrone Power made SECOND HONEYMOON, another comedy. Loretta remembered her first line of dialogue. "We're at a dance, and I'm wearing this beautiful white dress. I'm out on the balcony alone, and Tyrone comes out wearing a white dinner jacket and he looks marvelous. I look at him and say, 'Raoul!' That was his name, but I couldn't say it without laughing. It was such a funny name for Tyrone. It sounded like I was growling every time I said it. 'Raooooul'"

Loretta remembered something else about that first day. "They had plucked Tyrone's eyebrows. I had loved his eyebrows; they were like one great big beautiful bird hovering across his brow that had softened the blackness of his eyes. Now there was a large blank space between each brow. I said, 'Tyrone! What have they done to your eyebrows?' He said, 'Does it matter?' "Tyrone was so good looking, so nice, that he didn't have to do anything.

Life came to him and just carried him along. That's not good for a man. "

Loretta continued to see Tyrone. She related, "It was more than casual dating. It wasn't exclusive, but I dated Tyrone more than I dated anybody else for a couple of years. I'm sure that if he had asked me to marry him I would have."

John Ford would direct Loretta's next film, FOUR MEN AND A PRAYER. Loretta recalled, "I thought he was a man's director, and I don't think it thrilled him anymore than it did me to work together. I preferred a Frank Capra, and he preferred a Maureen O'Hara.

"He didn't like it when he thought I took too long to change costumes. One day, he grabbed the corner of the set dressing room which was on wheels and shook it. He only tried it once because, to scare him, I let out a yell, then moaned and groaned as if I'd fallen and broken every bone in my body. I kept it up for three of four minutes. Finally, I quieted down and said, 'I'd like the doctor to come over,' which he did. He found nothing wrong, of course, and finally, I came out to a very subdued director. We both knew that I was one up on him."

THREE BLIND MICE followed, co-starring Joel McCrea. There is a dancing scene in THREE BLIND MICE in which Loretta wears a white evening dress designed by Adrian. The gown features a low back. Watching the movie years later, Loretta recalled how the make-up people wanted to put make-up on her back. "Pancake make-up is dull and makes the skin powdery looking. Without make-up, your skin shines, and I liked the clean look of it, so I never let them put make-up on my back. I just wouldn't stand still long enough to let them get it on." Defending her willfulness, Loretta said, "You wouldn't last in this business or any other if you did everything someone told you to do."

Loretta wasn't reluctant to display her displeasure on the set of SUEZ. She recalled, "I was playing second lead to the French actress Annabella and I was furious. I only went ahead with it because I needed the money, and I was working with Tyrone again. I did some things on that picture just for meanness, just to get back at Daryl Zanuck. I had long fingernails and, of course, the costume designer wanted me to cut them because they didn't wear their fingernails long at the time of Empress Eugenie. I refused and in close-ups with Tyrone, I'd put my hands all over his face just so they could see these long fingernails.

"I also insisted on wearing a white dress with a huge hoop skirt at the royal tennis match, so that I'd stand out from all the extras.

Zanuck objected, but I prevailed. This rankled Daryl, and he issued a new ultimatum: 'After you make the wardrobe tests, you cannot change one single thing once those tests are okayed.' So to test him, I decided to carry a handkerchief in a ballroom scene which had not been tested and okayed. I said to the assistant director, 'Send somebody up to Mr. Zanuck's office. Tell him that Miss Young wants to carry a handkerchief in the ballroom scene, but that it was not tested and okayed.' My intent was to rankle him as much as he had rankled me. As it happened, Daryl was on the Polo Field that afternoon so, of course, they couldn't get me an answer until he returned. That suited me fine."

Tyrone headed to Mexico for a vacation after SUEZ wrapped. Annabella followed and became Mrs. Tyrone Power in a Mexican wedding ceremony. Loretta reflected, "At the time, I really was devastated because I thought he was going to ask me to marry him. We were both the same age; twenty-five is still very young for a man, and I thought he wasn't ready to get married. I think it was more destroyed dreams, what could have been with him that I saw go by the wayside, more than what actually was. I thought I was just very much in love with him, and he thought he was in love with me; but he couldn't have been too much so, or he wouldn't have married Annabella."

The big-budgeted KENTUCKY, a Romeo and Juliet story set against the bluegrass landscape of thoroughbred horse country, followed. Loretta recalled, "It was a Technicolor picture and we decided on a lot of blue ribbons in my hair hoping my eyes would take on a blue hue and they did. Irene made a very pretty suit for the races. It was very slick looking with colors that were different tones of my hair." This attention to detail did not go unappreciated by one reviewer. *The New York Times* said, "In color, Loretta Young is a beauteous Kentucky belle. Her lensing in tints will be accepted as the best of any actress to date."

WIFE, DOCTOR, NURSE with Warner Baxter had been a hit so writer Nunally Johnson quickly concocted another story titled WIFE, HUSBAND, FRIEND. Loretta reflected, "At the time, I thought I was just divine as a comedienne. You have to think that people like you or you can't do it." But, recalling WIFE, HUSBAND, FRIEND, Loretta states, "It wasn't anything. Come to think of it, I did an awful lot of pictures that weren't anything."

Anything is a relative word. Loretta's movies made money, and her contract was to expire in six months. Zanuck, knowing that Myron Selznick provided Loretta with the toughest representation in the business, was prepared to offer Loretta $2,000,000 for a five year contract. Loretta's response came in a crucial meeting in which Zanuck and Joe Schenck (the moneyman behind the studio) were trying to cajole her into signing the new contract. Myron Selznick was at Loretta's side. She recalled, "Joe said to me, 'Loretta, why don't you want to resign?' I said, 'I'll tell you why: it's because of Daryl. He's never ever raised my salary! He's never .... anything. Tyrone tells me that he's had four raises. I just don't want to go on being treated that way. And I don't like the parts. I'm sick of LLOYDS OF LONDON and SUEZ parts, all these little nothing parts. That's no way to build my career. I want to keep going up, and I know I can do that, but not under Daryl because he doesn't make women's pictures unless you're a six-year-old (Shirley Temple) or can skate (Sonja Henie). '

"Finally Daryl said, 'Loretta, you've never asked for a raise. Tyrone has gotten these raises because he fought for them.' There was no sense of honor in a contract for Daryl. That didn't mean anything to him. I said, 'That's exactly what I'm talking about. I don't want to have to deal any longer with someone I have to fight with all the time about everything. It's too discouraging.' Myron hadn't said one thing. Finally he said, 'All right, Loretta, that's enough. You can go now. We'll finish.' I got up and left the office. Myron simply told them, 'She doesn't want to re-sign with you, so that's it. '"

Loretta recalled a later visit with the Selznick brothers, Myron and David, while vacationing in New York. "David tried to talk me into reconsidering Zanuck's offer. He said, 'Loretta, it is a good studio, and Daryl hasn't done too badly by you so far.' I agreed, 'So far, but I see no real stardom in my future with him.' If I was ever going to make my move, now was the time. David warned, 'You know Daryl can be awfully cruel when he wants to be. He's a hotheaded man, and you've really hurt his pride.'

"The script for THE STORY OF ALEXANDER GRAHAM BELL had not yet received its final okay before my expiration date would arrive. When Zanuck became aware of that fact, he simply opened the picture two days prior to the last day of my seven year contract and hooked me into the picture. Then, three days later, he closed it to finish preparing for the real starting date three weeks later. A neat little trick, all spelled out in my contract, a crummy thing to do but not beneath Daryl's tactics."

One pleasant dividend of doing THE STORY OF ALEXANDER GRAHAM BELL was the opportunity of working with all three of her sisters. Loretta was playing Mrs. Bell, and they were playing Mrs. Bell's sisters. Loretta recalled, "I went to check on them when they were getting their hair done, and I didn't like what they were doing to Bet. Bet gave me a look that said, 'Butt out,' but I didn't because it looked so terrible. Later Bet said to me, 'I just think it's terrible because that hairdresser worked an hour on my hair.' I asked her if she liked it. She said, 'No, but she was working so hard.' Bet was and always has been more people oriented than me."

When THE STORY OF ALEXANDER GRAHAM BELL wrapped, Loretta's contract was finished. Loretta recalled, "Myron Selzneck told me, 'I'm going to get you $100,000 your first picture out.' I was delighted. Nevertheless, I remember saying, 'Great, if it's a good part. Remember, it's the part that I'm interested in. '" Loretta was twenty-six when she left 20th Century-Fox. She had been a leading lady for over a decade, and 3,000 independent theater owners had just selected her as their biggest box office star.

CHAPTER 10: CHOCOLATE COVERED BLACK WIDOW SPIDER

Loretta described her relationship with writer Joe Mankiewicz. "He was one of the cutest looking men I've ever seen. His major works (A LETTER TO THREE WIVES, ALL ABOUT EVE, SUDDENLY LAST SUMMER) still lay ahead of him when we dated in the late Thirties. Joe had been one of the men that I started seeing while Tyrone was still in the picture, but ultimately, I got tired of the battle at the door. He just couldn't understand why I wouldn't go to bed with him."

Flobelle Burden, a niece of Douglas Fairbanks whom Loretta knew from her days at Ramona Convent School, was married to Shirley Burden, a great grandson of Cornelius Vanderbilt. They were eminent Los Angeles hosts, and Flobelle persisted in Loretta's meeting a young man named Bill Buckner. She said, "He's from very good people. I don't think wealthy, but good, solid people."

Loretta agreed to go with him to a dinner party at the Burdens. She recalled,
 "He certainly had beautiful manners and clothes, and was a good conversationalist. He had connections and was in the bond business. Flobelle was right. I liked him a lot."

Bill Buckner was thirty-years-old and Loretta, twenty- five. He was handsome in a boyish way and Ivy League in manner; Loretta found herself more than intrigued. Bill Buckner seemed so different from the previous men in her life. He had nothing to do with the film industry, yet he had all the trappings of success that were so appealing. His base was in New York, so theirs was a long distance romance. That suited Loretta just fine as she was busy finishing up her obligations to Zanuck. She had the comfort of knowing that there was a promising romance in her life, and at three thousand miles away, he could appear all the more promising without reality disturbing the illusion. He would come to the coast just often enough to make Loretta's impressions seem tangible. The long distance calls were long indeed, and Loretta discovered the thrill of writing and receiving wonderfully romantic letters. The relationship became quite serious in the matter of six months. Loretta recalled, "We talked about marriage and, in fact, I was informally engaged to him. I thought he was just perfect for me. He was eligible; he was Catholic, and he hadn't been married before; he wasn't an actor; I had had it with actors. And, yes, he was handsome."

He was not what he appeared to be. The Securities Exchange Commission had had him under surveillance for some time, and upon return from a business trip to Europe, he was arrested and charged with mail fraud. The December 2, 1938, edition of *The Los Angeles Times* reported: "Buckner is accused of defrauding bondholders of the Philippine Railway Company of a total that may exceed $100,000. He is charged with fraudulently manipulating the value of the bonds by cabling a false report to Manila, which indicated that the bonds were being purchased at an inflated value in New York. Buckner was quoted as saying that the complaint against him was, ' ... nothing at all. It's all on the level.' He said he plans to marry Miss Young and fly to Honolulu for their honeymoon."

Loretta recalled her shock. "I woke up one day and read the newspaper headline: LORETTA YOUNG'S FIANCE ARRESTED FOR FRAUD. In a way, I knew it couldn't be completely untrue; they must have had some evidence, some proof, or they wouldn't have arrested him. But I didn't put it together with him because he never mentioned anything about his business to me, ever. If he had asked me, 'Want to buy $100,000 worth of bonds?' I'd have said, 'Sure', if I had it. But we never talked about business. In the course of the six to eight months that I had known him, I introduced him to an awful lot of my friends, motion picture people.

"Buck flew out three or four days later, and after a few hours of talk, I was convinced that he was more right than wrong. I decided to make a public show of my belief in him, so we made reservations at Ciro's, a table for two under his name. That alerted the press and, as we arrived at 8:00 p.m. prompt; the flash bulbs blinded us.

"Buck went back to New York and eventually stood trial. We had agreed that I would stay away. He said, 'It will be too gruff on you, Loretta. They are going to make their point with me.' I was crazy about Buck, but I was also embarrassed by the whole episode. I wanted to trust him as one in love is supposed to do, but I couldn't. So, I started feeling guilty. I never had the guts or honesty to simply ask him, 'Did you do it?'"

Between his trial and sentencing, Buckner was able to make another trip to Los Angeles. Loretta recalled, "After dinner one night, he said, 'I think if I had a $100,000 I could clear this whole thing up right now.' I said, 'Well, I haven't got $100,000. I have $10,000 that I know I can put my hands on, but not $100,000. I pay for this house. I have a lot of expenses.' He said, 'No, no .... 'I said, 'But I would be delighted to give you the $10,000.' I didn't want to go and get it out of the bank because I was afraid that some overly dedicated reporter might be following me, so I called my public relations man and asked him to go and get it out for me. I had that money from a couple of radio shows, and I was trying to hang onto some money because I never had been able to. Anyway, I gave it to him, and I didn't expect to get it back. And really, way down deep in my heart, I kept praying that he wouldn't take it, but he did. Of course, it didn't fix anything at all. He went to prison, the poor fellah."

Once again, Loretta threw herself into her work. Myron Selznick had negotiated a deal for Loretta to star in ETERNALLY YOURS for independent producer Walter Wanger. Her leading man was former house guest David Niven. He played a magician and Loretta his wife and assistant.

Zanuck had one last trick up his sleeve for Loretta. His ego had been wounded and he wanted retribution. It is unknown if he was cagey enough to wait for her to do one project before he put his plan into action, or if it was Loretta's sliding into her freelance career so easily with ETERNALLY YOURS that really goaded him. Loretta described Zanuck's revenge: "After I left 20th Century-Fox, or even before I left, every producer I'd see would say, 'Oh, I have a script I'm dying to send to you.' I was delighted that it was going to work out so well. To my amazement, nine months after ETERNALLY YOURS, I was still waiting. My amazement began to turn to panic that I would never work again.

"Myron came to me and told me he had heard I was being blackballed. He said, 'I know exactly what happened. In one of their Sunday night poker games, Daryl Zanuck asked if any of the big producers sitting around the table were interested in hiring Loretta Young. Falling in line, they all said no. That's all it takes (to set up a blackball), but it also takes only one guy to break it,' and Myron said, 'I think I know the man, Harry Cohn. Harry's got a couple of scripts over there; one of them I know he tried to get Irene Dunne. She's tied up, and he's looking around for a substitute. If I give him a price on you, give him a bargain, I think he'll go for it.' So instead of the $100,000 asking price, I think Myron settled for $60,000. Within two days I was signed up and ready to do THE DOCTOR TAKES A WIFE. Myron knew these men and their personalities backwards."

Eighteen months earlier, David Selznick had asked Loretta to test for GONE WITH THE WIND. Loretta remembered, "I said, 'No, I wouldn't be right for it, David. You'll end up wanting me to play Melanie, and I'm not going to play a second part to anybody."

John Hay Whitney, known as Jock Whitney, and his cousin, Cornelius Vanderbilt Whitney, were business partners to David Selznick. The initial Whitney millions had been made through astute investments in railroads, and when Jock Whitney's father died in 1927, he inherited a personal fortune of 60 million dollars (He would inherit another 25 million when his mother died in 1944). His business operation was based in New York, but he was often in Hollywood.

Loretta recalled, "I was crazy about Jock the first night I met him at a party at David and Irene's (Selznick's). He was a no-nonsense, masculine, big man. He either liked you and showed it, or he ignored you, no half measures with this one. He didn't ignore me, and I was flattered. He was married and I knew it. We both had a crush on each other, but that is as far as it went. I think I only had one dinner with him alone. The rest of the time it was always at parties, or evenings out with the Selznicks and the whole Hollywood group of that time.

"I was in New York on one of my publicity trips, and Myron called up and said, 'Jock wants to know if you want to go to Virginia to his house for the weekend. His wife is going to be there.' I said, 'Yes I would.' So Myron, David Selznick and I went down.
Liz Whitney was a charming hostess, but she and Jock didn't seem to get along; there was constant friction between them. He was not nice to her, and she was barely polite to him. I couldn't decide to be happy or sad about it. "

On another East coast weekend, Jock invited Loretta to a football game up at Yale, his alma mater. William Powell was also in his party. Loretta related the price of being a movie star. "The police came and said, 'We hate to do this, but Miss Young and Mr. Powell's presence is causing a riot.' Bill Powell and I left and waited in the car, the Whitney's private train car that so impressed me. That's how we had gotten to New Haven from New York."

Loretta's relationship with Whitney was bound to crash against reality sooner or later. She recalled a fateful conversation. "Jock and I had been to a party in Los Angeles. He came in for a drink and said, 'We really have to do something about this relationship; I'm falling more in love with you every day.' It was a sticky situation; his marriage was rocky, but he was married nevertheless. I really didn't want to talk about it because I didn't want to lose his attention nor his affection.

"Anyway, he said, 'Liz and I haven't been getting along for three or four years now, and it's not going to get any better.' I explained, 'You're married in your own religion. Until she dies, you're married to her, and she looks well and healthy to me. I've already been through one of these. I got married out of the Church at 17, and I was miserable. I would be all the more miserable now.' We had a long discussion, and he was very considerate. He did not walk off in a huff, the way most men would."

Director William Wellman would one day tell actor Stuart Whitman, "That little Catholic girl, Loretta Young, broke more hearts in Hollywood than anyone else." Loretta reflected on this subject, "Nobody was as romance-struck as I. I think I was in and out of love so much because it was more pleasant for me to be in love, or think I was. If I'd get the least bit of an extra look from a man, I'd think, 'Oh good, he likes me!'" Loretta continuously fell in love with men who, for one reason or another, really weren't available to her. Just like John Earle Young.

THE DOCTOR TAKES A WIFE co-starred Ray Milland, and was followed by another Columbia picture, HE STAYED FOR BREAKFAST. It co-starred Melvyn Douglas and was a NITOTCHKA knock off, only this time, Douglas played the zealous Communist who learns about life and love from bourgeois Loretta.

The rest of Loretta's family remained busy. Gladys continued her decorating, and Polly Ann continued to be a leading lady in low budget pictures. Jack Lindley graduated from Loyola Law School, and Sally and Norman were befriended by Orson Welles and the Mercury Players.

Loretta was doing a lot of radio and agreed to appear on an early episode of THE SCREEN GUILD THEATER which premiered on CBS Radio in January, 1939. Tom Lewis, the thirty-seven-year-old, fair-haired boy of Young and Rubicam's radio department, was the producer. In these salad days of radio, the advertising agencies were very powerful, not only representing the sponsor but actually producing the shows. Young and Rubicam was one of the country's top agencies.

A meeting was arranged to discuss the script, and to accommodate Loretta's schedule, it was agreed to meet at her home. Loretta recalled, "I was doing a portrait sitting that day with my three sisters, and we were posing at the bottom of the staircase. The butler led Tom and his entourage past us and into the living room, closing the doors behind them.

"When I finished I joined them. Tom was there with assistants. Advertising people always run in packs plus there were my agents, five or six people altogether. I found Tom very interesting. He was bright, and he was the boss of the whole thing. He did a lot of talking and he talked well. He had a lovely smile, and I was attracted to him right away.

"Two or three days later, I asked my radio agent, 'Why don't you ask Mr. Lewis to join us for lunch?' He arranged for Tom to meet us at the Brown Derby. Tom was late, but asked for a rain check for lunch the following day only to be late again. I realized that he had a lot of things to do besides going to lunch with the leading lady."

Tom was still based in New York, but he and Loretta started dating frequently when he was in California. Loretta wasn't Tom's first movie star girlfriend; he had a very close relationship with actress Glenda Farrell in New York, and he had dated Bette Davis on previous forays to the West Coast. Bette was to read in the newspaper that Tom Lewis and Loretta were an item. Reacting, Bette dubbed Loretta, "A chocolate covered black widow spider." When Loretta heard about this, she said, "I didn't like it but I understood it. It had happened two or three times. She'd be seeing someone, George Brent, for instance, then I'd meet him, and soon I'd be dating him. So it was with Spencer and then Tom."

Who was this guy who could swoop into Hollywood and attract the attention of two of its most fascinating women?

John and Josie Wayne married in the garden of Loretta's Sunset House, 1933. Loretta was Maid of Honor.

Traveling on the SS Ise De France in 1935. Loretta is pregnant with her secret baby.

Sally and Norman Foster's wedding day, 1935. The ceremony took place in the Sunset House. Loretta remained in her upstairs bedroom; her secret pregnancy was now to obvious.

Polly Ann and Carter Hermann's wedding day, 1936

Chapter 11: ALL THE RIGHT REASONS

When Tom Lewis was a young boy in Troy, New York, his policeman father sought the position of Police Chief. The local Democratic-political machine had initially promised their support but then threw their weight behind an opposing candidate. Some years later, Sergeant Jim Lewis sought the appointment a second time only to have the original scenario repeated. The whole family felt betrayed.

Tom had two older brothers plus an older and a younger sister. He often escaped across the street to the Perry house. Quite a contrast to the Lewis's rented home, it was one of the largest in town and included a library. Miss Perry, a spinster caring for her aging mother, became quite fond of Tom and through her books, introduced him to faraway places. Tom admired the people in these stories. What they did and how they lived seemed so much more important than the activities of working class Troy.

Years later, he was elected Class President of his senior year. Tom's father was Welch, his mother, Irish, and Tom was mastering the use of Celtic charm to get what he wanted. The year was 1920.

Tom worked his way through Union College at Schenectady, New York, collecting delinquent payments for the Singer Sewing Machine Company. Upon graduation, he headed for New York City and tried his hand at acting and playwriting. He returned to Schenectady three years later where he wrote, produced, and played in a fifteen minute serial broadcast three times weekly. His responsibilities expanded to include being the station's announcer and the male lead of a weekly soap opera.

Six years later, Tom moved onto the NBC owned radio station, WTAM, in Cleveland, Ohio. His producing talents were soon recognized by the parent company, and he became the station program director. He then set his eyes on Young and Rubicam in New York. He realized working for a major agency was the way to the top of the radio world of the Thirties. The president of the agency was Chet LaRoche. He liked Tom and hired him. THE KATE SMITH HOUR for General Foods was one of the first shows Tom produced. He soon became Production Supervisor of all the agency's radio programs.

Tom, now in his early thirties, was a handsome man with dark eyes and wavy brown hair. He parlayed his good looks by dressing exquisitely and established a smart address at the Russell Hotel on Park Avenue. He escorted his dates to the nightspots where one was noticed, and his name soon began popping up in the gossip columns as a man about town. Actress Glenda Farrell was the most famous of his dates, and they became a steady item.

Tom was the producer of THE SCREEN GUILD THEATER which required him to become bicoastal. Murray Bolen worked for Young and Rubicam in Hollywood. He recalled Tom's arrival on the scene, "He was superimposed on the rest of us working fools; Chet LaRoche set this boy in there! He was a very hot character, and he moved in the right circles. As far as the office, it took exactly that kind of gung-ho attitude to get everything to work well, and he was a master at it. I can't say that he actually had any production knowledge, but he had people to do all that. He did all the upper-structure stuff."

The more Loretta learned about Tom, the more impressed she became. He was Catholic and seemed to know a lot about his religion. She was fascinated that this man about town was also on a spiritual quest. The romance prospered even though it was often long distance. Loretta recalled, "Either Tom had some project to do out here, or he would fly out, maybe once a month, for three or four days. Then we'd write romantic letters back and forth, and it was all kind of make believe."

Reflecting back, Loretta admitted that she was feeling pressure. "I was sick and tired of reading in the paper, 'Oh, poor Loretta, her romantic life is doomed. Here she is twenty-seven-years-old and no man in her life.'" She also knew that she could only be happy in a marriage blessed by her church.

Loretta recalled, "Tom had asked me to marry him, and I had accepted him, but Mama had not given the engagement party yet. We were going to a Sunday afternoon cocktail party. While we were driving there, I said, 'Tom, are you sure you are enough in love with me to stay married to me for the rest of your life?' He said, 'Yes, indeed. Aren't you?' I said, 'No. I don't know. Not for sure, I mean.' Well, he hit the ceiling! I meant it as a serious and important question for both of us; I didn't realize at the time that his ego was bigger than anything else. He said, 'I'm going to tell you something: I'm going to be difficult enough to be married to if you're madly in love with me, and if you aren't, forget it!' We arrived at our host's, and Tom leaned over and opened the car door. I got out and he, simply nonplused, closed the door and drove off. I was very hurt and upset because there was absolutely no understanding of what I meant. What I meant was: 'I'm a movie actress and that wouldn't be easy for any man. Are you really enough in love with me? Because when we get married, that's it; both of us are Catholic and we can't marry anybody else.'

"I gathered myself together and went in, explaining that Tom would be back in a few minutes; he had gone to get cigarettes.' Somebody was leaving a half hour later, and I asked, 'Would you mind dropping me at home? I've got a big headache.' Then I said, 'When Tom comes, tell him I'll meet him at my house. '

"Tom never came, and he didn't call for two or three days. When he did call, he was back in New York, and he said, 'It was a dumb thing for me to do. I don't know what got in to me.' I said, 'Well, I don't think you are sure, and I don't think I am sure, so let's just let things go for a while.' He said, 'Well, fine. When I come out I'll call you.' The press knew everything in this town, so quite soon, they were saying, 'Poor Loretta, now she's not engaged anymore.'"

The period when Tom and Loretta were dating overlapped with the time that Loretta was also seeing Jimmy Stewart. She recalled, "One time I walked into some restaurant on The Strip with Jimmy, and Tom was there with somebody else. Tom came over to the table and said, 'I thought you were out of town.' I said, 'I was.' And Jimmy said, 'So what?' his voice rising, sounding just like he did in one of his movies. Jimmy was playing the field, but it was always very special when he asked me out. I could have been seriously interested in him. In fact, I was crazy about him. I prayed for a long time for Jimmy to ask me to marry him, but he didn't."

Loretta planned to attend a New Year's Eve party at Myron Selznick's chalet at Lake Arrowhead. She recalled, "I was packing to go, and Tom called from New York and said, 'I'm coming out.' I said, 'Oh, that's too bad because I'm going to be away for New Year's Eve.' He asked, 'Where are you going?' I said, 'I'm going up to Myron's in the mountains.' And he said, 'I'll be at the Hotel Marmount in case you want to reach me.' I said, 'Fine.' Anyway, I didn't get back until Tuesday, and he was leaving on Wednesday, and so he called me on Tuesday night and said, 'I cannot get over you.' I said 'Why?' He said, 'I thought you were going to call me on New Year's Eve.' I said, 'No, I told you I was going to Myron's. I didn't say I'd call you on New Year's Eve.' He said, 'Well, I just assumed you would. Perhaps I shouldn't have.' From that point on, he took an entirely different attitude towards me. Now it was, 'Oh, whatever you want to do,' and he simply ingratiated himself right back into my life and our engagement.

"Really, I think what actually turned me around was a letter I received from Mama who was in Mexico City. She was on a buying trip and had been away for about six months. She liked Tom very much because he was a Catholic and a very likable man. And she was so afraid that I was going to marry one of those poor acting fellows who had been married three or four times before, and I'd end up being excommunicated from the Church. I had written to her, and told her that I had broken my engagement to Tom. I had said, 'I don't know why except that I'm just not sure.'

"It wasn't characteristic for Mama to write a letter. When she'd write, it was a very, clipped little thing. This time she wrote a long letter back and said, 'I'm going to presume to do something which I probably shouldn't do, but I want to tell you this story. I was engaged to a man before I met your father, and I should have married him. He was a wonderful man for all the right reasons, but I met your father and your father swept me off my feet. There was nothing wrong with Earle except he was a charmer and wonderful looking, and he just loved the women, and the women loved him, and he couldn't leave them alone. I should have married the other man. If I had been more mature, I would have.' She continued, 'I feel the same way about Tom Lewis. He is solid'….and he's this and that and the other. She wrote over ten pages and it made sense as she always did."

Loretta reconsidered and concluded, "Tom will take good care of me. I'll have a good solid life and be happy as a wife and mother."

The wedding day August 1, 1940 arrived. The only member of Tom's family to fly out for the wedding was his brother, Charles, who acted as best man. Dr. Charles Lewis was Chief of Staff of a hospital in Troy. Charles had had some reservations about the marriage. Loretta recounted a conversation that took place between the two brothers at the time of their engagement that Tom would later relay to Loretta. "Charles said, 'Tom, I like Loretta very much, but can you handle a movie star? She will get all the attention. Can you handle that?'"

The ceremony was held in the priest's rectory at St. Paul the Apostle in Westwood. Loretta recalled." It was customary in those days for second marriages to be simple affairs, and there was the added consideration of privacy. Had it been held in the church, the public would be able to attend."

The Los Angeles Times reported that three thousand fans stood outside to get a glimpse of Loretta. Four women fainted in all the excitement and it took five policemen to clear a path for the newly married couple when they departed the rectory.

It was in the early morning hours of the following day when Tom and Loretta flew to Mexico for their honeymoon. Loretta remembered looking at Tom as he fell asleep in the seat next to her. "I asked myself, 'What do I really know about this man?' It was just a brief thought that came over me. My main feeling was that he was perfectly cast as Mama had observed in her letter: ten years older than I, a practicing Catholic, not in my business but in radio, and yes, I was in love with him. It was easy for me to believe, 'I've married him for all the right reasons.'"

They would spend a whole month honeymooning in Mexico. Irene had designed her trousseau in addition to her wedding dress, so there were lots of suitcases travelling from one destination to the next. Loretta was very popular in Mexico, particularly after RAMONA. They attended the bullfights in Mexico City, and Loretta was invited to throw the corsage to the matador. Loretta recalled, "Right after I did that, the whole stadium went wild, and a crowd started moving toward our box. Immediately, a wall of policemen strategically gathered around our box. Tom loved the attention."

The newlyweds settled in New York City to start everyday married life. Loretta recalled, "We took a quite large apartment at the Marguerite on Park Avenue with a living room, a dining room, three bedrooms and three bathrooms. I'm not sure what came over me; I was afraid of New York the first five days I was there and wouldn't leave the apartment. I don't know why. Maybe because all the times I'd been to New York, I had been there as a movie star, and now I was there as Mrs. Tom Lewis, a wife. The role was so unfamiliar to me and I panicked. Tom sensed my uneasiness and arranged for a woman from his office to take me shopping. After that I was all right."

Once they were settled in their new apartment, Loretta arranged for Judy and the governess, Miss Shankey, to join the household. Loretta recalled, "One night after they arrived, Tom and I had gone to the theatre with some friends. There wasn't a trace of snow going in, but when we came out, it was like a fairyland. I had never seen snow falling and everything was so white and pure. After we got home, I went to the window and just stood there gazing. Tom woke Judy and brought her in. He said, 'Judy, your mother is so impressed with this, I thought you would be, too. Isn't that beautiful?' She was only five at that time, but she was thrilled to death. I loved Tom all the more for wanting her to share that lovely moment with us. These were very happy days."

The future of her career as an actress was in an arbitrary stage of ambiguity for both Tom and Loretta. Would she continue her acting career? Was she to be the Manhattan wife of radio executive Tom Lewis? Could she have it all and do both? Tellingly, the subject was never discussed prior to their marriage. This allowed both of them to position themselves to get what they wanted without disturbing any illusions. Loretta recalled, "I went to New York because that's where Tom's job was, but somewhere in the back of my mind, I thought, 'Fine. This is where I'll go. This won't last,' because I knew that if I wasn't working, money wouldn't come in fast enough. How was he going to pay for that apartment, my clothes, our entertainment and Judy's schooling?"

Tom was equally duplicitous. He had sent Loretta house hunting in Los Angeles before they had married. Loretta recollected, "I called and told him, 'I've found a house on Camden Street (Beverly Hills) that Mama can redo. It's $10,000; do you want it?' He said, 'Fine, buy it. 'I think the $10,000 dollars was his entire savings. Then I put $60,000 more into redoing it. The ratio of how much each invested reflected their individual earning power at that time. Tom was in the $30,000 range, certainly respectable for 1940, but dwarfed by the $250,000 that Loretta was making annually. By having that house, in addition to the apartment in New York, Tom was able to lock in a working movie star wife, and at the same time, be able to say, "Well, my work is in New York."

The issue was settled quite simply when Loretta was offered THE MEN IN HER LIFE, a picture about the rigors of a ballet dancer and her love life along the way. Tom's response was, "Well, obviously you have to go home to do the picture. I'll come out when I can." The project offered the opportunity to fulfill

Loretta's childhood dream of being a ballerina. She started practicing twelve hours a day with an instructor from the American Ballet who came to their apartment every day for two months.

THE MEN IN HER LIFE was delayed, allowing Loretta to sneak in another project, THE LADY FROM CHEYENNE. The comedy, set in pioneer days, brought Loretta back to Los Angeles. She worked on that film during the day while continuing her dancing rehearsals for THE MEN IN HER LIFE at night in her garage.

Loretta had a frightening experience while filming THE MEN IN HER LIFE. She recalled, "It was an emotional scene. The dancing master played by Conrad Veidt was driving my character too hard on the bar, shouting, 'Faster, faster!' She obeys until finally she collapses onto the floor and bursts out crying. The scene was going well, but when I collapsed onto the floor as rehearsed, everything froze. My hand was still clutching the exercise bar and wouldn't move. I couldn't talk, and my eyes wouldn't close. Apparently, not enough oxygen was getting to my muscles. The thing that scared me the most was that I couldn't undo my hand. They called for the studio doctor who gave me a shot to relax my muscles. I went immediately to sleep right there on the floor, and they then moved me to the infirmary. The next morning I was fine, so we shot the scene again, but the director had printed all the film from the day before, and that's what they used in the finished picture."

Loretta's post marriage return to films set the template of her continuing career. Polly Ann decided to call it quits. She played Bela Lugosi's daughter in her last film, THE INVISIBLE GHOST. She recalled a scene where she was supposed to be sleeping and Lugosi, in a trance, stalks into her room with the intent of strangling her. "They had to shoot the two of us separately because I couldn't keep from laughing." It was a fitting sendoff. Polly Ann said of her career, "I enjoyed every bit of it, but I was busy with Carter and I didn't need to work."

Sally's focus was also on her marriage, and it was Norman Foster's career that was gaining steam. He had developed a working relationship with Orson Welles and directed him and Joseph Cotten in JOURNEY INTO FEAR.

Meanwhile, Georgiana began a career of her own. She recalled, "I was accompanying Mama to New York. Bob Taplinger, a writer and one of Mama's tenants, was on the train and we stopped off at Washington, D.C. Bob took us out to dinner, and Howard Hughes joined us. They both were asking, 'So, what are you going to do when you get to New York?' I said, 'Well, nothing. I'll just be with my mother.' They said, 'You should do some modeling.'

So, once we got to New York, Bob, who was on the make, thought it would help him by introducing me to the editor of *Redbook Magazine*. Bob knew the editors of all the fashion magazines. The next night, I got a call to go to the Harry Conover Agency and he arranged for appointments with *Harpers* and *Vogue*. I soon found out that if you worked for *Harper's Bazaar*, *Vogue* wouldn't use you, but it was better to work for *Harpers* because then you could also model for *Town and Country* and *Glamour*. I worked for six or seven months and I loved it, I was doing very well, several covers. I became the biggest model at Harry Conover's."

Gladys had insisted on Georgiana accompanying her on that trip to New York to nip a romance Georgiana was having with a married man. It was Loretta's responsibility now to finally end the lingering affection Spencer Tracy continued to express. She recalled, "Every year on my birthday, Spencer would send three dozen red roses. On the first year Tom and I were married, they arrived again with the note, "Love, Spence.' I could tell it rankled Tom so I wrote Spencer, 'The roses are beautiful, but I am a married woman now, and your sending me flowers upsets my husband very much. If you do feel as strongly about me as you say you do, please don't send any more flowers. I can't be thinking of five years ago. "'

Loretta's commitment to Tom Lewis in marriage included turning all financial considerations over to him. Loretta stated, "I never really thought about it; I would make the money, and I expected that Tom would know what to do with it. Mama had always handled it before my marriage, and did it extremely well. Now my husband would take over."

Gladys had invested Loretta's discretionary funds into the seventeen Beverly Hills homes that she furnished and rented. Tom didn't have a background in real estate, and it bothered him to carry mortgage obligations. Tom indicated he wanted to be totally in charge, so Gladys referred to him the myriad of monthly bills. Loretta recalled, "The first time I knew there was any problem, we had been in the Camden house for several months, and I heard Tom talking on the phone. I didn't know who he was talking to, but he was saying, 'I don't care what you say. I want it by the end of this month, or we'll take this to court.' I said, 'Who are you talking to?' He said, 'Your mother.' I said, 'My mother!' I put my hand over the receiver and said, 'You hang up that phone this minute!' She didn't talk to us for a year."

Sally got into the middle. She recalled, "I went over when Tom wasn't home and said, 'Gretch, Mama is crying because Tom is accusing her of stashing away cash in some bank account. You know that's ridiculous.' Before I left I said to Loretta, 'The way that he's treating Mama about this money, wait until you see what he does to you. It'll happen; you wait and see.'"

The net result was that equity in the houses was split and, at Loretta's insistence, Gladys kept eleven of them. Tom sold the remaining six houses and the Sunset house as well. The cost of this financial realignment spilled over into the personal venue. Gladys was not speaking to Loretta and Tom, and Loretta wasn't talking to Sally because of her harsh accusations about Tom.

Loretta didn't want an estrangement from her mother, and in turn, the rest of her family. She had been in that predicament before when she married Grant. What she did want however was something she had never had. She wanted to cling to the conventional view of a man taking care of her. Toward that end, loyalty to Tom came first.

Tom, too, had very traditional views regarding appropriate gender roles, and he had real misgivings about his mother-in-law. He saw her as a bad example to her daughters in the way that she had shed both of her husbands, and then became successful in her own right with no obligations to any man.

THE LADY FROM CHEYENNE and THE MEN IN HER LIFE were only lukewarm at the box office. However, the tally for

Columbia's THE DOCTOR TAKES A WIFE, and HE STAYED FOR BREAKFAST came in favorably, and Harry Cohn was anxious to nab Loretta for another formula comedy, BEDTIME STORY. It was now apparent Loretta's work would keep her in California, and the New York apartment was given up.

Japan bombed Pearl Harbor while BEDTIME STORY was in production. It propelled Hollywood into a new phase, and both Tom and Loretta would play their parts.

Chapter 12: WARTIME

Loretta was engaging in battle with studio head Harry Cohn weeks before Congress declared war. Loretta explained, "We started production on BEDTIME STORY and discovered we needed an extra dress for the next week. I had recently shopped for my personal wardrobe at I. Magnin's, and I said, 'I have a beautiful dress that I haven't worn, and I'll sell it to you for the picture.' The people at wardrobe agreed, and I called Magnin's to send the white dress to Columbia. The wardrobe man asked, 'What's it going to cost?' I asked him, 'What'd you pay Irene (the designer) for the other evening dress?' He said, '$750.' I said, 'Fine, same price.'

"A few days later my agent called me. He said, 'Harry Cohn is madder than hell. He says you're charging him $750 for a dress that you paid $165, and he thinks that it's disgraceful that you'd try to make money on him this way.' The sale's price was still on the dress, and a lady from the wardrobe apartment alerted Harry. I got furious, 'It's none of his business what I paid for it.' I explained that it was a sales dress from Bernard Newman, and because he's a friend of mine, he spent hours adding a scarf and redesigning the dress for which I paid extra. He called me back in a few minutes and said, 'I've just talked to Harry, and he says, 'No way is he going to pay you $750; he won't buy the dress. He's

sending it back to your house, and he'll have the wardrobe
department copy it.'

"This started us off. Overtime at the studio is very expensive,
and I knew it, so I decided I would not fit during my noon hour,
but only after I finished working at six. That put them all: the
beaders, the seamstresses, everybody, on overtime. We'd be in
the fitting room and I'd say, 'Oh, this beading is lovely, but it
should be down there, don't you think?' So they'd take it all off
and put it all back on again. I don't know how much money I ran
up on that dress.

"Harry Cohn was furious with me and sent word, 'Tell her she's
not to take her stockings home anymore.' For years at the studio,
when I'd put on a pair of stockings, I'd just wear them home. I'd
never bought a pair of stockings in my life, and nobody seemed
to mind. A star is not going to wonder, 'Who wore them before?'
The studio didn't supply your underwear, but anything you
could see was supplied, and stockings are something that you
see. So I said, 'Oh, okay.' So each night as I would take my
stockings off, I'd put my fingernails all the way through them just
so they'd rip. Then I put them in a cellophane bag and sent them
up to Harry's office, marked *Loretta*."

Now that Congress had declared war, Hollywood responded in major ways. Both the Hal Roach Studios and The Disney Studios were commandeered for the making of training films. Bette Davis and John Garfield organized the Hollywood Canteen where servicemen were entertained by stars. Loretta remembered observing Bette Davis at this time. "Oh, she was bright. Extremely so. And she had very little self-consciousness. She didn't expect too much from herself as far as looks; she never thought she was even pretty. Therefore, when she was talking about something she was interested in, she'd learn everything she could about her subject, no matter what it was. She did it so well, she scared the hell out of me. You didn't dare open your mouth, or she'd pin you right to the wall."

Tom Lewis received a direct commission as a Major to head the Army Radio Section. The idea was to provide radio entertainment for all army troops regardless of where they were stationed. Programming consisted of telecasts produced for the U.S. commercial stations, minus the commercials, as well as specially produced material. The programs were transcribed on long playing acetate discs that could be shipped all over the world. Major Carter Hermann, Polly Ann's husband, reported to Tom. He was the officer in charge of the Short Wave Operation's section. Short waving was used for live special-events like the World Series. Armed Forces Radio was an ambitious undertaking, and it was just the opportunity that would tap Tom Lewis's best resources. He could charm, cajole, and posture his position of authority with ease.

Director Frank Capra was making films for the military, and after successfully convincing his superiors that he needed improved facilities, moved his division to the Fox Studios on Western Avenue in Hollywood. Tom's radio division relocated from Washington, D.C. to join Capra. By this time, Tom had been promoted to Lieutenant Colonel.

Loretta was an excellent War Bonds salesperson, credited for selling seven million dollars in bonds. She also visited induction centers as well as injured troops in the hospital.

Loretta remembered signing a bomber that was headed for the Pacific. She wrote in large letters, LORETTA using a big paint brush. "I was up on a ladder, and it was at some base back east. Not too long ago, I ran into a man who asked, 'Do you remember signing a bomber? I was one of the crew.' I He told me he was the only one that survived. He had a picture of it which he carried in his wallet. There they were; all standing in front of this giant of plane with my name larger than life written all over it. They were all smiling and pointing to my name. I was deeply moved looking at the picture of all those young men."

The USO asked Loretta to go overseas two or three times, but as Loretta recalled, "Tom vetoed the idea saying, 'No, absolutely not. That's why I'm in the war to protect my wife and family, and she's not going overseas.' But nobody else knew that. I was allowed to go down to the canteen from time to time. Tom's attitude was, 'No sense in everybody getting into it.' The war was his."

Wartime audiences could not get enough of Hollywood entertainment. To accommodate the war workers' and servicemen's demand, many theaters operated 24 hours.

MY SISTER EILEEN, set in Greenwich Village, had done very well. Hollywood, never adverse to imitation, placed Loretta's next film, A NIGHT TO REMEMBER in Greenwich Village. It was billed as a comedy-thriller and co-starred Brian Aherne. Loretta had one of her favorite close-ups in this film. It appears very early, right after she steps out of a cab and is gazing at her new apartment building.

CHINA was surefire excitement for wartime crowds. Loretta played an American teacher to a group of Chinese girls who was trying to escape from Japanese soldiers. They combine forces with Alan Ladd who, as an American petroleum salesman, switches his allegiance after the bombing of Pearl Harbor.

Loretta was now thirty-years-old and extended Father Ward's admonition, about the power of example in her personal life, to what she did on screen as well. This tenet produced a clash with both the director of CHINA, John Farrow, and the Production Head of Paramount, Buddy De Silva. Loretta explained, "The teacher I played was to condone the suicide of one of the Chinese girls. I said, 'No, I'm sorry; I can't do this picture. I won't propagandize suicide as an answer to anything.' They said, 'Fine, we'll cut the scene.' We were three weeks into the picture when John Farrow, the director, brought me the blue pages and the scene was back in. I said, 'I'm not going to play this.' John said, 'Then you and I better go see Buddy De Silva.'

"We met with Buddy De Silva and he said, 'I understand that you refuse to do this scene.' I said, 'I've already explained all of this before I started the picture, and Myron Selznick got an okay from you. I am diametrically opposed to the theory that suicide is an answer to anything.' Buddy said, 'Well, it's only a movie.' I said, 'I'm sorry. It's not only a movie. If you read some of my fan mail, you'd realize how seriously some people take these movies.'

"He said, 'You and your Goddamn Catholicism! This is not a church; this is a studio, and we're making pictures to entertain people.' I said, 'You can always get a new leading lady.' Buddy stood up and pounded on the desk, 'You're not going to tell me how to run my studio!' I said, 'I don't intend to, Buddy, but I told you and the studio that I'd only agree to do this picture if that scene was deleted. Who put it back in?'

'Well, Mr. Farrow and the producer think it's important.' I said, 'Mr. Farrow never mentioned this to me on the set.' John (Farrow) was sitting right there, and he said, 'I thought it was the studio's business more than yours.' I said, 'Well, apparently not,' and then I said, 'Buddy, you can recast if you like, but I'm not playing that scene as it is now written.' John Farrow thoroughly enjoyed that escapade, but the scene was deleted."

A further complication on CHINA was that Loretta didn't like working with Alan Ladd. Loretta recalled, "He was a whiner and I hate that. It's bad enough for a woman, but in a man it's very unappealing. Any man who calls for his agent every time he doesn't get his own way and his agent happens to be his wife (Sue Carroll), there is something radically wrong. The least little thing that would happen, he'd be on the phone saying, 'Sue, you'd better get over here and straighten this out.'

"I remember one time there was a rain sequence. My dressing room was inside the stage, and his dressing room was outside the stage, and he didn't like that. So he called Sue and said, 'I'm going to get just as wet as she is; I can get pneumonia just as quick as she can. You'd better get over here.' There simply was not room on the stage for the set, the camera, the crew, and two dressing rooms. He would not work until Sue arrived so everybody sat around. When she finally came in, she went around quietly and talked to the assistant director. They didn't bring his dressing room into the stage, and I got a cold shoulder from Alan from then on."

LADIES COURAGEOUS was Loretta's second film with a war theme. It was based on the true activities of the Women's Auxiliary Ferrying Squadron.

Russell Bidwell was Loretta's public relations representative. When he came up with the idea for her to ride around Beverly Hills in a horse and carriage to promote the idea of saving gas, she thought it was time to look for someone new. Tom introduced Loretta to Helen Furguson, and her first project was for Loretta to pose in a Red Cross uniform on the cover of *Saturday Home Magazine.* Loretta felt this kind of positioning tapped right into her appeal, and her association with Helen would last for the next twenty-five years.

Loretta reflected on what she thought her appeal had been to movie-goers. "Compared to Joan Crawford or Bette Davis, I was more like the average woman. During my years there were a lot of awfully nice, pretty, sweet, average women. I don't know what the average woman is today, but she's certainly not like they were in the Thirties and Forties. My appeal wouldn't have been to the intellectuals or the neurotics. Nor to the shop girls and secretaries, that would have been Joan Crawford's market. But there were an awful lot of women out there like me: willing to play by the rules, didn't sleep around, and weren't very aggressive. A Loretta Young movie had a happy ending, a nice husband or lover, no abuse of any kind. That's what the heroes and heroines were in those days."

Norman Foster headed south of the border to make pictures in Mexico. Sally, and their daughter Gretchen, accompanied him. They met the young actor Ricardo Montalban who in turn introduced them to his family. Sally remembered his mother saying, "'Ricardo, if you can find a girl like Sally, get her and marry her fast.' I said, 'I have one sister left!' I decided that I would bring Ricardo to Los Angeles with me specifically to meet Georgiana."

Georgiana recalled, "I had just celebrated my 19th birthday, and Sally wrote, 'I have your husband all picked out for you and I'll send you a picture.' The married actor that I had been in love with was also Mexican, so I was expecting to see someone who looked like him. She sent me Ricardo's picture, and he didn't look like this other man at all. Ricardo was so handsome, so pretty and I thought, 'I don't like handsome men.' I was more for the John Garfield type. But then I met Ricardo! We went together for two weeks, fell madly in love, and went to Tijuana and got married before he went back to Mexico to do a picture. I was supposed to go with him, but didn't because I was pregnant right away. When he came back, we got married in a church; then he had to go back to finish another picture."

John Wayne and Carter Hermann were concerned about protecting their wives and children in case the Japanese invaded California. Together, they bought a 1,700 acre ranch outside of Fallbrook, California, in San Diego County, and built homes next door to each other. Everyone kept it a big secret so that woman and children could quietly disappear if need be.

Polly Ann and Josie were never to live in those homes. The Waynes' marriage would not survive the war. Josie speculated on the reasons, "I think success came too soon, too fast for Duke. He had had his big success in STAGECOACH, and I think that he woke up one morning and thought, 'I'm, married, I have four children, I'll probably have ten children before long, and I haven't really gone out and sowed my wild oats yet.' That was part of it, but I think that our break-up was a combination of a lot of things.

"When I was going through my divorce, Gretchen was absolutely marvelous. I remember feeling depressed and calling Gretch one night; it must have been 10:00 or 11:00, and Miss Shankey answered. She said, 'Oh, no, no. She's working in the morning; I couldn't disturb her now.' I said, 'Okay, fine.' Gretch called me the next morning and asked, 'Did you call me last night?' I said, 'Well, Miss Shankey told me .... ,' and Gretch interjected, 'And I told Miss Shankey that I don't care if it's 3:00 in the morning. If Mrs. Wayne ever calls, put her on the phone immediately.' I'll never forget that."

Loretta recalled, "Once, after their divorce, Duke had invited us to something, and I said, 'No way.' Tom disagreed, saying, 'I think that you're carrying things a little far. After all, Josie gets along with him.' I said, 'No Tom, I'm sorry. Josephine is my best friend, and if I were in her situation, I wouldn't appreciate it at all if she were buddy buddies with my ex-husband.' I realize now that the other woman had threatened a scandal if he didn't marry her.

Still, she must have had something that fascinated him, or he would have said no.

"I remember one time, I was just arriving at my house and I saw Duke's car coming up on Camden. Even from a half a block away, I could see he was looking at me. I hesitated at the driveway and he sped up, and I said, 'Oh, please, Lord, don't let him stop; I don't want to go through this.' This was after he was married to the other woman. Anyway, he stopped for a second; I looked at him, he looked at me, and I went in the house and he went on. And that's the only contact I had with him for the next thirty years."

By all accounts, Tom was doing a fabulous job heading Armed Forces Radio. He was an important man, the kind of guy he had felt destined to be. As for the future, only the sky was the limit.

Chapter 13: A SON FOR TOM, A SON FOR LORETTA

Loretta wanted another child. After 3 1/2 years of trying, including artificial insemination with Tom's sperm, Dr. Holleran had another idea. "I'm going to perform a D&C; it's not the chic thing to do, but it often works." Loretta was pregnant three months later.

Loretta's career pace changed after her marriage. She now only wanted to make two pictures a year. The catch was she needed two good scripts, and Myron Selznick's continuing drift into alcoholism had lessened his effectiveness. She gathered the courage to confront Myron and ask his help in obtaining a new agent. He directed her to Bert Allenberg.

Loretta had time to do AND NOW TOMORROW before her pregnancy became obvious. Alan Ladd would play the male lead. Paramount didn't care if they liked each other; CHINA had made money, and they wanted more of the same.

Christopher Paul Lewis was born at Queen of Angels Hospital on August I, 1944. It was a tough delivery, and after the baby came home, Loretta had a hard time enjoying him. She recalled, "I wanted whatever time I could steal with this child to myself, but nursing lasted only a few weeks because the baby nurse wanted to wean the baby off the breast and onto a bottle as quickly as possible. I felt cheated somehow, but she was the expert, and I was used to listening to the experts. Subsequently, I decided the reason she was in such a hurry to wean him was because she had to get up in the middle of the night and bring him to me from the nursery every four hours."

Tom was swept away with the joy of having a son. For Tom, Chris was like a reincarnation of himself, but this time he'd be starting out with all the advantages. Tom had been a very attentive father to Judy up to the time that Chris was born. She had been his little girl. Now, at age 9, Judy was dismissed almost as an outsider. Loretta tried to compensate, but Judy was a sensitive child and aware of her father's rejection.

Bill Geotz had been a good friend of Loretta's since she was a teen contract player at First National Studios. He was now president of a new studio, International Pictures, and he approached Loretta with a five million dollar offer. He guaranteed her that she would have approval over all of her roles and have a hand in developing projects that would further her career. It was the best of both worlds: a guarantee of financial wellbeing combined with artistic freedom. The first film that Loretta did under her new deal was ALONG CAME JONES with Gary Cooper in the title role. It was quite a change of pace for Loretta. After eighty films, she was dressed in gingham and talking cowgirl talk.

Loretta was at the studio doing some tests before ALONG CAME JONES went into production. Concurrently, there were casting tests for the male antagonist. Loretta recalled, "Just as I was leaving my dressing room for the set, the assistant director came in and said 'Miss Young, I think you ought to know that one of the actors testing for this part is, he kind of whispered it, Grant Withers.' When I reached the set and I asked, 'Where is he?' The assistant said, 'We told him to wait in the make-up room until we were ready for him.' I said, 'Oh, don't do that; ask him to come out on the set.' He came out, and I realized that people thought there was going to be tension. I looked at him and said, 'Grant, you're never going to get this part; you're much too nice, and it will show.' And he didn't. I don't think there was a mean bone in Grant's body."

International Pictures had invested a lot of money in securing Loretta, and they wanted to recoup their investment by loaning her out for THERE GOES LONA JOHNSON. The story would be built around her character, just the kind of project that Loretta sought. She recalled, "I had discovered that I was pregnant again and was delighted. I thought that I was just two weeks along, so even though the costumes were of a bustle period, which meant you had to have an hour-glass figure, I thought that by the time I finished the picture, I would still be all right because they would hurry up and do the picture in twelve weeks. They said, 'Fine,' they'd start right away.

"But after my first visit to the doctor I discovered I was four months pregnant. I called the studio, and said, 'I'm terribly sorry, I'm not going to be able to do this picture because I'm four months pregnant, not two weeks.' I expected them to postpone the picture until after the baby was born. Not at all. I think it was twenty-four-hours later that I got a call, 'Could I come and meet with the Board of Directors?'

"My agent, Bert Allenberg, and I arrived at the studio and went into this board meeting. It was the first time I had been invited to attend, and I didn't know why, but I thought it was scary. The Chairman of the Board, not Bill Geotz, was running the meeting. He pointed out that I had only done one picture under my contract, and that was right after Christopher was born. The Board felt that if I was more interested in having a family than I was in my career, they would have to cancel my contract. It was a big contract. Abortion was still illegal in those days, but it was clear that's what they had in mind.

"Bill Geotz was sitting there, and when I looked at him a couple of times, he was looking someplace else; he was too embarrassed. Anyway, the Chairman got all through, and I said to him, 'Well, is that all?' The Chairman said, 'Yes.' So I got up and left the room. Later that night Bert Allenberg called me and said that they would cancel my contract if I went ahead with this pregnancy, and they wanted me to return the money paid me since I had finished my last picture. My reply was,
'Tell them to DROP DEAD!' and I got off the phone." It would take several months before a settlement was negotiated.

Amidst the uncertainty, the Lewises needed a bigger home with a new baby on the way. They bought Constance Bennett's forty-five room mansion on Carrollwood Drive in Holmby Hills for $68,000. Loretta described the home," There were three dining rooms, a large formal dining room, one for the children, and one for the servants. There was also a projection room, a four car garage, swimming pool, and tennis court, all spread out on two acres of land."

The Lewises were now set up to entertain formally, and they did a great deal of it. That took a full staff. Loretta remembered, "We had a housekeeper, a baby nurse, relief nurses for the children, a governess, a cook, relief cook, upstairs maid, downstairs maid, a gardener, a houseman who took care of Tom's clothes and for a while, a night watchman."

Peter's birth was a much smoother affair than Christopher's. Loretta recalled, "We had just arrived at the hospital when Dr. Holleran came meandering in. He said, 'Well, let's take a look.' He started to examine me and he said, 'Oh! Get the cart!' The baby's head was right there. A minute later, we're running down the corridor, Josie on one side, Tom on the other, and the nurse pushing the cart. Then the elevator is out of order, and we have to run all the way back to the other end of the corridor. We slam into the Delivery Room. The baby came so quickly, just like that. I asked, 'What is it?' He said, 'It's a boy.' I said, 'Oh, Tom is going to be so thrilled, a friend for Christopher.' Then I went to sleep.

"When I woke up, it was so quiet and peaceful, and I had a marvelous sense of having accomplished something wonderful. The baby was perfect and my feeling of total contentment stayed with me that entire day. At that moment, babies seemed to me the most important, the purest reason for my being alive. It was the happiest day of my life."

Loretta was only home two days before Tom talked her into allowing Father Peyton to visit her. Father Peyton was trying to get a radio program together in which Catholic actors would say the rosary. Loretta found him very dear, but thought his idea naïve. She agreed, never thinking it would happen. It did. The friendship between Father Peyton and the Lewises grew and one afternoon, Father, Tom, and some of his creative associates, were brainstorming in the Lewises' living room. That's when the phrase, "The family that prays together stays together," originated.

Before Tom separated from active service in December, 1945, Loretta recalled a meeting that he held in the Carrollwood house. "There were four or five of his officers, and we were all in the library. I knew all of these men, and I was sitting there sewing. Tom was talking and it was quite a long story. He had a habit of exaggerating. Everything he saw was from his own point of view, and it was a very interesting point of view, but it wasn't always based on the truth. If it made for a better story, so be it. I remember sitting there and thinking, 'Boy, this isn't what happened at all!'

"About every four or five lines, he'd say, 'Isn't that so, Dear?' 'Isn't that right, Loretta?' Up to this time, not wanting to embarrass him, I had always said, 'Ah-hum; Oh yes; Sure.' Well, finally I had had enough, and I blurted out, 'No, that isn't the way it happened at all, Tom.' There was dead silence in the room, and everybody looked at me and looked at him. I felt so sorry for him; it was as if I slapped him in the face. H was furious and didn't speak to me for two weeks."

Tom returned to Young and Rubicam after he separated from the Army. It wasn't an easy adjustment. His sphere of influence had shrunk. In addition, he was ill-prepared to reign over a large home with servants. Loretta recalled, "I came home from the studio one night. Miss Shankey, now the housekeeper, asked to speak to me. She said, 'It looks like we're going to lose the cook. She says she's never been treated this way in any house she's ever worked in.' I asked, 'Well, what was it?' She said, 'Mr. Lewis was in the kitchen while the servants were eating ice cream. He asked them, 'Is that Will Wright's ice cream you're eating?' They said, 'Yes.' He said, 'You save that for the family. You get yourself some less expensive ice cream,' and then left the room. I said, 'I can't believe that, Miss Shankey.' She said, 'I'm sorry but it's true.' I said, 'If she goes, she goes. Buy a pint of lesser ice cream and let it live there, but give them whatever they want. What we eat, they eat.'"

Tom made a better impression on Miss Smith, the boys' nurse. Loretta remembered, "Miss Smith regarded as Tom lord and master, and did anything he said. I usually didn't get home from the studio before 7:15, and I had asked Miss Smith, 'Please do not have the children in bed before I get home. I don't see them in the morning when I go out, and I'd like to see them at least once a day.' Anyway, I got home one night, around 7:15, and I went right upstairs. And as I walked into the nursery she said, 'Shhhh, we must be quiet, the boys are already in bed.' I said, 'Really? I asked you not to put ....' She replied, 'Well, Mr. Lewis thinks they should go to bed by 6:30.' I said, 'I'm sorry what Mr. Lewis thinks. I haven't seen them all day, and I miss them. So I got them both out of bed and sat down on the floor, and, oh, they were delighted to see me as I was to see them. In the meantime, Miss Smith just sat there pouting. Finally, I said, 'Miss Smith, haven't you got something you can do right now?' and she left the room.

"Tom came in and said, 'I thought the boys were in bed.' I replied, 'They were and I've gotten them out of bed because I haven't seen them all day. Surely that's a mother's right to see them once a day.' He said, 'Well, Miss Smith gets upset.' I said, 'I don't care what Miss Smith gets upset about, but I do care about seeing my sons.' What was so frustrating was that Miss Smith and Tom had a much better run at the boys than I did. They were crazy about her, and they were crazy about him, and they liked me. They saw the least of me."

ALONG CAME JONES, released the week Peter was born, had done very well so the executives at International Pictures negotiated one last picture with Loretta before her contract was rescinded. THE STRANGER focused on a manhunt for a Nazi mastermind who, after the war, fled to the United States. Orson Welles played the Nazi; Loretta played his deluded bride; and Edward G. Robinson played the clever pursuer of Welles. Welles also directed, and John Huston was an un-credited contributor to the script. All the ingredients were there to make a huge hit and it was. In fact, it was the only Orson Welles directed film that made money on its initial release.

Loretta had tremendous respect for Orson Welles, but found his cherubic face a source of humor. Loretta recalled him saying, "'All right, Loretta, I know I'm putting on weight, but you don't have to make fun of me in front of the whole set.' I said, 'Oh, Orson, I wasn't making fun of you. It's just that when you get so serious, your face is so cute that it makes me laugh. Russell Metty (the cameraman) tells me that if I laugh too much, I'll have to go and change my make-up at noontime. I'm getting all these laugh lines around my mouth, and he doesn't want to photograph them.'

"He said, 'Oh. Well, that makes me feel a little better.' From then on when he wanted to give me direction, he'd come up behind me and he'd say, 'Loretta, no, don't turn around. In the next scene, I want you to be so uptight that a pin dropping on the floor would make you scream.' That's the way he directed me."

There's a climactic scene in THE STRANGER where Loretta climbs a long ladder in a clock tower. Orson's character grabs her by the wrist and pulls her up, leaving Loretta's feet momentarily dangling. In reality, it was a stunt man pulling Loretta's hand and she had a harness on her wrist from which a continuous wire ran from the harness and up the stunt man's jacket, and beyond to another man holding on in case the first man let go. Loretta recalled, "The top of that sound stage was probably three stories high, so that's why they were taking such precaution. But they tried shooting this scene three or four times, and each time they'd yell, 'Cut 'because they could see the wire. I asked the stuntman what were the chances of him dropping me. He said, 'Only if I had a heart attack at that particular moment. 'So, we shot it without the wire, and everything went fine. Orson nearly killed the stuntman when he discovered what we had done. I said to Orson, 'Don't blame him; kiss him. You got the shot.' "

Georgiana and Ricardo had settled stateside, and Sally and Norman returned from Mexico. Georgiana recalled, "It was Norman who introduced Ricardo to Jack Cummings at MGM. Jack was looking for an actor for a picture called FIESTA (a major

Technicolor musical starting Esther Williams), and Norman talked him into giving Ricardo a screen test." He got the part, and it heralded the beginning of a lengthy relationship between Ricardo and Metro Goldwyn-Mayer.

Loretta's next project was THE PERFECT MARRIAGE with David Niven as co-star. Virginia Field played the second female lead. Loretta was not a favorite of Virginia Field. She said in an interview several years later that she found Loretta to be sickeningly sweet, a pure phony, and that Loretta's two faces sent her home angry and in tears several times. Miss Field was asked in 1990 for confirmation, and she said that she would stick with that assessment.

Loretta responded, "I made THE PERFECT MARRIAGE some forty years ago, and I'm sure I was not as understanding, or compassionate, or even interested in anybody else, as much as I am today. Anyway, I'm awfully sorry if I did that to Virginia. I admit however that all women are in competition with all women whether they know it or not. If you're in second place, no matter what it is, you're scratching to get to first place, and you've got to put the first one out of commission before you can get there. This is automatic. I'm not talking about personal ties. I'm just talking about 'female'."

Producer Dore Schary visited Loretta on the set of THE PERFECT MARRIAGE, and brought her a script called KATIE. Loretta recalled, "He had offered it to Ingrid Bergman, and she turned it down. Why he thought of me, I'll never know. Anyway, after I read the script I told him, 'It's a charming script, but I don't have a Swedish accent.' He said, 'Why don't you let me find a coach for you and try it? Just see. '"

Loretta did give it a try. Although it was a simple little story, the film would be a watershed event in Loretta's career. It would be released under the title of THE FARMER'S DAUGHTER.

Chapter 14: HOT PROPERTY

Loretta recalled a pivotal phone call from Tom nine months after he returned to his civilian career. Calling from his New York hotel, he said, "'How would you like to have a husband out of a job?' I was so shocked, I thought, 'Oh my God, I'm going to be the breadwinner forever.' I said, 'What's the matter?' He said, 'I just had a big blow-up with the Chairman of the Board (Sig Larman). He thinks I'm too extravagant. He wants to know why I have three cars in my garage, and I finally told him to go to hell and that's where we ended it.' I said, 'Well, you don't have to take insults from Sig. Fortunately you've got a home here, and a family who loves you. '"

Eventually, Tom was more forthright about the nature of the disagreement. Loretta recollected, "Tom had redecorated his Los Angeles office in movie star style, and Young and Rubicam wasn't used to that kind of extravagance. Sig had asked, 'How can you justify spending $20,000 on redecorating your office when you only earn $30,000 a year?' I think he hit a nerve. I noticed with my husband, if he got awfully mad, it was because you hit a nerve."

To Loretta's knowledge, Tom wasn't being deluged with offers. "Believe me, if he had been offered any kind of a job, even if it meant moving to New York, I would have moved back there so quickly because you can commute and do pictures. A lot of people did it. I was willing to do anything at that time to make this marriage successful. The boys were one and two years old, so we were just beginning."

Tom must have been suffering withdrawal. His position at Armed Forces Radio
had been a real ego booster, and now he was out of work. Loretta recalled a postwar conversation with George Rosenberg, a writer for Armed Forces Radio, in which he described to Loretta how imperious Tom had acted in his glory days. "'Everyone was calling Tom *Hitler* behind his back. Tom was a nut; he'd march up and down on top of the conference table during a meeting.' Later I asked Tom if he had really done that. He replied, 'Yes. I wanted to get their attention, and I got it.'"

Loretta could now better understand an incident that had bothered her earlier. She explained, "I was terribly shocked. Danny Kaye, Jack Benny, and Bill Geotz were at our house for a birthday party I was throwing for Tom. It was during the war because I remember Tom wearing his uniform. When it came time to blow out the candles, these three were standing together, and they sang, 'Happy birthday dear Tom, happy birthday you bastard, happy birthday to you.' They all laughed and thought it was hilarious. I was upset with all three of them. Tom probably had done something. All the actors in Hollywood were making shows for the Army, and Tom called on anybody he wanted, and I think probably misused them or bossed them around too much."

The fact that Loretta was pulling $250,000 a year was a mixed blessing. They could afford to live luxuriously and they did. But how was Tom important? He had a lot of time to think about it.

Meanwhile, Loretta was busy. THE FARMER'S DAUGHTER was an RKO comedy with heavy doses of patriotism and politics intertwined. The story focused on a maid of Swedish descent who, while working in a Congressman's home, decides to run for Congress on the opposition ticket. Joseph Cotten, Ethel Barrymore, and Charles Bickford co-starred.

Ruth Roberts, who had helped Ingrid Bergman lose her Swedish accent, coached Loretta to obtain one. Loretta was feeling very proud of her accent and recalled her indignation when, halfway through production, Director Henry Potter said, "'You know, I've been thinking about this thing, and I think it's time now that you drop the accent. After all, you've (Katie) been to night school. ' I replied, 'Yes, for six months. Why, if I had always gone to American schools, and I hadn't lost my accent by the time I hit twenty-five, which was the youngest I could be and still run for Congress, why would I lose it with 6 months at night school?' Henry said to me, 'Well, I feel you should lose it'. I said, 'Yes, and the people will say Loretta forgot her accent.'

"We went back and forth and finally I said, 'You'd better get Dore (Schary) down here to settle this; it seems we can't.' Henry and I continued our argument, and Dore finally said, 'Loretta, I think your accent is charming, but if it bothers Henry that much, do you think you could just lighten it a little?' I looked at him and I said, 'No. If you want to, Dore, you can recast.' It was about 4:00 in the afternoon by this time. Dore said, 'Well, it's late, why don't you go on home?' I said, 'I'm going home, but I'll see you in the morning with the accent so prepare yourself.' We went back to the set the next day and, I must say, Henry never mentioned it.

"Dore used to come on the set every day after viewing the rushes from the day before. About four or five days after the *drop the accent* incident, he said, 'Come here. I want to tell you something. You just keep going the way you are, and you're going to get an Academy nomination. You may not get the award, but you will get a nomination. Don't let anything rock your boat.' I said, 'Fine, I won't.' I thought it was just a little pep talk to make me feel better.

"I had a miscarriage during the shooting of the picture, and they had to close the picture for ten days because I was practically in every scene. When we came back, we were working on location at an auditorium called the Ebell Club on Wilshire Boulevard, and we had our portable dressing rooms outside in the alley next to the theatre. Mine was first in line; they do it by cast system; the star, and then the leading man, and then the character people, and so on. When I got out of the car and was walking to my dressing room, Ethel Barrymore was standing there, and she walked over to me very slowly and said, 'My dear child, you've been through a great deal; you must rest now as much as possible. I'm going to put my chair right here in front of your dressing room door, and nobody will get by me unless it's vitally important.' I said, 'Oh, wouldn't that be marvelous.' Boy, for three days we were
down there, and nobody bothered me. I would hear her say, 'Oh don't disturb her; she's working so hard and she needs her rest.'"

The farm location shooting took two weeks and was done on a real farm near Petaluma, California, north of San Francisco. Loretta recalled eleven-year-old Judy coming for a weekend. "She travelled on the train by herself, and I picked her up in San Francisco. She had a ball." No wonder. Loretta's idea of roughing it on location was staying in a suite at the Fairmont Hotel in San Francisco.

Loretta bleached her hair to play Katie. She elaborated on the repercussions. "When the picture was finished, my studio hair dresser advised me, 'Let it grow back; don't dye it back.' I said, 'I can't go out of the house looking like this.' She said, 'You have to.' I walked around town for about a month, and I couldn't stand it, so I went into some beauty shop and asked them to dye my hair brown. They did and, of course, it looked just like I had a hat on; it was all one color.

"Then I was walking down the street in Beverly Hills one day and, in the window, I saw myself, and I thought, 'My God, I've got to do something about this hair!' I spotted a beauty shop about three doors down and went in.

"This poor hair of mine had been so mistreated that when the woman got it all up in these little tiny permanent things and turned the heat on, all of a sudden, I saw this look of panic on her face. The man in the place came tearing over to me and switched something off. My hair was falling out, and I had a big hole in the back. The man was shaking so; he was scared I was going to sue him and make a fuss. I said, 'Look, it's not your fault. My hair has been bleached until they couldn't bleach it anymore, and then I had it dyed back. I neglected to tell the operator, so don't worry about it.' I walked around with a kind of a turban on for two or three weeks, and sure enough, little by little, it just fell out. I lost a lot of it. Then it started to grow back in strong and shiny."

Her marriage wasn't strong and shiny, and a moment of reckoning arrived from which there was no retreat. Loretta recalled, "We were at a party at the Shirley Burdens, and my brother-in- law Norman offered to get me a drink. I said, 'No, I don't like to drink.' He said, 'Well, you don't know how to drink, Gretch, that's why. Just drink champagne, and put a cube of ice in it, and you won't have a headache.' I said, 'All right, I'm going to try it.' So all that night I was drinking champagne and having a great time, and finally Tom dragged me home about 4:00 in the morning. Once I put my head down on the pillow, the room went into a spin, and I got sick to my stomach, and so I sat right up. Tom said, 'What's the matter?' I staggered out of bed and headed for the bathroom. I don't recall how long I was in there, but finally I managed to return to bed, climb in and just started to settle down when I turned over to see Dr. Marxer coming through the door with Tom right behind him. He said, 'Tom called and said you're sick.' I said, 'Oh, for God's sake. I'm drunk! I drank too much champagne.' By this time it was about 6:00 in the morning, and he sat down on the bed, and Tom sat on the other side of the bed, and these two proceeded to have a long discussion about me. I tried to tune them out and go to sleep. All of a sudden I heard Dr. Marxer say, 'Tom, what do you really think about her? Is she a good wife?' Tom said, "No, she's a lousy wife!' 'Do you think she's a good mother?' 'No, she's a lousy mother!' He said, 'Well, have you got anything good to say?' He said, 'Yes. She's a pretty good actress.' I was so shocked.

"I remember lying in bed that particular morning and I knew, at that moment, that he didn't like me as I was. I hadn't met many people in my life who didn't like me. I was always liked by my family; I may have been a little headstrong but they loved me, really. Tom didn't. My family had always seen some compensation that balanced my faults, but the only compensation I was to Tom was that I was a pretty good actress. It was the first time that I realized that's what he really thought. I think that killed every bit of tender love I had for him. I looked at him and I thought, 'It doesn't make any difference what I do. That's what he thinks about me, and I don't think he'll ever change.'"

The way Tom treated Judy was equally troublesome. Loretta commented, "Tom was really terrible to her, little things that would just kill any little girl, particularly a sensitive little girl. There was a bracelet that she saw in a shop when we were vacationing at Lake Arrowhead. She had pointed it out to me saying, 'Mama, look at that beautiful bracelet.' I showed it to Tom and said, 'Judy's crazy about this bracelet.' Paul Henreid's daughter was having a birthday party while we were up there, and Tom bought that bracelet and gave it to her for her birthday present. We were all sitting at the table as she opened it. When I saw Judy's face, I thought my heart was going to burst. Tears started to fill her eyes; all she could do was try to keep them from falling. I looked at Tom, and his face didn't express anything. In the meantime I slipped my hand over Judy's and squeezed it hard. I got the saddest little smile back.

"It may have been on that same trip to Arrowhead. I remember Judy and me walking together on a path when Tom came up and pushed Judy back and said, 'She's my wife; you walk behind.' He laughed as he said it, like he was joking, but she knew better, and I did too. Every time something like this happened, I lost a little more respect for my husband and grew more protective of my daughter. I tried to talk to him, 'Tom, she's a little girl. She doesn't know what you're talking about.' I think that three fourths of the arguments I had with Tom in those days were about Judy."

Possibly, there was another cause for Judy's unhappiness, one which Loretta was unwilling to acknowledge even to herself. Sally recalled Judy at three or four. "She ran up to me in the upstairs hallway and asked, 'Are you my mother?' All I could say was, 'No, dear.' I think from a very young age she was on to something that she couldn't put her finger on." Loretta's response to Judy a few years later when she inquired about her biological parents was a narrative stating they had been killed in a car accident.

Loretta was an eager to please seventeen-year-old when she reported to the Samuel Goldwyn Studios in 1930, tongue-tied at the prospect of working with Ronald Colman. It was a much more assured Loretta who returned to the studio seventeen years and sixty films later. The film was THE BISHOP'S WIFE in which she starred with Cary Grant and David Niven. Loretta recalled an early run-in with the studio mogul, Sam Goldwyn. "I had already been dismissed for the day. The big stage door was open and I was talking to Cary while I was waiting for the car. All of a sudden, Sam walked right through the big doors and came up to me shaking his finger in my face, 'You are ruining my picture! I've just seen the rushes and your lips are too thick!' I looked at him and said, 'I'm sorry Sam, I was born this way.' He said, 'No, no, no.' Finally I said, 'You mean the make-up?' He said, 'They're too thick.' I said, 'Sam, we did a scale of about 7or 8 different kinds of makeup starting with nothing. By the time we got to 7 or 8, I had all the false eyelashes and everything else on. We agreed on #3.' He, and I, and the director, Henry Koster, everybody, agreed #3 was the right makeup, that it was just enough but it was not too much. I said 'That's what I have on now; that's what I had on yesterday. '

"Well, he started up all over again. Just then I saw my car drive up. I thought, 'Good. I'll fix you.' He started to argue and I said, 'Sam! I'm very offended that you would walk on the set and speak to me this way in front of the entire company. I'm going home! I've had it!' I walked off the set and got in my car and drove off. Henry Koster told me later that Sam watched me the whole way, just walk out, and there was a dead silence. Sam never knew that I had already been dismissed."

Jane Mullen Sharpe recalled visiting Loretta on the set of THE BISHOP'S WIFE. "A day on the set with Loretta was a great treat. We had so much fun. David and Cary had crazy games going all the time because, really, making movies was such drudgery: take, retake, sit, and all that. The scene they were working on that day was everyone coming into the dining room, and David was supposed to be quite irritable."

Loretta recalled the same day, "The director told David, 'I want you to be really cold to Loretta,' David nodded but whispered to me, 'Gretch, I just can't be mean to you.' I said, 'You better. You're getting paid to take direction from this man. Be cold or he'll jump down your throat.' At that point of his career, David was still more of a personality than an actor, so it was hard for him to go against his feelings. We had become very fond of each other having lived in the same house for over a year."

One of the memorable scenes from THE BISHOP'S WIFE was the ice skating sequence with Loretta, Cary, and James Gleason, who played the cab driver. None of the actors were accomplished skaters, and Loretta explained how they managed to film the scene so convincingly. "We skated a little but just to stay up, none of the fancy work. They did a very wise thing. They took masks of all three of us, and they put these masks on the doubles who were right out of the ice follies. There weren't any close ups and from a distance, they looked like us."

Dory Schary had another project with the kind of star role that attracted Loretta. RACHEL AND THE STRANGER was a frontier comedy-drama about the marriage-of -convenience between a bondwoman and a young widower. It takes a visiting stranger to awaken a romance between them. Two up-and-coming actors co-starred: William Holden as the husband, and Robert Mitchum as the stranger. Location shooting was done near Eugene, Oregon, and Norman Foster directed.

Robert Mitchum actually thought that Loretta was the producer. He recalled, "She was very knowledgeable about all the backstage work and the cameras and the lighting. I suppose it's a personal thrift; she doesn't see any point in wasting time. I remember one time standing around, and Loretta was talking to the electricians. She said, 'Put the shutter down on that and put a half of gauze on this,' and she's arranging all the lighting, and she turns to the gaffer, the chief electrician, and she says, 'I don't know why I'm worrying about him (Robert Mitchum), he's been working in nothing but leak light all his life. I don't think he even knows what we're talking about.' I said, 'Yeah, Loretta, I know. I just don't give a damn.' She said, 'Well, I do, Honey, so put a half apple on that ... '"

Robert Mitchum summed up the relationship between Loretta and her director/brother-in-law, Norman Foster. "Well, he was very, very conscious, acutely conscious, of her approval or disapproval. She just looked at him, and he nodded; that's all."

Loretta lived in a little rented house for the eight weeks' location shoot while the rest of the cast and crew stayed at a hotel. She recalled, "I took my own maid and then we hired a cook up there. On Saturday night I used to invite Norman, the Holdens, and the Mitchums for dinner. I think it was the second or third Saturday that we had dinner at my house, Bob and Bill drank a bottle and a half of Scotch between them. The next day I called them both over and I said, 'Listen you two, I've got a feeling you're going to be big stars, both of you, but not if you continue to drink the way you do.' Bill said, 'You're right. I should cut down. Next Saturday night just limit me,' and he walked away. Bob, on the other hand, just looked at me with his squinty eyes and said, 'Are you through, Mother Superior?' I burst out laughing and said, 'Yes, I'm through.'"

Robert Mitchum recalled, "Loretta would shake her finger and cluck her tongue. I wouldn't call it the imposition of morals, but she would remind us of our behavior. I didn't mind it; that's her, and it's rather endearing."

Mitchum saw Loretta on several different levels. "She projects a serenity and she is in control of herself, at least gives the impression that she's in control of her circumstances. That control is her armor. I should imagine the reason she keeps herself so collected is because she's so vulnerable. Every once in a while, if things weren't going right, you'd see that vulnerability. Rather than seeing a temper fly, she might become tearful."

THE BISHOP'S WIFE was selected to be shown at the Royal Command Performance in London, November 25, 1947. Loretta recalled one of their nights in London that week. "We went to the American Ambassador's home for cocktails; the theater was at 7:00. I had on a beautiful white dress and a full length white-fox-coat. We were guests that evening of Piggy Warburg, a darling man whom I had dated when I had been in England before I was married. His date that evening was a seventeen-year-old daughter of an American diplomat, who never stopped talking, never stopped bragging about her attachment to the royal family, her attachment to the film colony, and how much she loved all English actors. Piggy said to me, 'She's a pain in the neck, but I have to take her along with us to the theater.' I said, 'Fine.'

"I figured this little girl had probably never seen me in a picture, and I thought, 'I'm all dressed up so I will give her a taste of what Hollywood can be like.' The minute we got out of the car, there was a crowd 'oohhhhhhing and aahhhhing.' They knew from the papers that we were in town for the Command Performance. We walked into the theatre as the lights were just going down. I had learned a long time ago, you can either whip up excitement, or you can calm things down; it depends on the way you behave. I walked down the aisle first, and I made the most of this white dress. The whole theatre started to applaud. The girl was looking around to see what they were applauding about, and I said, 'It's for me, Honey; it's for me.' I smiled at her, and we went in and sat down, and her whole attitude changed."

Loretta was, indeed, an internationally recognized star. CHINA, AND NOW TOMORROW, ALONG CAME JONES, THE STRANGER,

THE FARMER'S DAUGHTER, THE BISHOP'S WIFE, and RACHEL AND THE STRANGER were all hits, and Loretta's career had never been so hot. She certainly had no regrets regarding her decision, almost a decade earlier, to break away from the dictates of Daryl Zanuck .

THE FARMER'S DAUGHTER had been released in early spring of 1947and challenged THE BEST YEARS OF OUR LIVES and THE EGG AND I as the top box office film of the year. Loretta knew that it was good prior to its release. She recalled, "Every Sunday night, Mr. Mayer, Daryl Zanuck, Bill Goetz, they all had houses along the beach, and they would have a dinner party and run a movie. One night Edie (Louis B. Mayer's daughter and Bill Geotz's wife) and Bill had invited Tom and me to dinner, and during dinner Edie looked at me and she said, 'Oh, Loretta, I'm sorry, I forgot.' They tried not to have pictures that their guests were in because usually everybody talked right out loud in the projection room, good or bad. You'd get all the dirt and everything else. And she said, 'I've got THE FARMER'S DAUGHTER to run tonight.' And I said, 'Oh, you don't have to worry, Edie. It's good.' And she looked at me and said, 'Oh my, aren't we humble.' I laughed and said, 'Edie, I haven't made that many good pictures. '

"We sat through the first two reels of it, and I felt that because I was sitting right there, nobody said anything, one way or the other. Finally, we just slipped out quietly, hoping our departure would relax the other guests enough to enjoy the picture. Edie called the next day and said, 'You were darling in it, and the picture is excellent.' I said, 'Thanks. I think it is, too.'"

CHAPTER 15: MOVIE STAR

The 1947 Academy of Motion Pictures Arts and Sciences nominations for Best Performance by an Actress were: Rosalind Russell, MOURNING BECOMES ELECTRA, Joan Crawford, POSSESSED, Susan Hayward, SMASH-UP, THE STORY OF A WOMAN, Dorothy McGuire, GENTLEMAN'S AGREEMENT and Loretta Young, THE FARMER'S DAUGHTER. Loretta asked Tom to write an acceptance speech for her. She explained, "It was not because I thought I was going to win; in fact, I knew I wasn't. But I had seen an actress, an important actress win the Academy Award, and all she could do was stand up there and cry. She never did pull herself together."

The nomination also allowed Loretta to go to Adrian for a new dress. Loretta recalled, "He chose some green taffeta and designed a great big dress with ruffles all over it. I was perfectly happy with a nomination and my new Adrian dress."

Rosalind Russell was the heavy favorite in the "Best Performance by an Actress" category with Loretta pulling up the tail end. Rosalind called Loretta the night before and said, "'Everybody but God and me thinks they know who's going to win this award, but when you get it, unscrew it somehow, and throw me the top or the bottom, I don't care which. ' I laughed and said, 'Everybody knows where it's going to go. '"

The ceremony was held at the Shrine Auditorium on March 20, 1948. Loretta recalled, "Polly Ann and Sally weren't coming because Mama had said, 'If she's not going to win, let's not go and embarrass her.' Georgiana and Ricardo ended up sitting a few rows behind us." Producer Armand Deutsch was sitting next to Loretta, and he remembered Tom continuously cautioning Loretta not to get her hopes up. Finally, he heard Loretta say, "'All right, Tom, you don't have to keep saying that.'"

Director Delmar Davis produced the ceremony that year, and Loretta recalled, "They had constructed a huge *Oscar* a couple of stories tall that took up half the stage. Several tiers were built into the pedestal where the real *Oscars* set. Now there was just one left. In those years, the last presentation of the evening was saved for the Best Actress. Then Freddy March said, 'Ladies and Gentleman, this is the award that *Oscar* loves the most, and if you listen very carefully - we're going to turn the lights down - you'll even hear his heart beat for this one.' They turned the lights down, and you could hear his heartbeat. It was very dramatic and very emotional. Then he said, 'And the winner is: LORETTA YOUNG!' The lights went booming up, and I was in shock. The whole place stood up, and I heard Georgiana scream, 'Oh, Gretch!!'

"I CANNOT TELL YOU HOW THRILLED I WAS!!!! I just kind of sat there, stunned and thrilled to death. Then Tom said, 'You better go and get it.' I remember walking up and thinking, 'Oh, I should have taken my gloves off;' thank God I didn't because, in the pictures, they looked marvelous with the dress. The stairs to the stage went up from the front aisle. The dress had a hoop in it, and as I lifted it up to walk up the stairs to the stage, it just looked like this big green butterfly floating up the steps; it was beautiful, at least that's what I was told later from people in the audience. Freddy presented me the *Oscar* and, thank God, that whole speech flashed back into my mind, and it went off perfectly.

"Everyone seemed so thrilled for me, not only because I had been such a dark horse, but I think because I had been in the business for twenty-years and never had been nominated before, never came anywhere near it. I stayed an extra half-hour talking with the press because being lowest on the totem pole, they hadn't bothered to prepare any history on me. Everybody was already gone by then, and I wanted to call Mama before I left the theater. It must have been midnight by then, and I woke her up. She was sure I wasn't going to win, so she hadn't listened to the program on the radio. I said, 'Mama! This is Gretch.' She said, 'Yes, Dear. What's the matter?' I said, 'Well, I won! She said, 'Wonderful. What did you win?' I said, 'The ACADEMY AWARD!' 'OH!' she said, 'That's wonderful, Dear. Congratulations. I'll come by your house for brunch tomorrow.' So we planned for the whole family to come over the next day for brunch.

"When we came out of the theater, the car that the studio had hired for us had disappeared. I guess the driver assumed we had left with someone else. There were some duplex apartments across the street from the Shrine Auditorium, and a woman was standing on her balcony. She was the only person around, and she said, 'Hey, Loretta, how's it feel?' I answered her, 'Marvelous, just marvelous, I just love it,' and we had a long conversation while someone found a taxi.

Tom and Loretta sat up and talked until 7:00 a.m., not wanting the excitement to fade. Later that day, after the family had left the brunch, Loretta received a phone call. She remembered, "It was from Sister Marina; she's the one to whom I said in the first grade, 'Oh no, Sister, I don't need to learn to write. I'm going to be a movie star, and movie stars have secretaries.' She was in the convent infirmary, but she had listened to the ceremony on the radio. She said, 'Oh Dear, I just knew you were going to win, and I stayed up all night! '"

Loretta could now truly think of herself as an actress after two decades of being a movie star. She had done it on her own terms. She had never played the part of a terrible person lest the audience might have confused her with the character. And, unlike Bette Davis, an actress Loretta admired greatly, she was unwilling to stretch herself in a role in which she looked unattractive.

A few months later, Loretta was starring in THE ACCUSED at Paramount and recalled a pleasant surprise. "I went off the stage one time, and there were some men constructing a set on the other side of the street. By this time, I had gotten over the thrill of winning. From way up high, one of these construction men yelled, 'Hi, Champ!' I heard it, but I didn't know he was talking to me, so I went right on walking. Then he said, 'Loretta! You are the champ!' I said, 'Oh! Yeah!' Then we both laughed, and I thanked him, and it occurred to me that it is all so fleeting. For a year you are, and then the next year somebody else is."

Loretta also had her family to keep her in check. Sally recalled, "After she won the *Oscar*, she was so uptight. She was this big movie star, and she wanted all of us to be conscious of our behavior. Polly Ann and Mama did behave, I guess, but I didn't. It made Loretta nervous when I was gay and laughing a little loudly at something. I just couldn't take her that seriously. She used to bug me if I was with her in public. The way she spoke sounded phony to me. As for those of us who were with her, we didn't matter. She was someplace else, playing the movie star, I guess."

On June 8, 1948, just months after Loretta's won her *Oscar*, *The Los Angeles Examiner* proclaimed on page one, "Father, Loretta Young Didn't Know, Succumbs". The story reported that John V. Earle, age 58, had been living in an Alhambra rooming house. He had married a second time to a woman named Rota who had died fourteen years earlier. His job history included managing an Alhambra music store, clerking in a stationery store in the same town, opening a hot dog stand in Redondo Beach which failed, selling drafting instruments, and working in the Los Angeles City College Book Store.

The *Examiner* also scooped a copy of a letter that Loretta's grandmother, Mrs. Laura Young, had supposedly written to her famous granddaughter. "Dear Loretta, I am obliged to tell you that a person who called himself John Earle died in the County Hospital of a stroke or heart attack yesterday and is to be buried in Woodlawn Cemetery, Santa Monica at 1:30 on Thursday. Please notify your mother and others who should know. Everything has been taken care of as the monthly check I received from the Good Samaritan (Loretta) has not been used for provisions, and I could save some of it. So again, Dear, you pay. All my 1ove, Grandma."

The newspapers reported that Loretta was unable to attend the funeral because of a picture commitment. Loretta didn't' remember if she was working or not but commented, "Even if I hadn't, I don't think I would have gone. I felt nothing for my father, and I thought, 'I won't go and make a public spectacle. All the cameramen would be there, and it would be a lie.' I didn't even know him, but I guess I felt that he must have been kind of a bum to leave Mama with all the kids. And I think I felt he shifted his financial responsibilities onto my shoulders because it wasn't too long after he left that I first worked and brought my salary home to Mama."

After John Young had re-emerged in 1936, asking financial assistance for his prosthesis, Sally had been the only one of the girls who had expressed an interest in seeing him. She recalled, "I talked it over with Mom and the girls and they all said, 'No, no, no. You don't want to do that. What are you going to say to him?' What was I going to say? 'Are you the man who went away when I was 6 1/2 and didn't ever give us any Christmas presents?' After he left, I remember thinking, 'I'm sure he'll be back by Christmas,' and then the next year thinking, 'We'll, he'll be back this Christmas,' and for several years, I was just sure he'd show up. But he was never there. For all I knew, he didn't even know if we had enough food to eat, if any of us were sick. What was I going to say to this man?"

Loretta and Gladys had made their decision not to attend the funeral, but Sally wasn't going to pass the opportunity to see her Papa one last time. She recalled, "I was four and a half-months pregnant, and I didn't want to go by myself; that's why Polly Ann went with me. I said to Polly Ann, 'Let's send some flowers just in case.' All we knew was that the service would be at a certain hour, and so Polly Ann and I got there early because I didn't want to waddle in. The only flowers that were there, besides our spray of red roses, were home-grown and scrounged down in Mason Jars with a fern thrown in. There were three of those.

"Polly Ann and I were saying the rosary, and Jack came in. As he had been walking in, a man had approached him, not even realizing that Jack was the son, and asked, 'Would you stay all the way through and help us carry the casket?' There were only a couple of men there, and they were old and Jack agreed. Jack and I were absolutely hypnotized by looking at Papa in the box because we'd always wondered what he really looked like. And I was so glad because he looked so much nicer than my Aunt Grace said he did. He was really a nice looking man. His hair was white by this time, but there were all kinds of things that you could recognize. The ears were set on the head like mine. And the forehead, I always said I had my mother's forehead, but it was his. Then I couldn't help but cry because he had the cheapest, worst suit on, tan with red stripes. I just cried. I loved men's clothes, always. I knew it was him, but I wasn't positive. I wanted to lift up the bottom of the casket to see if his right leg was missing."

Polly Ann remembered the Christian Science ceremony at the funeral home as being very brief. "Some man got up and talked for a minute and that was it." She remembered looking at her Dad in the casket, "He looked exactly like he did the last time I saw him. He didn't look much older. I was more moved watching my brother. Jack had never seen him to remember him. He stood there so long, just staring at his father. Papa was a good looking man, and Jack resembled him quite a bit. I thought to myself, 'Oh, there is something very strong between a father and a son. Jack didn't say a word, but you could tell.

"The other thing that impressed me was when this woman came in. As it turned out, she was Father's 'special friend.'" A newspaper account reported that Miss Laura Lund of Hermosa Beach had claimed the body.

Jack remembered looking at his dad, "I cried a bit because I really hadn't met him during his life. I didn't think I looked like him at the time, but later, I saw a picture of him when he was twenty-four, and that was me all over. At a distance, you'd mistake him for me; same build, same appearance of the head, same ears hanging out a bit."

Like Sally, Jack had been curious about his father. He reflected, "My mother didn't want me to get in touch with him, and I never pursued it. Still, I came close to meeting my father though I didn't know it at the time. I was going to Loyola Law School. Nearby was Dietz Engineering Supply Company. I was very interested in drafting, so I'd look at all the drawing instruments as I went by. And one time I saw this man inside looking at me with sort of a scared expression. At my father's funeral I found out that's where he had worked. I walked by many times during the three years of law school. He must have known who I was."

Sally found it bizarre that the three of them were the strangers at their own father's funeral. She recalled, "Dad's woman friend and her friends must have discussed it on the way to the cemetery because when we arrived, they came to us and said, 'Come sit where the family sits. '" Sally also recalled, "It was sad; somebody tried to give us each a rose from that spray, and Polly

Ann wouldn't take one. She wouldn't accept it. I took mine and Jack took his."

Sally and Polly Ann visited with their father's woman friend at the grave site. Sally recalled, "She was a schoolteacher, very refined looking. She told us that she had wanted to call us just before my father went into the County Hospital, but that Grandma had said, 'No, do not involve them in this. They've done enough.'

"After the funeral, we went over to Loretta's. She and Mom were huddling together, and Mom wanted to know just exactly what it was like. We told about the woman and what she looked like. She said, 'Oh, I'm glad I didn't go.'

"We went to see Grandmother Young and our Aunt Grace the next day. Grace said to Polly Ann and me, 'You girls certainly are the essence of your mother;' she always liked mom, 'and you're nothing like your father.' That wounded me a little bit. Grace also told us that Papa used to think that I was Loretta Young and that Gretchen was Sally Blane. He'd go and sit in the theater and come and tell Grace that he had seen me in a wonderful picture, and it was Gretch. He couldn't be convinced otherwise.

"A couple a days later, Dad's woman friend called my house, and she started in on me. She asked for money for taking care of Dad for all the time she had known him. I was pregnant and overly sensitive anyway, and Norman got on the phone and he really told her, in no uncertain terms, to go to hell."

Gladys summed up John Earle Young in this quote from *The Los Angeles Examiner* at the time of his death. "He was not a mean man, but he was a weak man." And, she added, 'He was handsome, much too handsome for his own good."

Loretta's personal life was again front page news two months after her father's death. This time, Loretta was the victim of a notorious burglar whom the press had dubbed "Raffles" Loretta recalled, "The Arthur Rubinstein's gave a big dinner party that night. Irene Selznick had on a gorgeous diamond bracelet; my guess is that it would be worth a half of million in today's market. I said to her, 'What is that?' She said, 'It's my consolation prize from David.' She and David Selznick had just separated. I said, 'Oh, Irene, it's beautiful!!!!' She said, 'I'd rather have David,' and dismissed it as if it was nothing. So kiddingly, I said, 'If you hate it so, let me wear it for tonight.' To my surprise, she took it off her wrist and put it on mine, and said, 'Enjoy.' I flashed it all over the party.

"I had forgotten all about the gorgeous bracelet when it was time to go home, and we were half-way down the driveway when Tom said, 'Oh, Lord! You've got Irene's bracelet on; we've got to take it back.' I said, 'Oh, I don't want to go back there and say good night all over again to everybody. I'll send it over in the morning.' He said, 'No. Give it to me and I'll take it back,' so I took it off, and he took it back and gave it to her.

"That's the night 'Raffles' broke into our house, and he would have gotten that bracelet. We were asleep when he came in. He had climbed up the side of the trellis, then went into my sitting room, and right into the safe and closets. He went to the drawer in my dressing room where I used to put good stuff and junk together. When I got up in the morning, I did not notice one thing out of place. It was Sunday morning, and I was getting dressed to go to Mass. The maid came in to get a coat out of the closet that I wanted to wear. She came back from the fur closet and she said, 'Mrs. Lewis, you'd better come in here.' So I went in and the Konar mink was gone. The Nutria, the one I wanted to wear, was gone as well. I don't know why he took that because there was a full length fox coat right next to it, and a brown mink coat right next to that. He probably could only handle just so much.

"We learned later how he knew our home so well. This good looking young man had come to the door several months earlier and presented a card to our housekeeper. He said that he was from a real estate company and that Mr. Lewis had asked him to appraise the property. She showed him everything including the alarm system.

A robbery notwithstanding, Loretta, professionally, was at an apex. But, there was a price to pay. Just what that price entailed would soon become clearer.

CHAPTER 16: PAYING THE PRICE

Loretta remembered picking up the phone one day. "It was Malcolm Smith, a friend from New York, and he said, 'Loretta, I'm so thrilled we've got your house. We're going to love living in it.' I was dead silent. He said, 'Well, you do know we bought your house, don't you?' 'Oh, yes; yes, I do,' I replied. Of course, I didn't at all.

"I said to Tom when he came home, 'Malcolm Smith called and said he bought this house.' Tom said, ' Yes.' I asked, ' Why? We just finished it. We've spent a year and a half getting it just the way we want it.' He said, 'Well, if anything happened to you, I couldn't afford to keep it up.' I said, 'What's going to happen to me?' He just looked at me. I said, 'Tom, you've done this before. When we were in the little house, you couldn't wait to get out of that. Now we're settled here, and you can't wait to get out of this. '" Quite possibly, dabbling in real estate gave Tom a focus, at least for the short term.

Tom had talked Countess Estelle Doheny into renting her home on the Doheny Ranch for $1500 per month. The Dohenys had built a fortune on oil and were one of Los Angeles' wealthiest families. There were three homes on their 410-acre ranch perched in the hills of Beverly Hills. Loretta recalled, "Our house was on a knoll, and you had to drive two blocks from the gate to get there. We shared a swimming pool with Larry Doheny and his family and a tennis court which we never used. The house was absolutely beautiful. It was an old home, and Countess Doheny had combined several small rooms into one great living room with a huge fireplace and an expansive bay window looking out onto the garden. It had six family bedrooms and four servant's rooms. It really was a marvelous house." Though considerably smaller than the Carrollwood house, a staff consisting of a housekeeper, a downstairs maid, a personal maid, a butler, and a governess was still required.

Meanwhile, a decade after Loretta left 20th Century-Fox, Daryl Zanuck was ready to make amends and offered Loretta the title role in MOTHER IS A FRESHMAN. It was a Technicolor comedy about a mother and daughter attending the same college and both falling in love with the English Literature professor. Loretta recalled, "When Daryl sent me the script, I read it and asked my agent to tell him, 'No thank you,' but to add, 'You have a story on your shelf that she would give her eyetooth to do called COME TO THE STABLE written by Claire Booth Luce. She's read it and thinks it's wonderful!' It had been on the shelf for a couple of years. Zanuck sent a message back to me: 'You're still trying to tell me how to run my studio.' We went back and forth and

finally Daryl said, 'You can do COME TO THE STABLE if you do
MOTHER IS A FRESHMAN first. '"

Loretta was thirty-five when she did MOTHER IS A FRESHMAN.
By this time in her career, she had done so many love scenes that
she cautioned co-star Van Johnson, 'Van, do me a favor: Don't
hurt my teeth and don't hurt my neck.' I was concerned that Van
was insecure and would feel the need to prove his masculinity."

COME TO THE STABLE was the story of two nuns, one American
who had lived in France and the other one, a French woman.
They come to America with the object of building a children's
hospital. While COME TO THE STABLE was in production,
Loretta invited a friend of hers, Sister Mary Winifred, to serve as
a technical advisor.

Once day, Sister Mary Winifred, Loretta, Celeste Holm, who
played the French nun, and four other actresses playing nuns
were having lunch together. Loretta recalled, "There we were
like little blackbirds, sitting around this table, and a man came in,
one of the writers at 20th. I can't stand him. Never could. Anyway,
as he passed our table, he said, 'Is this where you get nun?' Oh,
they (the extras) laughed; they thought it was the funniest thing
they ever heard. I looked at Sister; she went right on eating as if
she hadn't heard, but her face was as red as a beet. As quietly as I

could, I said, 'That's disgusting. Not everyone at this table is an actress.' 'Oh, well pardon me.' It was said with as much sarcasm as he could muster. Then he strolled off. From then on we decided to take our veils off before going to the commissary just so people could tell the 'actress nuns' from Sister Mary Winifred, as Sister was with us quite often."

It's not clear when the concept of "The Swear Box" was first introduced on the set of a Loretta Young picture. Quite possibly it was on RACHAEL AND THE STRANGER; Robert Mitchum remembered it being in place by then. The idea behind it was to minimize the blasphemies often sputtered on a movie set. Offenders were fined and a couple of muscular crewmen served as enforcers. All proceeds went to St. Anne's Home. Loretta was particularly appreciative the policy was in force while Sister Mary Winifred was on the set during the filming of COME TO THE STABLE.

There have been many stories told over the years about people who defied Loretta's Swear Box by stuffing it with bills and then letting out a stream of obscenities. Loretta replied, "The only person who did that was Henry Hathaway (the film director) and he did it as a joke; the others I've heard make that claim wouldn't have had the nerve." Also, the penalty was for blasphemies only, not obscenities. You could say "Fuck You" all day long free of charge.

Loretta was so convincing as a nun that it bothered the male lead, Hugh Marlowe. Loretta recalled, "Hugh played an atheist and he was also an atheist in real life. One day, I was standing in front of my mirror adjusting the veil, and he looked at me and said, 'You know, you are such a beautiful woman; I can't stand to see you in that outfit.' At first I thought he was kidding, but then I realized he meant it. It didn't bother me because it was part of the character he was playing."

Variety's review of COME TO THE STABLE stated, "It is drama of considerable charm in its devotion to the tenets to the Catholic church. It has moments of poignancy, but often it skirts the bounds of entertainment in telling too pointedly its story of Godliness and faith." But COME TO THE STABLE flourished at the box office, making it one of 20th Century-Fox's biggest hits of the year.

Loretta celebrated her thirty-sixth birthday while she was filming COME TO THE STABLE, and the company threw a surprise birthday party for her during the lunch hour. Loretta recalled, "Celeste Holm said to me, 'Oh, I saw your husband over there.' I said, 'Not my husband, not on the set.' She said, 'Well, I think so.' Then she said, 'Oh, I wasn't supposed to have said that. It was supposed to be a surprise.' I was very surprised that Tom was on the set. Wives and husbands just didn't come on the set to visit. But I think what really made me uneasy was knowing that Tom didn't have anything else he was supposed to be doing."

It wasn't an easy time for Tom. The war had been over for four years and, unlike his previous track record, he hadn't slipped into a slot that was propelling him upward. The glory days of "Colonel Tom" were fading as Loretta's stature only increased. She was making the movies that she wanted to make, and the movies she made, made money.

The combination of clout and success has always made people attractive in Hollywood, and Loretta was a valued guest on the social circuit. That didn't make things easier for Tom. Loretta remembered an incident at a party hosted by Elsa Maxwell, "This party she gave was for some English people. She had the movie stars: Hedy Lamarr, Loretta Young, Ingrid Bergman, and Joan Bennett all at a table for ten in the dining room with the Englishmen. Tom ended up in the third room at a table with the English wives, and that made him livid. In the middle of dinner he came in and tapped me on the shoulder and said, 'C'mon we're leaving. I'll tell you why when we get outside.' He looked at

Elsa and said, 'I'm sorry, we have to go.' He pulled the chair back and took me by the hand. We got in the car, and I asked, 'What in God's name is the matter?' He said, 'No one is going to put me back in third class. I'm not going to sit there and take any more of it.' I looked at him and thought, 'I'd better shut up.' We went home, and I just got my make-up off and went to bed as quickly as possible.

"It must have been impossible for a man like Tom to be married to a motion picture actress who got all the attention. If we walked into a restaurant, and he'd made a reservation for 'Mr. Lewis and party' and the maître d' said, 'Oh, Miss Young, come in,' and they gave us a better table, Tom would ask, 'Is this the table you reserved for Mr. Lewis?' And, invariably, they'd say, 'Well, no,' and Tom would say, 'Well, we won't take it then. We'll take the table you reserved for Mr. Lewis,' and we'd go back in the corner someplace. So it spoiled the party, not only for him, but for everybody else with us, and the maître d' was embarrassed as well. "

Loretta recalled saying during a quarrel, "'Tom, you married me because I was Loretta Young. You wanted a movie star. You never went with your secretary; you always went with Glenda Farrell, or Bette Davis, or somebody. *Somebody!* So if you went with people like that, what did you think we were going to do if you did marry one of us? That we were going to not be what we are, and just turn around and be your little slavery housewife? Why in the name of God did you marry me? I'm a lead horse. That's what the matter with us is. We're two lead horses pulling in opposite directions."

Nor had Tom fulfilled Loretta's pre-nuptial dreams. She reflected, "He was Irish and Welsh, and it is a very difficult combination. His moods were very high and very low, and it was difficult for me to live with it. My temperament is rather even, and it takes a lot for me to get up the courage to really blast somebody, and then I have to be so angry I don't make any sense. I don't like the feeling. I don't like arguing and Tom loved to argue. I asked him one time, 'In any conversation with somebody else, if I'm disagreeing with them, why do you always take their side?' 'Oh', he said, 'I don't think I do, do I?' I said, 'Yes, always!'"

Loretta's prospective about her relationship with Tom had shifted over the years. She explained, "I was probably in my mid-thirties when I really decided that I wasn't wrong all the time. The first few years of our married life, I assumed that because he was older and had gone to college, he was smarter than I, and he wasn't. He wasn't at all. He knew the outer edges of things, but he never went to the core of anything. My whole drive was going to the core, and the edges could fall where they may."

The Lewises sought counseling from a psychiatrist who told Tom, "'You have to get an office; no woman can stand a man around the house all the time.' Well, I wasn't even in the house, but the children were, and so were the servants, and with Tom home all the time, there was always tension. So Tom opened an office in Beverly Hills. He had a private secretary who, by the way, couldn't stand me, so I don't know what he had been telling her. He paid our bills from the office; that's all I could figure out he did, and it was costing a fortune. And it really didn't settle the problem. I'm convinced that the basis of our unhappiness was the fact that I was the breadwinner. And when the children asked him, 'Daddy, what do you do?' he'd answer them testily, 'What do you mean, what do I do? I go to the office every day.'"

The Lewises were partners in several properties with Irene Dunne and her husband, Dr. Frank Griffin. Loretta reflected, "Frank Griffin was a genius, and if Tom could have just gone along ... but he wanted to be the boss ... and he didn't know enough to be the boss. Frank Griffin got us all into the Beverly Hills Hotel, and it was Tom's vote that got all of us out. It was a gold mine, but he had never seen that much money and he was anxious to take his profit. It was a long time before Frank Griffin ever spoke to Tom again."

Loretta realized that she wasn't the mother she could have been. She reflected, "I felt as good as a movie star can feel who is not able to be around her children all the time. If I had grown up in a house where the mother wasn't there, then I wouldn't have known the difference, but I did know the difference. I grew up in a very secure home; Mama was there. Even though she was running a boarding house, we were living in the boarding house, and she was there. I knew what it should have been. Unfortunately, circumstances, most of the time, make up your mind for you, and it is the lesser of two evils which you choose. I was working as a successful actress making $300,000 a year. Tom, if he was lucky, might have made $50,000 (if he was working). It would have taken more guts than I had for most of those years to turn around to my husband and say, 'I'm going to quit, and we'll live on your $50,000 a year.'"

For some in post-war Hollywood, Communism continued to hold great appeal and these devotees were eager to share their convictions. Even Loretta had found herself on the mailing list for *The New Masses*. She remembered asking Tom, "'What is this paper, and where does it come from?' Tom said, 'It's the Communist newspaper. Half of your friends are Communist.' "Looking back, Tom was right. The picture business was just riddled with them, particularly among the writers. That didn't mean they weren't good writers and wonderful people. And some were my best friends. They clung to their convictions as I did to my religion."

Was Loretta's friend, producer, Dore Schary, a Communist? The FBI wanted to know and questioned Loretta about him a number of times. Loretta recalled, "They asked, 'Well, has he ever said anything ... ?' I said, 'Never,' and he hadn't. I'm afraid I shocked one of the FBI men when I volunteered, 'Well, if he is a Communist, then more of us out here should be because he's a marvelous man, a devoted husband and father, and a brilliant producer. '

"Anyway, I hadn't seen Dore for a long time, and one night at a cocktail party at Van and Evie Johnson's, Dore and I were sitting on a sofa talking our heads off. All of a sudden, I heard myself saying, 'Dore, you have got to give me a solid answer. The FBI has questioned me two or three times about you; prove that you are not an active Communist.' And he looked at me and said, 'Oh, for Heaven's sake, Loretta, if I were a Communist would I hire George Murphy (an actor known for his conservative views who would later become a Republican Senator from California)?' I said, 'You know, I asked the FBI the same question and they said, 'George Murphy was already at the studio when he took over.' And I said, 'Well, would he hire me?' And they said, 'You're the perfect clean skirts for him to hide behind in Hollywood.' The more we talked, the more I wondered. Suddenly, there was *heavy silence* in the room. We were getting all the attention. Then I laughed and said, 'Dore, it really doesn't make one bit of difference as far as I'm concerned.'"

Schary became MGM's Chief of Production in 1948 and paved the way for Loretta's next film. KEY TO THE CITY would be a light comedy, and Loretta would be starring with the still reigning king of MGM, Clark Gable.

Loretta and Judy

Loretta's bridal picture when she married Tom Lewis. The marriage didn't last but the picture lingered, hanging in Loretta's bedroom suite until she moved out of her Beverly Hills Home at age 84.

Peter's Baptism party. Left toRigh: Judy steadying Christopher,
Loretta holding Peter.

Chapter 17: FAMILY FIRST

Why would Loretta agree to make a film with Gable after the tumultuous events of fourteen years earlier? She replied, "It was a way to disavow the rumors. I thought that people wouldn't believe I'd have the guts to work with Clark again if those rumors were true." But also, Loretta now viewed him through more sympathetic eyes. She commented, "After Carole (Lombard) died, Clark was devastated. He was quieter after that, more serious. He was in shock for a long time."

Loretta and Clark concocted an arrangement for Clark to meet Judy. The pretense was a pre-production meeting at the Lewis's home on the Doheny Ranch. Z. Wayne Griffin, the producer, was also invited. Judy was entertaining her girlfriends with a swimming party that afternoon, and Loretta took Clark and Griffin down to the pool to make introductions. Judy squirmed with delight at meeting "The King" in the same manner as her friends. She had no reason to think that Clark Gable had any special connection to her. A second effort was made years later when Loretta and Gable arranged for him to stop by the set of her television show where Judy was working as an assistant. However, Judy had a doctor's appointment that day and was late getting to the set. By Loretta's account, the meeting at the pool prior to the filming of KEY TO THE CITY was the only time Judy saw her father in person.

There was an added irony to Loretta and Gable's reunion on KEY TO THE CITY. Loretta was pregnant and, this time, overjoyed at the prospect. Her joy soon turned to sorrow. Loretta recalled, "Clark and I were doing a scene on the back lot. I had felt very touchy all day. My stomach was jumpy and my back started to hurt. All of a sudden, I started cramping. Clark was looking at me and asked, 'What's the matter?' All I could get out was, 'I'm so sick,' and that's the last thing I remember. I just lost all strength, and he caught me before I hit the floor. He carried me to my dressing room on the set, and they sent for the doctor.

"An ambulance took me home. I had been in bed for about an hour and a half when I lost the baby. This miscarriage nearly killed me. I didn't get babies easily.

"They closed the picture until I was able to return. Everyone was very, very kind. The day that I came back, Clark sent some flowers to my dressing room, and the note said, 'I can't tell you how sorry I am. I know how you must have wanted this baby.' I thought that was very sensitive of him."

Clark had shown his sensitivity toward Loretta in another way five years earlier. Loretta recalled, "Tom and I had gone to Louis B. Mayer's home. It's not unusual when a host splits up a couple to different tables at a dinner party, so I thought nothing of it when Tom went his way, and I went mine. I had just sat down when Clark came walking up behind me and said 'Hello,' sat down next to me and started talking. Suddenly, I became so flustered; I realized 1 wasn't making any sense. Finally, I said, 'Clark, don't talk to me right now. I'm so nervous I really don't know what I'm saying.' He looked at me a moment, smiled and said, 'It's okay; I understand,' and immediately turned his attention to the lady on his left which gave me the time I needed to collect myself. In a couple of minutes, I was fine. But, also, I realized Mayer had put us together to give his party some spark. I didn't appreciate it."

The 1950 nominees for Best Actress by the Motion Pictures Arts and Sciences were Loretta Young for COME TO THE STABLE, Olivia de Havilland for THE HEIRESS, Jeanne Crain for PINKY, Deborah Kerr for EDWARD, MY SON, and Susan Hayward for MY FOOLISH HEART. Loretta voted for Olivia De Havilland and picked the winner. In a candid moment, Loretta observed, "They were never going to vote for me in the role of a nun, and any actress who played the heiress would have won that year."

Loretta tried to integrate herself into family life when she wasn't working. She recalled a particular afternoon when Peter was five-years-old. "I had taken him to the doctor to get a shot, and 1 had promised him that if he didn't cry, we would go to the Brown Derby for lunch, just the two of us. He didn't know what the Brown Derby was, but he knew it must have been something special. He didn't cry, so the two of us went to the Brown Derby and, of course, the head waiter was making a big fuss.

"As I had walked in, I saw Bill Geotz at one of the other booths, sitting with some other men. He saw me too, and we nodded. I hadn't seen much of him since I finished off my contract with International. On his way out, he stopped by the table, and I asked him to sit for a minute which he did. He kept looking at Peter, and I couldn't resist. I said, 'Well, do you think he's worth five million dollars?' And he said, 'Oh, Loretta, don't even talk about that. There was not a thing in the world I could do. I was out-voted on it.' I said, 'I know that, Bill,' and I did."

Loretta recalled about that same time, "I became aware of a big problem with Miss Smith, the boys' nurse. She was handling my five and six year old boys in the same manner she had when they were babies. We were still living at the Doheny Ranch, and my bedroom was right above the porte cochere where the school bus picked up the kids. I could look out my window and see them getting on. It was our moment to wave good-bye. This particular morning I watched Pete say good-bye to Miss Smith and climb onto the bus. Then I watched Chris. He said good-bye to her and was stepping onto the bus when she said, 'Oh, give me one little hug before you go.' So Chris came out and gave her another hug. She said, 'I'm going to miss you all day.' Well, she finally worked him up, so that he didn't want to get on the bus at all, but he did. I thought to myself, 'That's it; she's got to go. '"

Miss Smith was replaced by Miss Call. Loretta remembered her as, "the most beautiful thing I ever saw. She came into my house and spent most of her time swimming in the pool hoping to attract some producer's attention. She lasted about three months." Miss Coney, a Scotchwoman came next. It was the beginning of a relationship between Loretta and Miss Coney that would continue for the next thirty-eight years.

Loretta had been married to Tom Lewis for 10 years. She reflected, "By this time in our marriage I was honest enough to ask, "Why are you so miserable?' He said, 'I think it's your career. I think you're more of an actress than a wife.'" It wasn't long after this conversation that Loretta was returning from a publicity tour promoting KEY TO THE CITY. She recalled, 'Returning on the train, I had a couple of days to myself. During those days I searched my mind and my heart. I thought, 'Well, if it really is my career that is going to split our marriage and ruin our children's lives, then I have to do something about it.'

"When I got home, the first night after dinner, I explained to Tom I thought and prayed about it, and had made a decision. If it was my career that was causing all the havoc, then I was willing to quit acting and buckle down and be a full time wife and mother. He could take a job any place in the world that he chose. Chris, Pete and I would go with him. They were young enough to adjust, but Judy was sixteen and her life style was set. Mama, who loved Judy, would welcome her into her home. That would leave him free to actually be the head of his family. 'No more husband of the movie star which you hate.' He said that was the best news he had ever heard, that he was overjoyed. And I was relieved because I thought I'd found the key to our happiness. But that was the last he ever mentioned it. He never brought up the subject again.

"His fantasy was one thing, reality was another. The psychiatrist who was counseling us explained to me that my career had been a good excuse for Tom to be miserable, but once I took the excuse away, he panicked. That wasn't what he wanted at all. He wanted to marry a movie star, and he did. And he wanted me to take care of him, and I did. And he wanted his kids to have the best that they could have, and they did. And he felt bad about it. It was the dark side of a fairytale world."

Maybe CAUSE FOR ALARM would help boost Tom's fragile self-esteem. Loretta explained, "Dore Schary said to me, 'If there is anything you want to do, let me know.' I had first heard CAUSE FOR ALARM as a radio drama, and I suggested to Tom that he get the script and take it over to Dore. It was really a labor of love because I was hoping that it would launch Tom as a movie producer." Schary agreed to back the project.

Barry Sullivan co-starred. He played the dying but paranoid husband who terrorized his wife (Loretta) because he suspected her of infidelity. Joe Ruttenberg was considered MGM's best cameraman, and that's who Loretta wanted. She remembered, "Dore called me and said, 'Loretta, everything else is fine, but Joe Ruttenberg is scheduled to do another picture. You're playing an average little housewife, so it's not that important what you look like.' I said, 'I know, and I want to play an average but pretty little housewife. I think it adds appeal, and it certainly makes me more comfortable. There are a lot of heavy moments in this picture, and unless it's well photographed, it won't be very appealing.' He said, 'Let me think about it.' He called back in a little while, and he said, 'Okay, you've got Ruttenberg. '

A major part of the story had Loretta trying to stop a letter that contained damaging allegations from getting to the District Attorney There were several scenes of her running down a street trying to retrieve the letter from the postman. Polly Ann and her family lived on Alpine Street in Beverly Hills, and that street was chosen for the location shooting, so that Loretta would be able to have lunch with her.

Loretta took a nasty fall in one of her running scenes, and one day while shooting at the MGM studio in Culver City, she went over to the chiropractor's office in the Irving Thalberg Building. Loretta recalled, "I ran into Spencer, and I hadn't seen him in a long time. I was thrilled to see him frankly, and apparently, he was thrilled to see me. We stopped and talked on the steps. He had been to see Margot Fontaine dance the night before, and that's what we talked about." But it was another moment much like the visit he paid Loretta at the Sunset House in 1935 when she was bundled up in bed attempting to hide her pregnancy: they talked about one thing, yet conveyed something else. Loretta remembered it as "a wonderful moment, lightheaded and intimate, and very, very full of understanding." They would never have such a moment with each other ever again.

Tom was out to prove his worth as a movie producer and set a goal to bring the film in at an unassuming budget of $700,000.

Loretta had misgivings. She explained, "I knew the business well enough to know that unless you spend three or four million dollars, you don't get any advertising budget. We rehearsed for four or five days and then shot the whole picture in sixteen days. Tom felt that because he brought it in under budget, he would get a gold star from the front office and probably a contract to do more low budget pictures. He was used to radio budgets where the bottom line was vitally important to the sponsors. This wasn't the case with motion picture studios. I've seen producers deliberately string the shooting of a picture just to insure their ad budget. Anyway, Dore didn't offer him anything else to do after that. CAUSE FOR ALARM didn't launch his career because he wanted to do it his way instead of theirs."

Variety summed it up: "CAUSE FOR ALARM is still a secondary feature not likely to cut a swath at the box office. Miss Young provides it with marquee value and her usual thesping excellence, but the film reflected the difficulty of trying to stretch a thirty minute radio idea over a seventy-four minute celluloid course."

Loretta's own review was much more enthusiastic as she wrote two inscriptions to Tom in the front of a bound script that now belongs to their son Christopher:

"To Tom, our producer. With my deepest appreciation for a wonderful script and a perfect job of producing. Result, my favorite picture! Loretta Young"

The second inscription read: "To Tom, my beloved husband. Happy birthday, Dear, and may our dear Lord continue to watch over you and love you. Another year of full fulfillment for which I am increasingly grateful. Forever, Me"

If only Loretta's written sentiment had any connection with reality. CAUSE FOR ALARM's failure to bring attention to Tom made him feel all the more restless, and the Lewises were on the move again. This time they were buying Huntington Hartford's home in West Hollywood; the extensive renovation would take two and a half years. In the interim, they rented Harry Warner's beach house in Santa Monica.

Beatrice Dudley had been Loretta's personal maid for three years, and she depended on her a great deal. Loretta found a note from Beatrice right in the midst of the move from the Doheny Ranch. Loretta recalled, "The note said that Tom had dismissed her at two in the morning. She'd just gotten in from the Doheny house at about one thirty, and he was waiting up for her. He said he wanted her out of there by six, so she just packed and left. The note went on to say, 'I think it really is better this way; it's been coming on for a long time.'

"I took the note into Tom and asked, 'What's this about?' He read it and said, 'I don't want her around anymore.' No real excuse, he just didn't want to have servants in his house that he didn't trust. I said, 'Tom, there's nobody in the entire world you could trust more than Beatrice.' He replied, 'You may, I don't. Anyway, she's gone, and that's it. I feel much happier, and you should, too. You'll get over it.' There was no reasoning with him."

The Lewises traveled to Troy, New York, for the 1951 Christmas holiday. Loretta recalled, "We stayed in the house where Tom had grown up. His sister Ruth gave Tom and me the master bedroom, and she set up cots in the basement for the two boys. They liked it because it was kind of a playroom, and it was warm; the furnace was down there.

"Tom bragged a lot about his brother, Charles, who was Chief of Staff of the hospital in Troy, and his other two brothers were bankers; they all did very well. But Tom was considered the star of his family because he had worked at WOR in Schenectady and then made it big in New York, and he married the movie star. He was the big shot who lived in a big house and drove the big cars. I never became part of that family. They all considered me as

Loretta Young and treated me as such. I used to try to help clean around the house as all the women did, but not with the cooking because they were experts at it; I wasn't. They were surprised I knew how to clean.

"Ruth never married nor ever lived outside the family home. I used to send her clothes at Tom's request. If I'd get a new dress from Irene, he'd say, 'Oh, after you wear that for a while, send that to Ruth, it would look marvelous on her.' I would have loved to have gotten a thank you note from her just once. I think it would have encouraged me to continue sending things to her without feeling disgruntled.

"I had to go into New York City on Christmas day to do a radio show for Hallmark. I would have preferred to stay in Troy and enjoy Christmas with my family, but it was that radio show that was paying for our trip. I remember resenting Tom's family for assuming that that's what I preferred doing. They felt that the glamour associated with my work more than made up for any effort on my part and said so."

Back in Los Angeles, Tom and Loretta continued to be very social. They saw a lot of Irene Dunne and Dr. Griffin; Irene was Peter's godmother. Rosalind Russell and husband Fred Brisson were also frequent dinner guests. They were close friends without being deep friends. As Loretta explained, "We didn't talk about personal problems because we were all playing a part. We were all playing 'Movie Star' and we knew that. We were supposed to have perfect lives. Of course, nobody did."

Even five-year-old Peter was aware that there was something magical about his mother. He recalled, "She was sort of like a fairy Godmother to me. We would go and watch her get dressed when she would be going out somewhere, and it was like dazzling to me. And if my parents were entertaining at home, I remember lying in bed at night and hearing these people down in the living room. As they'd laugh and talk, they would laugh so loud, it would just sort of scare all the shadows away. These people sort of had a super human quality."

The boys also met Grant Withers. Loretta recalled, "Tom and I and the boys were having ice cream at Chapman's on Santa Monica Boulevard. The boys must have been four or five. Tom spotted Grant coming in and pointed him out, and we were all staring at him. He saw us and I said, 'Grant, come over here.' He was so sweet, no animosity, no jealousy, and he was charming with Tom. The boys just thought he was wonderful because he told funny stories, and he sat down and had a dish of ice cream with us. He said, 'Gretch, I'm so glad you've got such a lovely family, and I wish you all the happiness in the world,' and he was sincere."

Loretta and Harry Cohn hadn't made up since the brouhaha related to the $750 dress. She recalled, "Over the years, we'd go to parties, and I'd see him, and I'd have to be mad at Harry Cohn all night. Finally, one night at Mervyn Leroy's house, we walked in and Harry's back was to me. I thought, 'Oh, this is stupid.' So I walked up behind him and said, 'Don't turn around, Harry; it's Loretta. I don't know about you, but I'm sick of being mad at you. If it will make you feel any better, you were right, and I was wrong, so let's just stop this nonsense. If you don't want to, just walk away, and I'll understand.' He took a long pause. Then he turned around and gave me the sweetest smile and said, 'Yeah, I'm ready to make up.' From then on, we never mentioned it again, and we remained great friends until the day that he died."

Harry Cohn was one of the studio giants who loomed over Hollywood during the glory years of studio preeminence. But, power was shifting, and an uneasy transformation was in the works. Loretta, too, would feel the vibrations. Ever resourceful, she would follow a new path.

Chapter: 18. TRANSITION

HALF ANGEL got off to a bad start. Loretta explained, "My brother in law Norman Foster first brought the script to me. He said, 'I think you'd be marvelous in this.' I didn't go a step further to think, of course, he wanted to direct it. I still had a picture left on a three picture commitment to Daryl Zanuck, so my agents took the script to 20th Century-Fox. They were all for it because MOTHER IS A FRESHMAN and COME TO THE STABLE, both light fares, had been profitable.

"The studio signed Joseph Cotten to co-star and Jules Dassin to direct. Norman never said one word to me about directing it. All I would have had to say was, 'Put Norman Foster on it,' but it never dawned on me. Finally, after Norman died, I said to Sally, 'You know, every time I think about it, I realize now that Norman intended to direct that picture; that's why he brought it to me. But I was so concerned with me, I never even thought of him.' She said. 'Oh, I know, Gretch. I cried over that. We needed the money at that time. '"

Jules Dassin had just completed NIGHT AND THE CITY, a story about a crooked wrestling promoter that would eventually be considered a minor classic. Loretta was unfamiliar with his work, so she viewed NIGHT AND THE CITY. She recalled, "I said to

Julian Blaustein, the producer, 'This is heavy drama, HALF ANGEL is a little sex comedy, nothing like this.' He said, 'Oh, he's a very clever young man.' I said, 'If you say so; okay, we'll try him.' Everyone said, 'Oh, he's a pleasant little fellah,' but I didn't find him to be. The board game Monopoly was the rage back then, and he kept talking about how terrible it was. He said, 'It's just a game for capitalists, and I wouldn't have it in my house. It teaches kids to be pigs about everything.' I said, 'Oh, I can't get too upset over that.'

"I was to play two personalities of the same character in this picture. The conscious part of her was a prude, and whenever she was around Joe Cotten, she was so self- conscious that she couldn't even talk to him. But when she was asleep, she was a tart who would sleepwalk and try to climb in bed with him as quickly as she could. The idea was that when she married, then these two personalities would mesh, and she'd make the perfect wife.

"We started out shooting the prudish character which was fine with me because I had become very uptight working with Jules Dassin. Everything about him seemed to rub me the wrong way. I began to worry that when we got to the tart part, I wouldn't be able to do it with this director. I needed all the self-assurance I could muster to feel 'tarty,' and by this time, I was feeling mostly insecure. We were ten days into production, and we were on location in downtown Los Angeles. There were all these fans standing around, besides the crew, and Jules called me. I said, 'Yes, I'll be right there;' I was still doing my face in front of the mirror, the rich kind of self-indulgent stuff he hated, all the pampering. He called me again, and I said, 'I'll be right there, Jules. I'm just finishing my make-up,' and he said, 'Loretta! You get yourself over here NOW!' It stopped me cold.

"Suddenly, I was back on the set of LAUGH, CLOWN, LAUGH. I was fourteen, and the director Herbert Brenon was yelling at me, and I was terrified. Once again, I was fighting back the tears. This time they weren't tears of fear, they were tears of anger, at me mostly, for allowing this director to treat me in this abusive manner simply to accommodate his own ego. At any rate, all the nasty little insults and insensitivities of the past ten days boiled over, and I heard myself say to the assistant director, 'Please ask Mr. Dassin if he would mind coming to my dressing room for a moment,' and I left the set. When he arrived, I said, 'Jules, we can't work together any longer. One of us is going to leave this picture, and I have a hunch it's going to be you because at this moment in our careers, I sell more tickets at the box office than you do. I've already called for Julian (the producer) to come down. I've told him that it's an emergency.' Jules had such a look of disdain on his face that it gave me chills, and then he just left my dressing room without saying anything.

"Julian arrived about three in the afternoon. After I'd explained my situation, he said, 'Yes, I have seen the tension in the rushes, but didn't know quite what to do about it. I spoke to Jules, and he didn't see any problem.' I continued my venting, 'I don't thrive under bullying; I dry up completely; so Julian, it's your decision: It's Jules or me. I'm going home now. Call me if I'm to report to work tomorrow.'

"The moment I got home, I was sick to my stomach. Frankly, I thought they might call and say, 'We're getting Joan Crawford,' or anybody else to do the part. Because they could have, and it would have been a very difficult thing for me to swallow because I had never walked off a set before, but now I'd stopped production at three in the afternoon. Julian called about 7:30 that night, and all he said was, 'Loretta, would Richard Sale be acceptable to you as a director?' I said, 'Yes, he would.' Julian said, 'Fine. Be ready at nine tomorrow morning.'

"I understand that a lot of actors thrive under a critical director; it makes them mad and they work better. I don't. I don't fight well. There's not that much anger in me that I can use it in my work in order to get rid of it. What talent is there is best wooed out of me. Some actors don't seem to need much direction, but I do, gentle but firm direction. After every scene, my eyes fly to the director for his approval. But it's direction, not coaching, that I need. There's a difference. When somebody tells me how to do something, that drives me crazy; I say, 'You do it then. It will only be secondhand best if I do it the way you want me. '"

Tom bought property in Ojai, California, for a vacation home. They already had equity in the Ojai Inn which was next door. Tom had time on his hands which allowed him lots of interaction with the children. Loretta reflected, "You'd think this would have been healthy, but it wasn't. Whatever Peter did was wrong. Whatever Judy did was wrong. Whatever Christopher did was right. I can remember Tom telling Pete, 'No, Pete, your brother's right; he's your older brother, and he knows best. '"

PAULA was Loretta's next picture. It was produced by Columbia and directed by Rudy Mate whom Loretta greatly admired. She recalled, "The best scene in PAULA is in the beginning where she has the baby and loses it. Rudy said, 'No make-up, just put a little oil on your skin. 'And he was right. It was absolutely beautiful and real looking. The bone structure and everything was marvelous."

Loretta met couturier Jean Louis while doing fittings for PAULA. She recalled, "Harry Cohn had stolen him from a top design house in New York. He had great taste, not motion picture taste, but New York taste. I said, 'I want to look very soft and very feminine. ''Oh,' he said. 'Fine', and that's just the way I looked in the picture. He was very talented.

 "At the time I was reading a little book about St. Martin de Pours, a black saint. Elizabeth, Jean's top fitter, was a very attractive black woman, and she was a genius as far as fitting clothes. She wasn't a Catholic, but I'm telling her the whole book and Jean was in the background. They're doing their work and I'm just babbling. I had it all figured out that I was going to convert Elizabeth. However, Elizabeth had her own ideas.

"I went to Mass at St. Victor's not long after that and saw Jean Louis walking down the aisle. I waited for him outside after Mass. I said, 'Jean, how marvelous, I didn't know you were in this parish.' He said, 'Oh, yes, I've lived in this parish for some time. 'I asked, 'How come I've never seen you before?' He answered, 'Because I didn't go to church until you started talking about St. Martin de Pour.' I was thrilled about that."

PAULA was a little picture. Filmed in black and white with all location shooting done in the Los Angeles area, it was able to turn its predictable profit. But profits were no longer as predictable in Hollywood as they had been in the heady war years of the Forties. The Federal Court mandate for studios to detach themselves from their own theater chains had complicated the situation.

Social mores were also in flux. Frank Capra's important films were all behind him as feel good stories were being replaced by a wave of postwar realism. Loretta was a hold out from the Golden Era; the newer stars exuded a more blatant sexuality. Jane Russell, Jayne Mansfield, Mamie Van Doren: all would hit their stride in the Fifties. No one epitomized the new sexuality better than a young girl coming on strong at 20th Century-Fox, Marilyn Monroe.

Loretta recalled the only two times she saw Marilyn Monroe. "I was over at the wardrobe department at 20th Century-Fox. I was coming out of a fitting room as Marilyn was coming in. David Levy, head of Wardrobe, said, 'Oh Loretta, I want you to meet a new actress who we have on the lot; she is going to go very far.' She said, 'Oh, how do you do?' Dave felt sorry for her. All men did. I had seen her once before with Johnny Hyde. Johnny was an agent, twenty years older than me, who came up to about my shoulder, and here was this blonde hanging onto him as if he were Clark Gable. It was just so obvious. My impressions of

Marilyn are that she was a little misfit who looked voluptuous, and I think, in a way, very beautiful. But she learned early to use people because she had been used herself, extraordinarily badly, and I guess she learned to maneuver."

Loretta was honored by LUX RADIO THEATER for making her twenty-fifth appearance on the program in the spring of 1951. She was the first and only movie star to achieve that record. Radio, too, was undergoing a transition and would share a common enemy with the motion picture industry: television. Advertising revenues were being diverted from radio to the new medium, and total motion picture revenue continued a steady decline from its apex in 1946. The cloud represented by television loomed much larger over the movie business than all other factors stirring up the industry. And the cloud would keep getting darker for another decade before the movie industry redefined its place in the new order. Movies would never again be king of the mountain in terms of revenue generated and the power of influence.

However, as television was just beginning, its future was far from clear. Many in Hollywood saw it as an upstart, distasteful at best, and vowed they'd never have a set in their homes. Loretta was more of a realist and one of the first to own a television. She remembered the first evening after the set was installed. "Tom and I and the kids were in the living room after dinner, and I had told the cook and the maid and the gardener, and anybody else who was around, to come in. So, the little bunch of us was watching a suspense show. The boys were little. There was a shot of a woman, fully dressed, walking into this room. She started to undress; the camera was on her face as she pulled her slip over her head. Finally, she turned around and two hands closed around her neck and choked her to death. Ahhh! She's dead. Well, of course, the kids screamed and everybody screamed because we were watching a murder right in our living room. Tom jumped up and turned the television off and we talked about it all night. I was horrified.

"My first impulse was to ask, 'Do I want this thing in my house if the kids are going to be scared to death by it?' But then I thought, 'This is the medium for me to get into. If I have a show, I'll take up one half hour where at least I won't' scare anybody to death.' Tom's reaction was, 'You're leaving a lucrative business to go into something unknown.' He had a point. I'd be leaving a career that was paying me over $200,000 a picture."

Loretta realized that she was at a juncture in her career. She had strived to be a movie star for many years and, in her mind, she had reached that pinnacle when she won an Academy Award. She realized, "I had made my goal, but I still wanted to become a better actress. I thought that if I had an anthology series, that it would stimulate my imagination and stretch me. The idea of playing a different character each week excited me."

Loretta's agents at The William Morris Agency didn't share her enthusiasm. They pointed out that, instead of making $20,000 a week while she was working, it would be more like $1,500. But, Loretta recalled, "I finally said to Abe Glasvogel, 'I can't wait around until there's enough money because I'll be too old to do what I want to do.'" It would take Loretta two years to talk him into making a deal.

Word got around that Loretta had set her sights on television and, to many, it seemed like a betrayal. Recalled Loretta, "Both L.B. Mayer and David Selznick, in separate meetings, warned me, 'It is the enemy of our industry, and if you go into it, you'll probably never get another script as long as you live.' I responded, 'I've made a lot of money for you and a lot of money for myself in films, but I'm going into this business because I know this is the next thing that is going to shape the world. I want to do this because I want to get one good idea into the mainstream of life once a week. I could never do that in movies. I will on television."

Later in life, Loretta acknowledged the debt that she owed to the studio system and the men who ran it. She reflected, "I wasn't that flamboyant a personality. I had to have a studio behind me and just wean me onto the public. If I had been bad, I would not have lasted, that's true. But, if you're just good enough, then you can get better with practice, and that's what happened to me. And after so many years, the soil was prepared. I didn't have to sell myself. Both the audiences and the producers knew what they were getting with *Loretta Young*."

There was another motivation behind Loretta's desire to get into television. She wanted to create a situation where Tom could have another fresh start, and in doing so, save a marriage that was becoming more and more fragile. However, the transition was going to take some time and until the deals could be worked out, Loretta continued making movies.

BECAUSE OF YOU was next. She played a dope peddler's moll sent to prison as an accessory. While serving time, she becomes a nurse, and then later, marries without telling her wealthy husband about her past life. Only after they have a daughter does her past come back to haunt her.

This would be Loretta's first film for Universal since she was a child extra. Her attraction to Universal was that old friend Bill

Geotz was now running the studio. In negotiations with the studio, Loretta had asked that the Deanna Durbin bungalow be made available to her. Loretta explained, "That dressing room carried a certain status. It told the whole studio what the boss thought of whoever was using it."

Jeff Chandler was Loretta's leading man in BECAUSE OF YOU. He was 6'4", 210 pounds, and with his chiseled good looks, Chandler was fast becoming a Fifties heartthrob. He was five years younger than Loretta. She found Jeff Chandler to be very attractive, and apparently, the feelings were reciprocal. Loretta recalled, "We'd been rehearsing a couple of days, and I started to go up to my dressing room, and Jeff said, 'May I walk you out to the bungalow?' I said, 'Yes, delighted.' So we were walking out and he said, 'I have to tell you something. I don't understand what's happening, but I think I'm falling in love with you.' I got very flustered, very flustered. I said, 'That's not necessarily bad ...' The minute it came out of my mouth, he kind of looked at me and I said, 'No, I didn't mean that exactly.' He asked, 'What did you mean?' I didn't know how to put it. What I meant was, 'Well, it's all right. I'm married and you're married, and nothing could ever come of it anyway, so it's not too terrible, but keep it that way.' Anyway, once you even admit anything like that, it makes it a little more difficult, but it makes for very nice love scenes."

Loretta theorized, "It's easy for a woman to be a faithful wife if she is happily married. But, if she is unhappily married and she's at all attractive, it's very difficult. Very! I managed in my marriage but, believe me, it was no picnic. I learned very quickly that you don't even hold hands. You don't even smile too long at each other, and you certainly don't kiss each other because the next thing you know, you've slipped into that euphoric state of sheer bliss where nothing else matters."

Loretta's distinct advantage was to be an actress. She laughingly said, "I could kiss Jeff Chandler while the cameras were rolling and actually get paid for it. Even with innocent kisses, I was deeply touched by Jeff's nearness and his sensitivity and, of course, his masculinity." Loretta knew she was playing with fire. She reflected, "Jeff never so much as held my hand outside of those scenes, but I think until he died, we both felt it. If I'd see him on the street, I'd walk the other way because I didn't want to spark anything. I said to him, 'Jeff, we're just bad news for each other so wave at me across the room but don't come near me.' I think that he was at our house a couple of times, at big parties because I didn't want to penalize him in any way. His wife was charming. I don't think that she ever knew that there was a crush."

BECAUSE OF YOU was a sleeper hit, a film that performs way beyond expectations, and was held over a couple of weeks at the Roxy Theater in New York. A *New York Times* reviewer must have sensed the attraction between the two stars. He wrote, "Jeff Chandler and Loretta Young make a fine romantic team. Sex angle is introduced with unusual prominence and played for all that it's worth. Miss Young is an eyeful and an expert in the clinches."

Loretta's second picture for Universal was IT HAPPENS EVERY THURSDAY. John Forsythe, a newcomer to film, co-starred. Loretta remembered working with Forsythe. "He was cute and very sweet, but he wasn't real clear on what kind of picture we were doing. I remember one day we were doing a scene, and I was sitting on his lap, and I was laughing about something. When we were through, he said, 'You know something. I think I'm the only person on the set that doesn't know this picture's a comedy.' I said, 'That's right, you and the producer.' The producer, Anton Leader, had produced the radio show *Suspense* and he wanted more drama. Joe Pevney was directing and he agreed with me, saying, 'I think we're taking ourselves too seriously.'

"We got to one scene that was all charged with drama, and I said, 'I'm sorry, I really can't do this seriously.' It was noontime, so I went over to Bill Geotz's office and said, 'Bill, you make fifty pictures a year, so you can afford one or two duds, but I really can't. This is a very nice little picture, but it's not a drama. If anything, it's kind of a sweet family comedy. You're going to have to get a comedy writer around here someplace, or you can stop and get somebody else to do the picture because I can't go ahead with it like this.' He said, 'I've been watching the rushes and I agree. Give me some time.' Bill called me in my dressing room after lunch and said, 'There's a young man we've got on the lot by the name of Dick Morris. He's quite a good writer. If you stay there, he'll be over in your dressing room in about 20 minutes. I asked that the director and the producer come over as well.'

"We were sitting around, and this kid wearing white bucks and a tee-shirt comes in. He had blond hair and looked about 25. I thought, 'Oh boy. He's too young to know anything.' Anyway, he sat down and got out his little pad of paper, and we all talked, and he made notes. We talked for about two hours, and he hadn't opened his mouth. Finally, he said, 'I have to think about it.' It was about 3:00 p.m. and the producer said, 'We might as well all go home.'

"About 7:30 the next morning, I was in my dressing room, and they came in with some pink pages. There were a couple of scenes we were supposed to shoot that day, and they were good, not hilarious, but at least they had a light touch and some humor. I got a call from Bill Geotz's secretary. 'Mr. Geotz wants to know if the re-writes are acceptable to you.' I said 'Yes, they are. At least I can do them.' They put Dick Morris on the project, and he just re-wrote all the scenes. When we were through, I thanked him. The picture didn't do anything, but it didn't break anybody either, and at least, I wasn't embarrassed by it."

IT HAPPENS EVERY THURSDAY was a rather inglorious ending to a film career of ninety-eight movies that spanned a period of thirty-six years; a career that reached back practically to the beginning of Hollywood movies and then rode the crest through the peak years of the Thirties to mid-Forties. Loretta personally reached her zenith in films from the mid-Forties to 1950, as the industry was waning in the wake of a changing world and the advent of television.

In the early Fifties BECAUSE OF YOU was Loretta's only major hit. Audiences were changing and so were their tastes. Were producers shying away from Loretta for another reason? Murray Bolen thought so. He had worked with Tom at Young and Rubicam back in the Thirties and also worked with Loretta on radio shows where she guest-appeared in the Forties. He opined, "Some producers were growing weary of Loretta's theological bent. I think Loretta had a reputation among the big moguls of being slightly difficult because she was religioso (Murray's slang word). She had a reputation for impinging her beliefs into the stories she was making. I think the reason she went into television was because she could guide the whole thing."

Chapter 19: WALKING THROUGH THE DOOR

Loretta was holding her ground for an anthology series, a format that had been popular on radio. There were no continuing characters from week to week. The host was the one constant.

She reflected, "My experience had taught me a lot. I knew that a true story worked best, and that you wanted to make just one major point with that story. I had learned a lot about make-up, so I was willing to play Japanese, Chinese, and other international characters. I knew clothes, so I could dress in anything I wanted. I could go to my own closet or borrow friends' clothes, and I knew I could go to 20th Century-Fox, and they'd give me anything I wanted.

"I would be the hostess and once the audience saw me at my best in the introduction, then I could play anything I wanted: ugly, old, young, whatever. As long as I looked great coming through the door, my ego would be satisfied. The three components of the show were: coming through the door, the story itself, and the quote at the end of the show."

Tom and a writer friend of his came up with an idea to embellish the format. The show would be titled LETTERS TO LORETTA. Loretta explained, "Supposedly, somebody would write me a letter, and I answered the letter with this little show. I knew it didn't make any sense. I remember Mama asking me after she watched the first show, 'What was that first part about?'"

Loretta surmised, "The crew was first class because that's all I knew. I had never made B pictures, only A pictures, so the people that came into television with me were people that I had worked with and were tops in their field. Norman Brodine who had photographed Jean Harlow was the cameraman. "

William Morris Agency put a deal together with Proctor and Gamble. Proctor and Gamble paid $30,000 per show, and that entitled them to the airing of a completed show on prime time NBC, plus the right to replay that show one time. After that, the show was owned outright by Lewislor, Loretta and Tom's production-company. Loretta's salary would be $5,000 per episode. Since the budget was so tight, Tom Lewis agreed to work without a salary. Tom's confidence was coming back in full stride. Loretta recalled, "He told me that the reason Proctor and Gamble had agreed to sponsor the show was because of his reputation in radio. And he meant it."

Loretta knew that they would need good stories and plenty of them. She recalled a fortuitous inspiration, "Ruth Roberts had worked with me on my last several films, and she came right along with me into television. One day I said to her, 'Whatever happened to that kid who did the re-writes on IT HAPPENS EVERY THURSDAY?' Two days later she came back and said: 'Universal let him go, and he's back in New York.' I said, 'Find him and ask if he wants to write for this television show.' She came back and said, 'He's thrilled to death, and he'll be on the plane tonight.' The next morning he walked into the studio. He was a natural. He knew how to get to the point."

LETTERS TO LORETTA premiered on September 20, 1953, 10: 00 p.m. E.ST. There were many shows airing that season now also considered classics: I LOVE LUCY, DRAGET, YOU BET YOUR LIFE, THE MILTON BERLE SHOW and THE JACKIE GLEASON SHOW.

Loretta whirling through the door and greeting her television guests is one of the most enduring images of early television. For those who remember television from the Fifties, to say that "Someone walks through the door like *Loretta Young* conjures up a very sophisticated image of a beautiful woman floating into a room wearing a gorgeous gown. It became Loretta's trademark, a signature far beyond anything her ninety-eight movies had accomplished.

The exact way that Loretta came through the door was developed to please a disgruntled designer. Loretta explained, "My manager had made an arrangement with the designer Marusha: if she would supply the clothes that I wore coming through the door, she would get exclusive credit in exchange.

"Marusha was a darling Hungarian and very volatile. The first dress she designed was a simple evening dress draped toward the back. I was to come through the door and walk down and say what I had to say at the desk. I tried it and the cameraman said yes and the director said yes. I looked over in the corner and Marusha was pouting. She said, 'No one is ever going to see the back of the dress.' I said, 'I can't back into the room.' She said, 'Oh, I know, but if I'd known this is the way it was going to be shot, I would have done something with the front.' I saw her point so while the crew was lining up the shot, I started to play around with the door to see if there wasn't someway she could view the back of her dress. Finally, I tried opening the door, stepping into the room, making a full turn, and then simply closing the door. Because it was a wide door, I had to step wide, both coming into the room and closing the door. I studied dancing as a child, and when I closed the door my feet automatically went into 5th position before I took off for the desk. The 5th position starts off every dance step known in ballet. I tried it a couple of times;

then I called Marusha to watch. She responded, 'It's better than nothing. '"

Murray Bolen, who had worked with Tom and then Loretta in radio, reemerged into their lives. He recalled, "I was back working for Young and Rubicam, and P&G was our number one client." He recalled, "P&G wanted to sell Tide on LETTERS TO LORETTA and they wanted Loretta, after she had whirled through the door, to come up to the desk, reach over to the announcer and take the box of Tide into her hand. They weren't even asking to see her face in that shot, just her hand, but I knew I could never get her to do it. She thought it was beneath her dignity. In those days, it was very sensitive stuff because the movies were still frowning upon movie stars connected with television, and Loretta was the number one movie star in television."

Lewislor had a repertory of actors signed to play various roles, but only Loretta appeared in every single show. The schedule was all consuming, which meant she saw very little of the boys. Loretta explained, "Monday and Tuesday were early days because we rehearsed and I got home usually around 6:00. But often on Wednesday and Thursday nights, I slept at the studio because it allowed me about two additional hours of sleep. On Saturdays I would write the format, find the quotes, learn thirty pages of dialogue and dress the show for the following week. But, at least on weekends, I did most of the work at home so I saw them then."

Loretta's consolation was that the boys had such a good relationship with Mary Coney. Loretta reflected, "A lot of nurses vicariously live through the children, but there was none of that in Mary Coney. She loved them, but did not try to possess them. She did everything that a mother would do with the children except there wasn't quite the intimacy."

The hopeful scenario where Tom as a producer would feel empowered and their marriage would flourish did not unfold. Dick Morris had written an episode called "Big Jim" which told the story of Big Brothers. Loretta recalled, "Dick Morris brought in the script and I said, 'It's perfect. Don't change anything.' But Tom made a lot of changes, and when the blue sheets came in to me, I just crossed them all out and said, 'No, I'm sorry, I don't like these changes; I want the original script.' Then all hell broke loose."

Tom regained control in the cutting of "Big Jim". He cut out one of Loretta's major scenes and replaced it with a shot of the kid walking up and down in his room waiting for his mom to arrive. Everyone, Loretta, Dick Morris, the story editor, disagreed, but

Tom was firm. He was in charge. This was a harbinger of many fights ahead when he would either choose stories with only bit parts available for Loretta, or he would edit her performance down to a bit part.

One very positive thing developed from "Big Jim." Dick Morris asked if he could direct, and it was the first of many shows that he wrote and directed for Loretta. An interesting note to that episode: Loretta was playing a woman with a shady past, and she went to 20th Century-Fox Wardrobe Department to borrow an outfit that a prostitute would wear. It ended up being a skirt, jacket, and floppy hat that Marilyn Monroe had just worn in one of her pictures.

Murray Bolen reflected, "I don't think Tom was very happy producing the TV show. I have to say that I really thought that Tom was essentially a phony guy. Of course, that impression goes back to when I first worked with him at Young and Rubicam. Tom was not too sure of himself in some way. There was something funny about him, a psychological problem, but I could never quite figure out what it was. He wasn't easy to work with because he was high-handed and overly important."

Tom's sense of self-importance also annoyed Sally. She recalled seeing him on the set, "He'd be walking around with a drink at the end of the day; that isn't something a producer would do. They don't walk around with a drink when everybody else, the cameraman, and the director, and the assistant director, are without a drink. You just don't do that. And he was talking as though he was responsible for everything. He had terrible pride."

Judy had completed high school and, at age 17, was sent to Duschesne Finishing School in New York. It was a rocky year. Loretta received this note in December, 1953.

"Dear Mrs. Lewis: Judy has an innate resentment against discipline of any kind and feels that rules and regulations inhibit her in a very disagreeable way. She has accumulated more demerits than any girl in the school. When Judy receives demerits, she has an air of injured innocence, a kind of martyr complex, instead of seeing that she made a mistake and determining not to make the same one again. In view of these attitudes, it would not be possible for us to accept Judy back after Christmas unless she writes me a letter saying that she is ready to cooperate.
Very sincerely, C. Krim R.S.G."

Judy sent the following letter to her mother as soon as she became aware of Mother Krim's note.

"Mom Darling, First, I want to start by saying that I love you so very much, Mom, that is seems impossible a daughter could love her mother with such a warm and deep hearted emotion and tenderness as I do you. It was because of this love that I had not previously mentioned any difficulties I was having. There are many reasons why I find it difficult and ones that I feel are very important. However, time doesn't allow the explanation of these. I have tried to model my life after you and the Blessed Mother. If I ever thought I was hurting either of you I would die. I love you Mom, darling, more than you know and would never do anything to disappoint or hurt you. I miss you. Your daughter, Judy"

Judy was determined not to return to Duschesne after the holidays and sent all her things home before she personally arrived. However, a persuasive Loretta convinced Judy to return and finish out the year.

Judy's problems had to be incorporated in Loretta's very busy life. Work was the focal point of her attention. The LETTERS TO LORETTA opening format proved too much of a contrivance and the show's name changed to THE LORETTA YOUNG SHOW. Lewislor moved over to the Samuel Goldwyn Studios at the beginning of the second season.

Loretta took Peter to Disneyland for a weekend shortly after the second season started; Christopher stayed home after refusing to do a chore. Loretta recalled the outing, "We were standing at the desk of the Disneyland Hotel and Marshall Workman, the manager of Samuel Goldwyn's studio, was standing there with his wife and their little boy, who must have been five or six. He introduced me to his wife and to his son, Jimmy. Marshall said to him, 'Miss Young is a big Movie Star!' The boy looked up at me then looked at his father and said, 'Don't you have to be any prettier than that?' His poor father nearly fainted. I burst out laughing and said, 'No, Honey, you really don't. "'

Loretta was in need of a good laugh. Tom was even more difficult as they progressed into the second season. An episode titled "Thanksgiving at Beaver Run" illustrated the problem. It was the story of a family with the emphasis on the father and children. Loretta was relegated to playing a bit part. It was one of Tom's favorite shows. Loretta recalled her reaction. "I kept saying, "Tom, this is wrong. This is THE LORETTA YOUNG SHOW, and you can't keep putting unknowns in it and having me playing bit parts. You have to merchandise me!"

Tom also ebbed away the people supportive of Loretta. He fired an assistant director, Loretta's make-up man, and he pressured

John London, the production manager, to seek a different project which he did by going over to CBS.

In the midst of this pressure-filled second season, Loretta recalled attending a party hosted by William Hearst, son of William Randolph Hearst, "There were place cards for everybody, and I was seated next to Tyrone (Tyrone Power) now married for the second time. I noticed a girl on the dance floor, one of the most beautiful creatures I'd ever seen. She had soft dark hair that fell a little below her shoulders in the back, and she had on a nude-colored beaded dress that clung to her exquisitely shaped body. Tyrone was talking, and I was listening but looking at the dance-floor at the same time. He said, 'What are you looking at?' I said 'That's the most beautiful girl.' He turned and said, 'Oh, Gretch, that's Linda (Linda Christian), my wife,' and he went right on. He had, absolutely at that time, no interest in her whatsoever. They were supposed to be happily married.

"We continued to talk and a little later, he said, 'Oh Gretch, if you had just pushed a little harder.' Even then, with both of us married to other people, my heart jumped and so many memories floated back into my mind. It stopped me for a moment and then I said, 'I was waiting for you to push harder.' He smiled and said, 'Well, that was yesterday but it's too bad.' I said, 'Maybe; who knows.' But I do know that it would have been an entirely different life for both of us."

Family members had watched the Lewises' personal relationship deteriorate over the years. Ricardo Montalban recalled, "When we were first married, often times we had dinner with Tom and Loretta. Tom was very pleasant and witty, and would carry on the conversation with anecdotes, and Loretta would sit very placidly with a very sweet smile. Now, as time progressed, sometimes the stories became a little repetitious, and Tom would talk and talk, and after a period of time, Loretta would Interrupt, saying, 'All right Tom, that's enough.' This went on for many years."

Proctor and Gamble, if not aware of the Lewises' personal problems, was certainly aware of the problem with the show. Loretta recalled, "They asked for a meeting in which they made their position clear. 'We bought THE LORETTA YOUNG SHOW and we want Loretta Young.' Ruth Roberts was the story editor and when Tom came up with a story that featured a little boy, she confronted Tom, 'I'm sorry. We've already been told by Proctor and Gamble that the show has to showcase Loretta.' Tom's reaction was to fire her."

The tension between Tom and Loretta was unceasing both at home and at work. The sound of Tom's deep-speaking-voice that Loretta had found so attractive during their early years, now made her cringe, even if he just mentioned her name. Dr. Markster encouraged Loretta to find some kind of resolution. She recalled,

"One evening when we were at home, I said, 'Tom, we can't continue working together because our problems at work are destroying our marriage. We've got to decide. Either you take this show, and I will go and get another one, or I'll take this show and you go and get another one. We cannot work together.' He said, 'For once, you're right.'"

The William Morris Agency got a quick reply from Proctor and Gamble stating that it would have to be Tom Lewis who would leave the show. Loretta remembered, "A few days later, I asked him, 'Has William Morris called you?' He said, 'Yes they have and I will look for something else.' I brought up the subject a couple of nights later, and Tom said, 'Don't butt into my business, and I won't butt into yours.' I said, 'That's fine.' Little did I know that he was already working on a *little piece of paper* that was going to turn my life upside down."

The Lewises moved into the Huntington Hartford residence on Flores Street. They also bought a luxury thirty unit apartment next door as an investment property.

Outside of these real estate investments, Tom was, once again, adrift. Loretta reflected, "I guess the poor man thought, 'What's the point in working if you've got a wife who can make six times as much as you can so I'll just take care of her affairs.' But he was just playing businessman at his office."

It was how Tom thought the outside world perceived him that brought him so much pain. Loretta recalled the evening in which they had gone to see Judy Garland and James Mason in A STAR IS BORN. It was a remake of the perennial story of a Hollywood couple, where the wife's star was in ascension as the husband's fortunes declined. "We didn't even get out of the theatre before Tom started to cry, just sob. I think he saw himself in this part, married to the star and getting kicked around. I couldn't budge him. I finally said, 'I'm going to sit down, Tom, because if I stand here any longer, we're going to cause a scene.' He said, 'I'll be all right in a minute.' I went down and sat in a seat, and he finally got a hold of himself. He said, 'Come on, let's go out to the car.' He didn't talk about that one. Didn't have to. Neither of us said anything on our way home."

The Lewis's discontent with each other was evident to anyone who spent time with them. Jane Sharpe recalled, "Tom so badly wanted to be domineering, but Loretta was the important one, and boy, did he resent her for it. I've seen her in tears so many times that it would just break your heart. But it was almost a marshmallow-covered cruelty. You couldn't believe what you were witnessing; it was a psychological cutting her down ... chop, chop, chop. Not unlike Chinese water torture, he was always belittling her one drop at a time. It was really subtle: GASLIGHT (title of a film in which Charles Boyer attempts to isolate his wife, Ingrid Bergman, and drive her crazy.)"

Sally used the same analogy when she speculated why Tom, a few years earlier, had rented Harry Warner's beach house. "He took Loretta down there and kept her captive from us. He didn't want our family around; he'd alienate us, one at a time. He tried to lock her away from everybody. It really was terrible. It was GASLIGHT if I've ever seen it."

Tom had moved out of their bedroom early in the second season of the television show. Loretta remembered that, after several weeks, she gathered the courage to discuss it. I asked "'What is the purpose of your moving into that bedroom? It's dismaying everybody in the house, including the children.' Tom replied, 'I don't think there's any purpose in pretending to be husband and wife if we're not.' I said, 'Indeed, we are husband and wife.' His response was, 'I just don't feel that I want to play that role anymore. '"

 Loretta was nominated as "Best Actress in a Regular Series" for the 1953/1954 season. Her competition was formidable: Lucille Ball, Eve Arden, Ann Sothern and Gracie Allen. Norman Brodine was also nominated for photography of THE LORETTA YOUNG SHOW. Loretta recalled the evening: "We were all at the same table. Tom was very anxious that Brodie get the award, but he didn't that year; he would in future years. Anyway, that night they announced the category for Best Actress and the presenter said, 'LORETTA YOUNG!' Of course, I was delighted, and I got up to go get my award. When I came back I leaned down toward Tom; I thought he was going to give me a kiss on the cheek. He did but then he said, 'The wrong person got it.' I sat down and said, 'What did you just say to me?' He said, "The wrong person got it. You don't need it. He needed it.' I said, 'Well, thanks a lot.'" Tom was cavalierly disregarding a Hollywood historic moment. Loretta was the first major movie star ever to have won both an Academy Award and an Emmy in the Best Actress category.

Chapter 20: DARK CLOUDS

Loretta recalled a recurring dream that began in the Fifties. "I'm lying down and this thing comes to me. It looks like the world glowing in color, but I'm holding it up because if I don't hold it up, it will squash me. I was so familiar with this dream that when it would start, I'd say to myself, 'Now this is only a dream, so it doesn't have to worry you,' but it always did." Even the most rudimentary dream analyst would conclude that Loretta was under intense stress.

One of Loretta's biggest frustrations was that she wasn't the nurturing parent that Gladys had been for her. And just as Tom resented Loretta's power in the world, Loretta resented his power in the home. Loretta recalled, "I worked Saturday mornings preparing for the following week's show, so Tom and the boys would drive up to Ojai, and Mary Coney and I would come later in the day. I resented the fact that Tom wouldn't wait so that we could have all gone up together. Not only did I have less time with the boys, but Tom was teaching them to be pure and utterly selfish in not considering I might be tired and would want to relax and ride with them." Loretta saw a male chauvinist pig attitude prevailing. Tom saw it as The PCT Club.

The PCT Club was made up of Peter, Chris and Tom. Peter recalled, "The whole wellbeing of our little family had to do with a willingness to be in this PCT Club where you were part of the group."

Loretta often found it a welcome distraction to be with other people outside the family. She recalled, "I saw Jean Louis walk into mass one morning with a perfectly beautiful redhead, exquisitely dressed. I couldn't wait until they got outside, and I invited them back to the house for breakfast. Her name was Maggie and when I got her alone, I learned that she and Jean had known each other earlier in New York and then stumbled across each other in Los Angeles. This was shortly after his first wife died." Maggie Fisher would soon be Jean's second wife and become an important friend to Loretta.

Tom and Loretta's relationship had reached a new plateau. No more was said about Tom's move to his own room, but to emphatically demonstrate his feelings, he began locking his door whenever he was in.

It was Tom's theory that Loretta always became upset over the holidays. Loretta concluded that she became upset over the holidays because Tom didn't want any interaction with her

family. She had her way, Easter 1955, and invited the
Montalbans to join them at their nine bedroom Ojai home.

Loretta recalled, "Georgiana and I were in Ventura buying Easter
candy and while walking down the street, I felt a crushing pain. I
thought it would go away, but it didn't. Finally, I asked Georgi to
get the car, and we got home around three in the afternoon. She
practically had to carry me in, and I asked Tom to call Dr.
Marxser.
Neither Georgi nor I heard Tom's conversation with the doctor,
but Tom came in and said, 'Doc says there is really nothing
wrong with you, Loretta; it's just that you get upset. He said to
stay in bed and put a hot water bottle on it.' "

Georgiana recalled that night. "I was so afraid for Gretch. I
thought that Tom behaved abominably. He kept sipping his
vodka and water in the garden and, basically, ignoring her while
she was throwing up with the pain. Miss Coney was afraid of her
own shadow, so I was the one who was caring for Gretch."

Loretta's memory of that evening continued, "Georgi kept
checking on me. About nine in the evening, I told her, 'I'm getting
weaker and weaker. You've got to get a doctor to come.' She
talked with Tom, and he said, 'Oh Georgi, she's all right; she just
gets emotional over the holidays.' Georgi said, 'Tom, if you don't

call a doctor to come and see her, I will.' So Tom contacted a local doctor in Ojai, and he came over. When he walked into my room, you could almost see a sneer on his face. He said, 'Maybe if you'd wash your hair you'd feel better.' I said, 'It isn't my head that hurts, Doctor. It has nothing to do with my head.' He said, 'I'm going to give you a pill, and I'll leave another one in the bathroom for you to take if you wake up later and have any pain.'

"About an hour and a half later the pain hadn't subsided, and I went into the bathroom and realized what he left was a sleeping pill. Tom must have convinced him that I was a hysterical actress who was throwing a fit. This time, I didn't call for Tom. I said, 'Georgi, get me to a hospital.' So at 5:00 in the morning, an ambulance arrived and took me to St. John's Hospital in Oxnard. They took some tests. Peritonitis had already set in, and they started me on penicillin.

"Sister Mary Rose Cristy was the Head of Nurses and assumed my direct nursing care. She also arranged for a lady gynecologist, Dr. Chess, to take over my case. She looked over my charts and explained that during my monthly ovulation, as the egg broke through the uterus wall, it hit a tiny blood vessel in the vaginal cavity and caused an infection of the lower intestine.

"Dr. Chess asked my family, 'Call before you come because sometimes all she's able to do is cope with that pain and company doesn't help.' I don't think Tom liked her very well because she would say, 'No, you can't go in and see her now, Mr. Lewis. She is not well enough for any more stress, and you cause her stress.' Or she'd say, 'The boys can only come in for two minutes, then give her a kiss and go right out again.' Judy was the easiest on me because all she'd do was come in and hold my hand, give me a kiss, and then just sit quietly.

"One day Judy told me she had signed with an agent. She was nineteen at the time.
I said, 'Judy, think very carefully if you want to become an actress because what you've seen is only the gravy.' That was true, all she saw were the clothes, and the houses, the cars, and all the attention. I continued, 'Unless you just love to act, unless that's where your heart and soul is, and you're just thrilled to death at every moment at that, it just isn't worth it; no matter how good you think you are.' And I added, 'Look at me now. I'm forty-one-years-old, they're probably going to cancel the television show; your father isn't working, and the money's going to stop. If I can't work, I don't know what I'm going to do.' 'Oh,' she said, 'You will.' I said, 'I hope I do, but, look at me now. Take a good look; I only weigh 82 pounds. This isn't all fairy tale stuff.'"

"The pain never seemed to be gone for long, and after fighting this infection for three months, and eleven doctors consulting, Dr. Chess came to me one day and said, 'I think you should have a hysterectomy. It's the only way I know to end the pain.'
I think that operation took her about three and a half hour. When I woke up, Tom had one hand and Judy had the other. That evening, about five, Tom said, 'I'm taking the boys to Troy, tomorrow. I don't want to bring them by because I don't want to upset them.' I said, 'I'd like to see them.' 'No,' he said, 'I don't think that's wise,' and I didn't see the boys for another month until I got out of the hospital."

A daily bulletin was issued from St. John's for the entire four months of Loretta's hospitalization. The William Morris Agency had even more direct access with the hospital and knew the nature of Loretta's illness and its encouraging prognosis. Her agent Norman Brokaw came up to Oxnard and told Loretta that Proctor and Gamble was willing to go ahead with guest stars and keep the show on the air until she got well.

"Norman went back and met with Tom. Tom wanted to close the show down and sell the first two seasons. Norman told him, 'You need at least five years of film to sell to a syndicator for reruns.' Tom was adamant, and they had a terrible fight."

When Tom had put together the Lewislor Production Company, he distributed 49% of the stock to himself, 49% to Loretta, and 2% of the stock to Bob Shewalter, the company accountant. Loretta hypothesized, "Tom must have thought that if he and I ever reached an impasse, he could influence Bob Shewalter to vote with him. But Bob was not the stooge that he was supposed to be." Bob Shewalter joined his 2% vote with Loretta's, and THE LORETTA YOUNG SHOW would go into production for a third season.

Loretta clung to the hope that if only Tom had a job, their stormy marriage would be given a new lease. Polly Ann and Carter were friends with Rosalind Russell and through Rosalind they knew Chet LaRoche, Tom's old mentor at Young and Rubican. His wife Claire was Rosalind's sister. Chet now ran his own agency in New York. Carter called Chet to see if he might have a position for Tom. Chet made Tom a very generous offer, asking him to create a television department in his new agency. Stock, as well as money, was included in the offer.

Loretta recalled, "Somehow Tom found out about Carter talking to Chet. Tom was so furious. He said, 'Tell your brother-in-law to butt out of my business. None of you have any right to go out and tell my friends that I need a job.' I said, 'Tom, take the job.

Please!' But he wouldn't. He said to Chet, 'How can I? I have a very sick wife and two kids who rarely see their mother.' To which I would have added, 'Two kids who were not allowed to see their mother!'"

Tom was also in competition with Loretta for her friends. Josie Wayne was the only friend Dr. Chess encouraged to come and visit. Loretta recalled, "Tom called from Ojai one day, and I told him that Josie was coming that afternoon. He said, 'Fine, I think I'll give her a call.' He called her and said, 'Come by here, and we'll have a regular dinner around 8:00.' About 7:30 she called Tom and said, 'Tom, it's getting late, and I have to drive back home, so I won't be able to get over.' He started to argue with her. He wanted to know why she had stayed so long with me. When she got off the phone she said, 'He must be drunk.' I said, 'Why?' She said, 'He said I should be over there visiting him. No way! I came to visit with you.' Josie would later tell me, 'It was the first indication that there was really something wrong with your marriage.'

"In early August, Dr. Chess discharged me. I chose the Ojai house to recuperate, and I asked that Miss Coney come up and bring the cook. Tom was furious with me. He had brought his sister Ruth back with him from New York, and they didn't want to be in Ojai with me and the nurses, but they also didn't want to be without a cook. I said, 'That's too bad. If you want to be in Los Angeles, then you and Ruth will have to cook for yourselves because I'm sick and I need the attention.' So they all stayed up in Ojai, and I used to sit in my bedroom and listen to those two, sitting out on the swing, discussing how awful I was. He said how I was crazy, nasty, even diabolical.

And Ruth agreed with it all. She worshiped Tom. He could do no wrong.

"I heard him on the phone talking with Jane Sharpe one day. 'No, Jane, I don't think you'd better come up here. I don't think she's emotionally up to it.' I overheard this and I said, 'Give me the phone.' He hung it up. I called her back and said, 'Jane, I'm all right, and I'd love to see you.' After I hung up, I said to Tom, 'Everybody else who's near to me, you've gotten rid of; you're not going to get rid of Jane Sharpe. I've known her since we were nine years old, and she's one of my best friends.'"

Jane did visit and came away deeply concerned. She recalled, "Loretta was in such pain, and Tom would come into her bedroom and sit on the bed and just bounce. He did that all the time. I don't know whether it was lack of consideration, or whether it even occurred to him how painful that was to Loretta, or if he did it on purpose. The more I got to know him, the more I thought he did it on purpose."

Finally, Josie invited Loretta to stay with her at her home in the exclusive Hancock Park section of Los Angeles (Hancock Park had been developed by Jane Sharpe's uncle, Richard Hancock). Josie's care was the tonic Loretta needed, and after several weeks, Loretta was ready to return to the townhouse in West Hollywood.

The third season of the show was underway. Loretta had many high profile friends willing to host for the first part of the season including: Joseph Cotten, Barbara Stanwyck, Ricardo Montalban, Merle Oberon, Van Johnson, Irene Dunne, Dinah Shore, Ann Sothern, Joan Fontaine and Claudette Colbert.

Loretta recalled visiting with Merle Oberon at the studio, "I liked Merle very much. She was a very feminine female. I remember walking onto the set looking for her, and someone said, 'Oh, she's in her dressing room; she's always in her dressing room.' I went to see her. She had been doing needlepoint, using a very big needle, nothing that would cause eye strain. After we got to talking a little bit, I asked, 'Merle, don't you find it dull in this room?' 'Oh no,' she said and continued, 'if I'm out on the set, I'd be laughing and talking and getting more wrinkles in my face. No, no, I just come in here and I do my needle point and I try not to strain my eyes.' She was so conscious of how anything might affect her appearance."

Loretta made her return appearance to the show on Christmas Eve, 1955. She swirled through the door and said, "Oh my, it's good to be back; I've missed you. In fact, one of my nicest Christmas presents is to be able to walk through that door and say hello to you." The audience could hardly appreciate just how sincere those sentiments were. Loretta would host the remaining twenty shows of the season and appear in seven of them. John London was hired back from CBS as producer, and Ruth Roberts returned as story editor and associate producer. THE LORETTA YOUNG SHOW became more focused on its star, and the ratings confirmed that the audience was pleased.

Other family members were busy with their careers. Norman Foster had moved to television and was directing DAVEY CROCKET for Walt Disney. He would later direct ZORRO. Gladys could hardly keep up with her own successful career as a decorator. Her client list included Bogart and Bacall, Ray Milland, John Wayne, Bing Crosby, and Bob and Dolores Hope.

Tom wasn't working, but he had a plan. He had an agreement prepared for Loretta to sign. In essence, it stated that all assets that each of them owned, regardless if it was acquired before or after their marriage, was to be split evenly. Loretta recalled his argument: "'It's only to protect you, Loretta, from all the people who want a piece of you. They're going to have to come through me first', and other such excuses. My accountant, Bob Shewalter, advised me not to sign it. 'Why would you want to give him half of everything, your furniture, everything you had before you were married?' To get away from the pressure, I went out to New Jersey and spent a couple of weeks with George and Oppie Gallop. They had a charming farmhouse near Princeton, and they were wonderful friends. Tom kept calling and asking, 'Have you signed that legal paper yet?' Finally, I said, 'For heaven's sake, Tom! Okay.' I signed it and sent it back to him. '"

Actually, what Loretta signed in April, 1956, were two agreements. The first eliminated Tom from further participation in the affairs of the corporation, the second dealt with their community property. It was signing the second agreement which Loretta referred to as the *one little piece of paper* that opened the door and ushered Loretta into the darkest passage of her life.

Chapter 21. THE STORM

Loretta returned from her trip to the Gallops, and shortly thereafter, Tom accepted the offer Chet LaRoche had made the year before. He would be working in New York and Loretta remembered thinking, "This separation will give both of us time to breathe." She just assumed that Tom would be commuting, spending at least one long weekend a month back in Los Angeles with his family, as he had the first year of their marriage.

Tom had other ideas which became clear when Loretta realized he had taken the butler with him. She recalled thinking, "'A man intending on coming home to his family and living in an apartment alone doesn't need a butler.'"

The Lewises' Huntington Hartford property on Flores Avenue included their ten bedroom townhouse and four luxury apartments. Gladys had built the apartments and supervised them. It was her intention that they would serve as Loretta's nest-egg after she retired from acting. Joan Crawford was one lessee. Miss Crawford was married to Alfred Steele at the time, Chairman of the Pepsi Cola Company. Their main residence was in Manhattan, but she still wanted to keep her foot in Hollywood.

Loretta recalled, "Mama furnished all the units beautifully: the best of linens, sterling silver, and hand woven materials. The apartments were in the back; it was all one complex. One day, Mama said, 'Gretch, I have rented the one bedroom apartment.' I asked, 'Are they nice people?' I was concerned because my kids were living there. She said, 'I don't know. The person's secretary and another man came and said that the person was so well known, they would prefer not to tell me the name, but that she wanted something nice and private.' I said, 'I don't like the sound of this.'

"Anyway, I went home that night, and Miss Coney told me that the new tenant was Marilyn Monroe. This was after Marilyn Monroe had split with Joe Dimaggio. I called Mama and said, 'Mama, that mysterious person that you rented to is Marilyn Monroe, and I can't have her in this building, not with the publicity that she's been getting. I will have reporters all over this place, and I don't want my children in that atmosphere.' Mama said, 'Dear, you have no control over her personal life.' I said, 'Indeed I don't, but I do have control over my building.' 'Oh,' she said, 'I've already told her she can come.' I said, 'You've haven't told her; you've told her secretary who neglected to tell you who his boss was which was manipulative on his part.' Rock Hudson had lived in the front apartment for a year and a half, not one bit of a problem. We had all sorts of people there, but this was a unique publicity attraction that I simply didn't want to get wound up with.

"At eleven the next morning, two men -- one was Marilyn's hairdresser, the other, her secretary -- were ringing my front doorbell to get the key. They came into the living room and we sat down. I said, 'I'm Mrs. Lewis and I own the building. My mother rented you the apartment, and unfortunately, she didn't realize that it has already been rented by my husband in New York. Therefore, I'm sorry, but it's not available.' The secretary said, 'She's coming in this afternoon.' I said, 'I think that it would be much wiser if you would tell her right now that it's not available.' The secretary looked so upset. He said, 'Can't she even come in for one night?' I said, 'Yes, certainly she can come in for one night, or two nights if she wishes, but not more.' They had a big painting of her that they were going to hang, and I said, 'The apartments are furnished already, and I would prefer really that you didn't hang up a heavy painting on the wall.' Marilyn Monroe did come in and stay a couple of nights, but I never saw her.

"My mother never understood why it would make any difference. She said 'Well certainly it wouldn't make any difference to me.' Mama was wonderful in that way. She never judged people; their behavior, yes, but never people. "She was a Mother Confessor and everybody went to her with everything, including many of her clients. Lauren Bacall was crazy about Mama."

THE LORETTA YOUNG SHOW had a successful fourth season; it was now an ingrained part of America's Sunday evening like ED SULLIVAN'S TOAST OF THE TOWN. Again, Loretta was nominated for an Emmy. This time the category was "Best Continuing Performance by an Actress in a Continuing Series". And, once again, Loretta was victorious. However, not everyone was tossing accolades toward Loretta. Proctor and Gamble was feeling pressure from people writing and complaining about the religious undertones to many of the shows and voicing that her themes were inconsistent with how people lived in modern society.

Loretta and Jane Sharpe returned from a European trip that spring. Jane recalled, "I left Loretta in New York. She was so hopeful about reconciliation with Tom and confided, 'I just know that we are going to make it go.' But Tom had no interest, and a few days later Loretta came home in tears." Loretta and Tom were able to resolve summer plans for the boys. They would spend a month with Tom, then a month at a camp. Chris was twelve and had just finished the seventh grade, and Pete was eleven and had completed the sixth grade. Both would be celebrating birthdays that summer of 1957.

Loretta recalled, "I was in bed with hepatitis. I had gotten it from a needle when I was given a vaccine prior to my trip to Europe. I remember the day the boys were leaving on their trip to New York. They couldn't come in, even to hug me or kiss me, or anything. Peter said his good-byes, and he went to help Mary do something. I remember Chris standing at the door. He looked at me and said, 'You mean I can't even come in and kiss you good-bye?' I said, 'Honey, nothing I'd love more, but you stand a chance of getting hepatitis, and then you couldn't go to New York.' He said, 'I sure do want to kiss you good-bye, Mom.' I didn't know then, and neither did he, that he'd never come home again.'

"I received a letter from Tom six weeks later. He said that he and the boys had talked it over, and that they were going to go to school at St. David's in New York for the next four years. I was in such shock, and I flew down to Cardinal McIntyre's (of the Archdiocese of Los Angeles) office. He was a close personal friend, and he often counseled me. This time he said, 'You just write Tom and tell him that he has to send the boys home.' I wrote but nothing happened. As summer was coming to an end a few weeks later, I called the Cardinal again, and he said, 'Get on a plane to New York and bring those boys home. '"

Meanwhile Peter remembered, "Dad told us why we couldn't be together as a family. He explained that there was a lot of unhappiness between him and Mom, and that most of it was Mom's fault. I don't know if it was always in Dad's mind that once we got to New York we would stay there. But, to give him credit, I think he did it in good faith. He believed that if we stayed in California, we would have to take whatever we could get as far as parental guidance while Mom worked. And my brother hated the military school, so for him, it was a good deal. I really didn't feel like I had much of a choice. What are you going to say when your dad asks, 'Do you want to go to school here?' If you're with your dad, you say 'Sure. '"

At the time, Ricardo Montalban was starring on Broadway with Lena Horne in JAMAICA, and he and Georgiana and their four children were living in Mary Martin's apartment. Loretta stayed with them when she came east to reclaim her sons. She recalled, "I had decided not to call Tom and the boys until after I arrived. When I did call, Tom was out, but Chris answered the phone. And I felt so sorry for him because he didn't seem at all happy to hear from me. He sounded scared to death. He said, 'Oh, Mom ... Dad isn't here right now.' I said, 'Well, that's all right, Honey, I'm talking to you. I'm here at Aunt Georgi's and if you're going to be home, I'd like to come over.' He repeated, 'Dad isn't here right now.' I said, 'Well, can't you open the door?' He said, 'All right.'

Pete got on the phone, and I said, 'Honey, I'm going to see you in a few minutes.' He said, 'Oh, great, Mom! Great! Hurry up!'

"Tom was there when I arrived, and after visiting with the boys, the two of us went into another room. I said, 'Tom, you can't do this. All their friends are at home. They are just out of their element here. They also need their mother.' He said, 'No, both the boys belong with the father. They're better off here; they've known California, and now they'll get a chance to know New York.' As far as Tom was concerned, the fact that he wanted them there was enough reason, end of discussion.

"Still, we must have talked for three hours without any of the real issues being aired. Tom's refusal to discuss things in a straight, honest, manner was a familiar pattern. He had never admitted to me that he was leaving me. He said that he would go to New York and come home on weekends. The reason for his evasiveness, for his not stating his true intentions, was that the checking account would have been stopped. He never admitted to me that we were even separated. And he never had the courage to say to me, 'I'm taking the kids because you don't have any time for them.' He was never that honest with me.

"I said goodbye to the boys. It was drizzling when I left the building, and I looked up at the kids waving from the window.

And I remember wondering, 'What must they think? Their mother has just been pushed out of their father's apartment, pushed out of their lives, really.' And there was nothing for me to do. I didn't have an umbrella; I didn't even have a coat, so I just walked out in the rain. I looked back at the boys again, and they were leaning over as far as they could until I got out of sight. My tears started.

"The next day I could see that Chris was handling it much better than Pete. Pete was falling apart; Tom had always shown partiality toward Christopher. I said to both of them, 'If either one of you wants to come home, you just call me and I'll make arrangements.'"

The boys began their school term at St. David's, a college prep school with an upscale student body. Peter was aware immediately that things weren't clicking for him. He recalled, "It was horrible; I was just lost. I had developed what they call school phobia. I wasn't able to concentrate. I realized St. David's was supposed to be a good opportunity, and that if I took advantage of it somehow my life would be on track. But I just couldn't, and I felt that my life was over for some reason. Of course, the realization I had *chosen* to stay with Dad, and not return with Mom, made me feel all the more responsible for this dilemma."

St. David's was more academic than St. John's in Los Angeles had been, but Pete wasn't overwhelmed by the studies, as much as he was by his sense that he just wasn't fitting in. Up to this point, in relation to his peers, he had always been able to handle himself. It was Chris who had had adjustment problems at St. John's, and now the tables had flipped. Peter recalled that first day that they came home from school. "I looked at Chris as he sat there, and he was able to do his homework, and I just wasn't. Right then I felt this big sense of loss. Chris and I had always been close, but now he was able to make this adjustment. He was going to be able to move ahead, and I knew that I wasn't. I felt that it was over between the two of us; we'd never have the same relationship again.

"That school drove me crazy in three days. I was sitting in Mr. Cleary's English class and feeling panicky. I asked Mr. Cleary if I could go talk to the principal. I just needed to get out of that classroom. He said no, and on the spur of the moment, I ran out of the classroom, down the circular stairs until I got out the door. Eventually, I went home. Meanwhile, the school had called my Dad and he and his friends were looking for me. I thought about killing myself, about going up on top of the garage and jumping. That's where they found me."

A few days later, Peter decided to go home to Los Angeles, and Loretta quickly arranged for his flight. He didn't stay long. Loretta recalled, "The poor kid felt so guilty; he was on the phone all the time with his dad. I called Tom and pleaded, 'Tom, please leave him alone and maybe we can work it out.' He said, 'No, I've decided that I'm coming out to get him tomorrow.' So I told Peter, 'Your dad's going to come out, Honey, and you can decide yourself whether you want to go back with him or whether you want to stay here. He had made up his mind. He knew that his father was expecting him to return, and early the next morning his bags were packed and ready to go."

After Peter returned to New York, He recalled, "I went back to St. David's, but I couldn't sit in the classroom. I had anxiety attacks, and I'd run out of the building but now they would always catch me. Dad would say to me, 'Man, you don't have what it takes to cut it.' He had to think that I was the one who couldn't cut it because he wasn't able to examine if he had done the right thing about breaking up the family. I know that he didn't mean to hurt me, but when he'd say that I couldn't cut it, that upset me more than anything else. I guess I really believed him and in a strange way, I was just fulfilling his prophecy.

"My school phobia worsened. I got to the point where I totally refused to go to school. Dad didn't know what to do with me. One night he told me that he was taking me to get a physical examination. I thought that it was weird that I'd be going to get a physical at night. He took me to a doctor's office at a hospital, and the doctor gave me a shot, and the next thing I remember was waking up in a mental ward, and all my clothes had been taken away from me. I discovered that the door was locked, and I couldn't get out of there, so I just sat on my bed. Of course, the patients around me were all crazy people with shaved heads, the whole thing. The doctor said, 'Until you agree to go back to school, you're going to stay in here.' I knew I didn't want to hang out at the nuthouse, so I went back to school and sat there, but I didn't learn anything.

"That Spring we went to Nassau for Easter break. After we returned, the panic returned, and I wouldn't go back to school. I'd just hang around the apartment. One day I was sitting there watching television and the maid and her son came in. They told me they were taking me to an amusement park I was familiar with. We drove in that direction but we passed it, and I asked, 'Where are you taking me? 'Instead of the amusement park, they took me to the Ark Farm in Hartford, Connecticut. It was a place for kids that were difficult or had emotional problems. I made a deal to get out of there by agreeing to go to a tutoring school. That worked out much better for me; they knew how to handle kids who were dealing with a lot of anxiety. I finished the 7th grade there, and the following year, one of the teachers started her own school at Beekman Place, and that's where I went and finished the 8th grade.

"Then Mom was coming through from a trip to Europe, and asked me if I wanted to go to Hawaii, and that's how I went back to L.A. It's not that I wanted to go back there; it was just too fucking crowded for me to stay in New York. I can get petty and say, 'Well, there wasn't enough room for me.' It's not that Dad or Chris were trying to exclude me, but that's the way it was, and that's one of the reasons I was freaking out. The PCT Club was no longer working for me."

New York was working for Chris, He reflected, "1 loved it. I had been conditioned by Dad to more or less expect that things would work out if I stayed with him. The kids at school were a real change, and I thought New York was exciting. We saw all the great shows, and I remember watching Castro riding up to the U.N. in a motorcade.
I liked that Dad would take me around and introduce me to everyone. He loved me. I think he loved us both, but I was the oldest.

"As far as Dad's and Mom's problems, that was between them. I never felt like Mom and I were estranged. I talked to her every week or two on the phone, and we'd see each other from time to time. Dad wanted what was best for me. I was never a good student, but Dad would go on my behalf and tell the teachers they were nuts. And in order to get my grades up, he hired the headmaster at the school to tutor me. He would do whatever he could."

THE LORETTA YOUNG SHOW was now in its fifth season and garnering its highest rating to date. Judy, too, was acting on television with a recurring role on KITTY FOYLE. Judy's life was blossoming in all appearances. Louella Parsons announced in a February, 1958, column that Judy Lewis, 21, was engaged to marry Joseph Tinney, television producer and director. Joe Tinney had grown up in an Irish Catholic family in Philadelphia and had met Judy through Jean and Maggie Louis.

The same month as Louella's scoop on Judy, the *Hollywood Citizen News* ran a front page article with the headline: "Loretta Young's Husband Sues to Dissolve Firm" It read in part, "Television star Loretta Young's husband accuses her and their business partner of dishonesty, mismanagement and unfairness. Advertising executive Tom Lewis, whose 17 1/2 year marriage to the actress has been considered one of Hollywood's happiest, filed a civil suit yesterday to dissolve their company of Lewislor Film, Inc. He alleged that Miss Young and their partner Robert F.

Shewalter have exercised complete control over the corporation to his complete exclusion. Unless the corporation is dissolved promptly,' Lewis contended in the complaint, 'he will be deprived of his rights as a shareholder due to the continued and additional dishonesty, mismanagement and unfairness of Miss Young and Shewalter.' In New York City, where he is vice-president in charge of television for the C. J. LaRoche Advertising Co, Lewis said the suit is "a corporate matter" and has "no personal implications". In Hollywood, Miss Young was not available for comment. Her press agent said she knew of no trouble in the marriage."

Tom was reacting to certain accounting procedures that Bob Shewalter had recommended to avoid paying taxes on capital gains. Loretta was greatly distressed at the suggestion of impropriety, but this would just be the first. There would be seven lawsuits in total that Tom would initiate against Loretta and take the next eleven years to resolve. The basis of all of Tom's suits would always be that *one little piece of paper* that Tom had cajoled Loretta into signing which gave him half of everything that was hers, before and after their marriage.

Loretta's havens through this difficult time were: her faith, her belief in herself, the support of family and friends, and, not the least, the opportunity to walk through "her" door and absorb herself into THE LORETTA YOUNG SHOW.

Publicity shot of Tom Lewis and Loretta during the early years of the television show. The smiles were only for the camera.

A break on the set of "The Loretta Young Show" with the star seated in profile. The episode was titled, "The Hollywood Story" which first aired on January 31, 1954.

Judy, Loretta, Peter and Christopher. Little did Loretta know that the boys would soon leave home; Christopher never really to return.

Loretta wearing fan pleasing haute couture during her television years.

A "Walking through the Door" dress.

Loretta in character as Queen Nefertiti for "The Loretta Young Show."

Chapter 22: HAVEN

Tom's second lawsuit soon followed; this one charging that Loretta and Bob Shewalter were misusing his money. Georgiana, on the day that news hit the papers, was giving Judy's engagement an Announcement Party for New York friends. Tom then sent word through his lawyer that neither he nor the boys would attend the wedding.

The wedding took place on June 21, 1958, with Carter Herman giving the bride away. Judy's gown was designed by Jean Louis, who also designed the dress worn by the mother of the bride. Loretta originally was to wear a dress designed by Jimmy Galanos. She tried it on for Jean a few weeks before the wedding and Jean decided that, indeed, she looked too stunning. After all, it was to be Judy's day.

Loretta's work schedule was consuming but she never found her work more exhilarating. She reflected, "I loved every minute of it. I was always the first on the set and ready, not in curlers, but ready to go. And if I was there, the whole television company took their cue from me; nobody dared be late. We'd start at 9:00, and we'd finish at 6:00, and that was it.

"I was out on the set all the time. I liked every part of it, all the mechanics of it. I remember saying to the director, Dick Morris, one time, 'I want you to come from a long shot up to this close on me;' he said, 'No way I can; it will be too sharp.' I said, 'You can use a sliding disc all the way, and it will be just gorgeous.' And it was. I knew about this because I had paid attention. One time while I was making a film I asked, 'How come it's sharp back there, and when you get up close, I'm still soft and gauzy and beautiful?' He said, 'Because I used a sliding disc.'

"I loved doing that show for another reason: I had the attention of about sixty men who were just darling to me. We were always playing games and by five in the afternoon because I'm an owl by nature and my energy was at its peak, I was playing music and dancing and ready to go. Of course, everybody else was winding down."

Loretta continued, "We were on such a tight budget that I couldn't afford good sets if they called for sophistication. So I'd call Mama up and say, 'We're having two shows in a row calling for upscale sets.' She'd take everything out of her house and my house and out of her garage, and decorate the sets. She had the best of everything, so the sets were beautiful. She'd still be decorating just before the director said, 'Roll em.' She'd say, 'Just a minute,' and she'd go and move this or push that. She never charged me anything, and she even paid for the truck that was hauling everything around. Money was never important to Mama, only what you could do with it.

"Both Johnny London and Ruth Roberts worked like dogs, but because the budget was so tight, they received only a pittance of what they were worth. So I decided to give each of them 5% of the show. I'm awfully glad I did because that set them both for life. We were like a family, and they supported me all the way through."

Robert Mitchum recalled visiting Loretta on the set one day, "I have never, never, seen such a mass display of devotion as I found on that set to her. And I'm sort of one with the crew, and they would tell me if they had any sort of beef, or any criticism. Not at all. Everybody loved her."

Professionally speaking, Loretta was at the height of the crest: in popularity, in influence, and in her own view, professional satisfaction. She explained, "My television experience interested me more than all the motion pictures because I had a variety of roles that I would give myself, roles that no producer in his right mind would give to me. The thing you have to offer on an anthology is variety. So I glommed onto any make-up, any wigs, any padding, anything I could do to make myself feel different, as well as look different.

"I was happiest while the camera rolled. I didn't like the interviewing. I could tire of the still photographing and the fittings. I definitely didn't like the arguments. But I just loved it when the camera rolled. I was then in my own world. Whoever I was playing, I was that person. It was almost a second life. You can be something on the screen that you don't dare in real life. The anthology format allowed me to express a lot more feelings that would have otherwise been smothered.

"Acting is play-acting all the time. It's showing off; otherwise it would not please me most when the camera is going, knowing that everybody is going to look at me, big and blown-up. But no matter how many times you've gone in front of the camera, you're never kind of settled in and sure because if you are, you lose your eagerness. There must be a certain amount of tension and insecurity, a certain amount of being scared spitless. It takes a lot of guts to stand up in front of a camera and crew and make a damn fool of yourself."

Dick Morris directed most of THE LORETTA YOUNG SHOWS in which Loretta appeared. She reflected, "I felt perfectly comfortable with Dick. I could turn somersaults on the floor and have my skirt fall over my head; it wouldn't have embarrassed me at all with Dick Morris. He would have said, 'You did that soooo beautifully. Do that again, but do it a little slower.' He knew me very well. In the guest shows, a script would be 35 or 40 pages, but for the show I'd be doing, Dick would only write 17 or 18 pages because he knew I'd improvise on the set.

"Dick knew how to woo the best performance out of me. We did a show based on a true story about a woman war correspondent who had been in solitary confinement in China for four years. In the first scene, she has just gotten out of prison, and she's at the airport in Taipei, and all the reporters are flocking around her. When I arrived on the set the first day, I said, 'I know just where I'm going with this woman. I saw a picture in *Life* magazine of a woman who had been in solitary confinement for four years, and she looked absolutely dead. Dick looked at me and he said, 'Oh no, I think she cries at card tricks.' I said, 'No, I'm sure how I want to do it.' He said, 'Okay, you're the actress.'

"So we did a long shot of it, and I answered all the reporter's questions and didn't cry. Anyway, Brodie came in closer, did a master shot and I still didn't cry, and he kept moving in, closer and closer and finally, he said, 'I can't get any closer on her or she won't let me photograph her.' I had no make-up on her, the woman was just raw, and just a rag on for a dress. But Dick kept saying, 'Go ahead; go in closer.' So Brodie got in right up next to me. I was bored now with playing the way I was playing it, so I said, 'Dick, oh come on, now!' He said, 'Give me one more, please, Honey.' So he finally moved in, and I thought, 'What have I got to lose, I've done all this other stuff, so I'll try it Dick's way this time. When one of the reporters asked, 'Where are you from?' - I said, 'Milwaukee,' and I started to cry and couldn't stop.

"Now, Dick had cautioned all the other actors, 'No matter what she does, don't stop. Give her all the time in the world; she'll come back to you.' He had worked with me enough to know that I would. The scene was shot. When I saw the thing in the projection room, I asked 'Dick, how did you know? You were so right.' Now, had he, in his efforts to get what he wanted, started a fight with me, he would have made me mad and then we wouldn't have had anything. Rather, he knew how to work with me. It was a wonderful collaboration."

Many in Hollywood were astonished that Loretta's shows, with their pointed ennobling themes, could hold such a large audience. Murray Bolen confessed his surprise at the show's durability, "I f you saw her scripts on some other show, you'd throw them out. My boys would read these scripts and say, 'Yeee gawds, where's this junk coming from? It's awful.' Except when Loretta did these stories, she always filled them out. She just kept plowing through, and frankly, we were amazed."

Silent star Mae Murray's career momentum had ended thirty years earlier. Loretta recalled, "I was driving along Sunset Boulevard, and I saw a woman sitting on a bench wearing a Moline hat, big black thing that they used to wear fifty years ago. She was sitting there posing, and as soon as I passed, I realized that it was Mae Murray waiting for a bus. I didn't stop but my heart sank. A few months later, Miss Coney came to me and said, 'A Miss Mae Murray on the telephone, do you know any ... ?' I said, 'Indeed, I do.' I picked up and she said, 'Oh, dear little Gretchen, how are you?' I said, 'Oh, Maestie, how are you?' She said, 'Well, I'm staying at the Hollywood Hotel in Hollywood.' I said, 'Would you like to come for lunch?' We made plans for the next day, and I told her I'd send a car for her. When she arrived, she had on another big black hat and a dress that was all ruffles, and she was wearing her little net gloves. She looked around and said, 'Oh, my Dear, your house is so beautiful.' I looked at her and thought, 'Oh, how things have reversed.'

"During lunch we exchanged pleasantries, 'Oh, I watch you all the time, and I remember how dear you were when you were little.' I could honestly say, 'I remember how kind you were to us, too.' She finally said, 'I want to ask you a favor. Some friends of mine, a man and his wife and their three children, are trying to get back East, and they haven't any money. I was wondering if you would help me to help them.' I said, 'Yes, I could do that. How much do you think it would cost to get them back East?' She said, 'Well, at least $2500.' So I said, 'Yes, I can do that, but I haven't got it here. I will call my office and tell them to issue a check to you. When the driver takes you home, he'll take you to the office first, and they'll give you the check.' She said, 'Oh that would be wonderful. Because it means so much to them.' I don't know whether I doubted her or believed her; it didn't make any difference to me. The driver came and we said our good-byes.

"When the driver came back, he said, 'I think you ought to know what happened. When we got near the Hollywood Hotel, she said that it was awfully busy in front of the hotel; she told me just let her out on this side, and she'd cross the street. I told her it wouldn't be any problem, but she insisted. So, I let her out and then, without her seeing me, I just crept along to watch that she didn't get hit by a car as she crossed the street. Well, she didn't go into the hotel. Apparently, she wasn't staying there.' When the driver had gone to pick her up, she had been waiting outside for him; it was all for appearances. I never saw Mae again. A few years later, I read in the paper that she died at the Motion Picture County Home."

Grant Withers, too, had fallen on difficult times. The March 28, 1959, edition of *The Los Angeles Times* reported with a headline, "Grant Withers Found Dead in His Home." A subhead was written below, "Suicide Note Written as Farewell by 55 Year Old Star of 1920's."He had taken an overdose of sedatives. A suicide note found on a bedside night table read, "Please forgive me, my family. I was so unhappy. It's better this way. Thanks to all my friends. Sorry I let them down."

The ensuing article stated that Grant had been married four times and made note of his 1930 marriage to seventeen-year-old Loretta Young. The article went on to note Loretta's reaction. It said, "Told of Withers' death after she returned home from Good Friday church services and approached in her driveway, Miss Young appeared shaken, 'Oh, I'm so sorry,' she repeated a few times."

Michael Wayne, oldest son of John and Josie Wayne, reflected about Grant, "He was a good, close, personal friend of my father's. My father told me that Grant never really recovered from that break-up with Aunt Loretta, that in a way she ruined his life. Grant was much more mature than she was when they married, and so he did it with much more knowledge, with much more feeling, with much more experience than she did. Grant and my father used to sit and talk, over not just a few drinks, and they probably had discussions all about it. I think that my father always respected Aunt Loretta, but he was sensitive to what she had done to Grant. Grant was one of his best friends and continued to be through all the years. My father loved him because he saw the good side. I think he saw Grant as nice but weak, and that he needed a little help. That's why he kept getting him into his films. I think, at the end, Grant was unbalanced because of the medicines he was on. I think he had cancer and it was like a death sentence to him; he didn't want to suffer. It was a terrible shock to everybody."

Meanwhile, Loretta continued to gather accolades. That spring, with her sixth nomination, she won her third Emmy.

All of the dire warnings, that if Loretta entered television, she would never be offered another movie role, proved false. Old friend Dore Schary offered Loretta the role of Eleanor Roosevelt in SUNRISE AT CAMPOBELLO. The story focused on Mrs. Roosevelt's brave entrance in the political arena after her husband contracted polio. Schary had written the original play in 1958 and was now bringing it to the screen. Loretta recalled, "I said, 'Dore, I really don't want to play Mrs. Roosevelt. First of all, I'm not properly cast for her. As a woman, I find her fascinating, but we are so diametrically opposed in our politics that I wouldn't do justice to her.' Dore just thought the sun rose and set with her. Anyway, I really didn't have the time to do the film with my busy television schedule. Loretta had turned down SUMMERTIME a few years earlier, again because of her tight television schedule. The role then went to Katharine Hepburn who won praise for her performance.

After Lewislor's five year contract with NBC expired, two new contracts went into motion. Loretta's then current production company, Toreto Productions, signed a contract, with a mutual option clause, directly with Proctor and Gamble. The same clause was in the new three year contract with NBC. The expiration of Loretta's original contract with NBC allowed Loretta to sell the shows produced under that contract. NBC purchased them, reportedly paying four million dollars. They packaged it as THE LORETTA YOUNG THEATER and ran it weekday afternoons.

Loretta's friendship with Jean and Maggie Louis had deepened, and she spent much of her social time with them. She recalled, "I was staying with Maggie and Jean in their New York apartment, and we got fourth row tickets to see THE MIRACLE WORKER. As we walked down the aisle, all of a sudden, you could hear a rumbling noise going throughout the theater. By the time we were seated, applause had started. Maggie was looking around, and Jean was looking around, and finally, the woman behind me leaned over and said, 'My Dear, why don't you get up and let them have a nice look at you.' I didn't realize it was for me. So I looked around and stood up, and, well, the whole theatre just shook! It was one of the biggest thrills I've had in my entire career. And it wasn't from the motion pictures; it was because of a television show.

"I experienced that same thrill a second time when Jean and Maggie, Chris and I went to see THE UNSINKABLE MOLLY BROWN. I was so glad that Chris was with me because I don't think he really knew what I did. Tom didn't let the boys see me in movies, and I don't think they watched my television show after they went to New York. When I received the standing ovation, Chris was impressed, and that delighted me because he could see it for himself."

Loretta decided that she wanted to open her new season with a story about Lourdes, a small community in the southwest of France where the Blessed Mother is said to have appeared to a peasant girl named Bernadette in the year 1858. Loretta recalled, "Dick Morris wrote a marvelous script, and all the arrangements were made, and I get a call from Albert Halverstadt, the manager of Proctor and Gamble's television advertising. He asked to have a meeting with me. I had just won another award, The TV GUIDE AWARD as the 'The Most Important Female Personality,' and I thought he wanted to congratulate me. I said, 'I'm packing for my trip, but you can come to lunch tomorrow.'

"We had a lovely lunch and then he said, 'I have to speak to you about something. I'm out here because the Chairman of the Board has asked me to speak to you personally. We have received so many negative letters about your show that he's worried.' I asked, 'Such as?' He replied that some had said, 'Please get that religious fanatic off the air or I'm not going to buy your soap anymore.' I thought to myself, 'All anybody has to say is that they're going to spend their money someplace else, and they've got a company like Proctor and Gamble scared. It's all about money, money, money.' And he went on and on about all this mail. They all objected to my attitude toward ethics and morality. I replied, 'Halv, you remember when you first signed me to do LETTERS TO LORETTA six years ago, I asked for a meeting with the Board of Directors and your Chairman? I went to Cincinnati and spent three days meeting everybody, and I stated several times, 'I'm here to tell you one thing: you are going to get such terrible mail on me. Of course, I'm six years more successful, and now having just won this latest award, it's going to get even worse. You go back to Cincinnati and tell them that.'

"I went to Paris, and Norman Brokaw (her agent) called me the first night I got there and said, 'Proctor and Gamble has cancelled.' That meant I had no sponsor, that I had to borrow money to make a picture that I couldn't get on the air. I was shocked and scared but not for long. Norman called the next day and had lined up 'Toni Home Wave' and 'Listerine' as alternate sponsors."

Murray Bolen was quoted in an interview that summer, "Loretta's done-in at least six good shows opposite her. When some of them came on and got very hot, such as the $64,000 CHALLENGE, Loretta slipped a little. Then she gradually crept back and clobbered them."

Loretta embarked on her regular schedule of filming for season number seven. Once again she was embraced by her company, mostly men, whose concerted effort was to film Loretta at her very best. As an actress, she never had it better, never felt so secure. But the course of Loretta's career would soon make some precipitous turns, and then come to an abrupt stop.

Chapter 23: OUT OF CONTROL

After selling her old shows into reruns, Loretta was more secure financially than she had ever been. The show was running every weekday in the United States, and her international audience was growing. It had been showing in Europe for some time and now was airing in such diverse markets as South America, Australia, and Egypt.

Tom Lewis had also benefited from the sale into reruns. He had not participated in producing sixty of those shows but the *one little piece of paper* paved the way for a split of their assets 50/50.Tom's first payment of $450,000 was linked with a written understanding that he would send Christopher home to Los Angeles for Christmas or Easter vacations as well as half of his summer vacations. But as Loretta stated, "Once Tom got his money, I never saw Chris unless I went out to New York."

Loretta did have Peter, and she recalled an incident that summer: "Pete and I spent a few weeks at Lake Arrowhead. Tommy Del Amo, Jane Sharpe's son, and Bill Paton, another friend of Pete's were with us. They wanted to go to a skating rink one evening, and I ended up chauffeuring. I had a new Imperial. It was a beautiful car, very heavy, and it looked like a dragon coming down the street. I was watching the boys skate, and three bullies, at least five years older and a lot bigger than Pete and his friends, would skate right up to them and then turn quickly. I could see that Pete and his friends were feeling more and more intimidated as the evening went on, and I was getting madder and madder.

"One of the kids said as we were leaving, 'There are those guys (the bullies) on the motor cycles.' I said, 'Hurry up and close the doors;' I thought to myself I'd just give them a taste of their own medicine. They pulled out, and I got right on their tails, four or five feet away. Pete said, 'Mom, you're too close!' I said, 'That's right, and they'd better hurry up, or I'm just going to nudge them right along.' They kept looking back at me, and with terror on their faces, yelling, 'Lady, what are you doing!' I didn't back off of them for a couple of miles, and then finally, I pulled around them, rolled down my window and yelled, 'Never do that again in the skating rink.' Pete and his friends were horrified. They were used to seeing kids terrifying grownups, but not the other way around."

Loretta's escapade with the bullies might have been a way to vent her own frustrations. Peter had enrolled at Loyola High School after returning to Los Angeles, but Loretta recalled, 'I couldn't handle Pete. He wouldn't go to school. He was a big kid, six foot by the time he was thirteen, and there was no way I could force him. I decided to board him at Loyola. His reaction was, 'I don't care whether I board or whether I don't; I hate school anyway.' He hated anything that confined him.

"He hadn't boarded for long when I got a phone call at 4:00 in the morning from the police department in Ventura. Peter and a friend had been joyriding in my station wagon, and they thought they'd be back in the dorm before the bell went off at six. Instead, they ended up in jail because Peter let the other boy drive, and it was apparent he was underage.

"Six weeks later, Pete was joyriding again, this time with another friend. They had driven to Las Vegas and were picked up for mooning pedestrians. I called the other boy's father and asked him to go get them. It would have been a circus for the press had I gone.

"At different times, I warned Pete, 'They're going to kick you out of Loyola.' One time he responded, 'You're too important; they wouldn't dare.' We were in Honolulu after the spring semester ended, and we got a letter. Pete was not being invited back the following semester. I said, 'Here, Honey. I want you to sit down and read this.' He looked at me and said, 'I don't believe it!'"

Loretta continued to have her recurring dream in which the world was descending upon her. There were other symptoms of extreme stress as well. She began suffering from migraine headaches and, not surprisingly, there were sleep problems. Sally recalled, "That poor little thing would have to take sleeping pills. She had to. She'd get into these griefs with somebody, and she had to plunk herself out to be able to get up and look okay for the camera the next day. Loretta commanded everything. It was her little head that put everything together, but running that show was too much for her, too much."

Loretta's overwhelmed state was caught in a painting by Simon Elwes. She recalled how this portrait evolved. "Sherril and Flobell Burden introduced Simon to me. He developed a crush on me and said he wanted to paint me. I said, 'No, Simon, I haven't got the time,' but little by little, my resistance broke down. I'm glad I did because it's the only painting of me that I've liked. The rest of them look like candy box covers.

"Simon had been injured in the war, and he had to learn to paint with his left hand. The way he did it was wonderful, just lots of dabs. But, oh, what he was able to capture with those dabs. When you looked at the painting, what you saw were eyes with a misty quality, just on the verge of tears. I was so upset at that time, and Simon saw that. Looking at it scared me to death. I thought,

'Everybody in the world is going to see how unhappy I am.' Here I was at the highest exposure of my career, I was supposed to look like I was a happy movie star and in control. If people could see that I wasn't in control of me, then they'd wonder if I was in control of my business or my children, or my house, or my clothes, or even my mind.

"At that time, people would say, 'I just love to see you coming through that door.' It was because I looked happy and on top of the world. People wanted that lift. If they knew that this woman was depressed, they'd think, 'What a fraud.' When I read those quotes at the end of the show, I wanted people to think that I lived by them and that everything was perfect. Maybe people saw through it anyway, I don't know. But, I was presenting the values that I did, and still do, believe in. I was afraid if they saw how miserable I was, they'd think, 'What good has any of that done her?'

"I remember thinking that everything was dragging on for so long; I didn't think that time would ever pass. I know now everything passes. I was really so worn out mentally, physically, and emotionally. I couldn't drink alcohol because I didn't like its effect or taste, and besides, it would show. I couldn't take dope because then I couldn't work, and if I couldn't work, I was in limbo."

Loretta worked herself to exhaustion in her attempt to get beyond her family problems. This left her all the more vulnerable to family problems such as dealing with Peter. It would take many years before Loretta would look back and see the experience with Peter as a leap for her. She explained, "Someone said to me, 'You know how much you love a person by how much you're willing to give up for them.' The only person that I've really had to give up anything for was Peter. I gave up peace of mind. From the time he came back from New York through the next eight years, it was pure chaos. He took a part of me, but he needed it."

Loretta approached a potential ninth season with increased ambition. She explained, "I wanted to go to an hour show because, too often, it seemed we were cutting too deeply and ruining the whole thing. I went back to New York and saw Bob Ketner, president of NBC programming. He said, 'You are going to have one big problem. When the sponsors buy THE LORETTA YOUNG SHOW, they want Loretta Young. They don't want you introducing the show, and then a guest star appearing in it. And nobody, playing a different character each week, can make twenty eight hour shows a year and have them good.' My reaction was, 'We can manage somehow.' Two weeks later Bob came back with a firm offer to do ten Loretta shows per year. I was very foolish. I said, 'No. I want the twenty eight, and I'll star in half and have guest stars in the other.' He knew exactly what he was doing, but I didn't listen.

"Once I heard my agent say in front of me, 'When it comes to herself and her career, don't question her because she's infallibly right.' Unfortunately, I believed it. By the time I woke up and decided to grab the ten hour shows, they had already signed BONANZA." THE LORETTA YOUNG SHOW came to an end after eight seasons.

CBS sent Loretta the script for CHRISTINE'S CHILDREN for the following season. All the impediments to a series that Loretta had avoided when she first entered television were still there. She agreed, anyway. She would play Christine, a widow with seven children, who works as a free-lance writer. Of course, there would be romance.

There was no romance in Loretta's personal life as she adhered to her church's teachings that the sacrament of marriage is a lifetime commitment. Loretta reflected, "My options were to beg Tom on my hands and knees to come back to me, or accept the fact I would never even think of another man until he died."

Tom's return to the advertising world proved unsatisfactory. He wrote of those days, "Things had changed. The agencies didn't have the power to produce as they had during the radio days. There weren't enough creative avenues; I did not like the situation because I could not find enough scope. And I had to deal with people like Charles Revson (The Revlon Company) who was arrogant and unpleasant." Chet La Roche eventually moved Tom from direct client contact to an inside position as Vice President in Charge of Personnel. It wasn't surprising that when Chris chose to return to Los Angeles for college, Tom moved back with him.

Tom garnished half the money Loretta earned during his four years in New York so he was well able to afford a life of leisure. He invested in the Beverly Wilshire Hotel but, as had happened before, he would sellout right before a major burst of appreciation. Basically, he was a socialite around town, his working days behind him.

Tom invited Loretta to dinner at the Beverly Wilshire Hotel. She recalled, "When we walked into the dining room, we caused quite a stir; we always did when people saw us together during those years. Tom seemed to enjoy that kind of attention. We had a very nice dinner, and then we went someplace for a drink. The evening got longer and longer. Finally, I said, 'Well, what motel would you like to take me?' He said, 'Oh Loretta! Stop that!' I don't know why I kept being so surprised, but it seemed so unlike him. I said, 'Well, perhaps you'd better drive me back home. So we went back home, and I was still thinking that he was going to come upstairs; I was in a big house alone, the perfect set up. But, he said, 'Good night. It's been very pleasant, and I'll call you again.' I said, 'Yes, please do, Tom,' and I remember watching him get into the car and drive away, and thinking, 'Boy, you're not the man I used to know. '"

"The programming people at CBS changed the title of CHRISTINE'S CHILDREN to THE NEW LORETTA YOUNG SHOW. Even though it was a series where she played the same character week after week, Loretta would come walking through 'her' door again, wearing a lovely gown, and introduce that evening's show. America had come to expect that from her.

Peter was now part of a musical group called "The Cornells" and Loretta thought it would be fun to feature him and his group on an episode of THE NEW LORETTA YOUNG SHOW. Loretta recalled, "Poor Pete, he was soooo nervous. We tried putting a close-up on him, and his mouth couldn't even move. He said, 'I can't do this; I can't do this,' so we backed off."

Loretta had always found her work a place to escape from the pain of her private life. Now even that would slip away. After they had filmed nineteen episodes, Loretta remembered producer, John London, coming to her and saying, "'Well, CBS isn't picking up the show for next year.' I thought it was joke because, frankly, I don't ever remember being fired. I've always walked away from it, and now CBS was walking away from me. Johnny asked, 'Shall we tell the crew?' I said, 'I'll tell them, Johnny. Ask them all to wait after work this evening.' So I said to them that night, 'I have some sad news. CBS isn't picking up our show for next year.' With that I started to cry. Nobody said anything. Nobody came near me. I just stood there and finally collected myself. Then I said, 'I hope that the remaining seven shows will be as good as the others have been. Please, for all of our sakes, let's work hard on it. Good night and thanks.'

"I just left the set. I heard later that they sat around for a long time. They had all worked together for nine years, an eternity in this business where crews are often slapped together with each production. It wasn't the show I would miss. It was boring for me to play the same part week after week. But these people were so important to me, every one of them. Working with them really was the joy of my professional life."

Ratings arithmetic suggests that THE NEW LORETTA YOUNG SHOW had fallen victim to being placed in too good a time slot. Airing on Monday at 10:00 p.m., E.S.T., Loretta followed THE ANDY GRIFFITH SHOW which finished the season at number six, and that show in turn had followed THE LUCY SHOW which registered at number five. The number seven show for the season was BEN CASEY opposite Loretta on ABC. Viewers were switching channels to watch the brooding young doctor.

Throughout all of her television years, Loretta had always ended with saying to her audience, "See you next week?" On the final show, she said, "Goodbye for now." Surely, she couldn't have imagined that it would be twenty-three-years before she would step in front of the television cameras again. Her future had never been more ambiguous.

Chapter 24: RESTLESS

The New York social scene was fresh enough to tantalize Loretta, and she flitted back and forth between coasts. Besides, Jean and Maggie Louis were spending much of their time there, and it was only with Jean and Maggie that she didn't feel like a third wheel.

Loretta recalled one particular return trip to Los Angeles, "I was waiting for my luggage, and another passenger asked, 'Is someone meeting you?' I said, 'Oh, yes, my sons.' So all the people on the plane were alerted that Loretta Young's sons were going to meet her, and of course, they were all interested to see what they looked like. Then I saw the two of them through the glass. Christopher had put Peter in a wheelchair, and Peter was acting like a spastic. I looked at these two and thought, 'Oh my God, they're not.' It took me another ten minutes to get out of there, and by this time, they were acting up a storm. Chris would say, 'Mom will be out in a minute, don't worry, ' and Peter would make some kind of pathetic response. I came out red as a beet, and all these people are looking at me to see how I'm going to respond. I put my carrying case on Peter's lap to hold him down, and as we were walking down the corridor, all these people kept walking behind us. I thought, 'I better make a joke of it because these people are going to feel so sorry for poor Loretta, and who wants that?' At the baggage center I had to show my luggage receipts to get out the door, and as I was doing this, I watched Chris roll Peter right out onto the curb and dump him into the street. After we were all in the car, they were still laughing. They thought it was so funny, and I went along with it to keep from crying.

"Two or three years later, one of them brought it up and I said, 'I'm going to tell you something right now. I was so embarrassed I nearly died, and you two were so insensitive that you couldn't see that.' I think it must have rung a bell with them because ever since then, their attitude toward me in public, at least in public, is very protective."

Loretta remembered a moment she and Peter shared, "He came into my room and said, 'Mom, I've just seen you in a movie on television. You know, a guy could fall in love with you.' I laughed and said, 'Yeah, well, a few of them have.' 'No,' he said, 'I mean, really.' I replied, 'Yes, I mean really, too.' Anyway, he was very impressed. I don't know when he started to look at me through somebody else's eyes rather than just as the mother who was yapping at him all the time."

Peter graduated from St. John's Vienne High School in the spring of 1963. He opted not to go to college. Peter recalled, "I let my hair grow long and started looking for a band. At that point I was living with my mom, and she got sick of my long hair and my attitude because I was more or less incoherent at that point. I would spend a lot of time just listening to "The Byrds" and another group that was around called "The Lovin' Spoonful". I would just listen to these albums day after day. At some point my mom said, 'Your hair is too long.' I said, 'Well, I'm not going to cut it.' She said, 'You're going to have to leave,' and I said, 'Good-bye.' So I got out on the strip and looked for a group to play in. I didn't find anything, so I started my own band called 'Peter and the Wolves'. We played up and down the California coast at sort of dumpy places. I eventually ended up getting a gig at Gizarri's on the Sunset Strip."

Christopher was studying film at USC. He made friends with George Lukas, another hopeful filmmaker to be.

Judy now had a daughter, Maria. She continued her acting career and assumed the lead role in Jean Kerr's, MARY, MARY on Broadway. Next, Judy decided to audition for a role for the soap opera THE SECRET STORM. Sally recalled, "Judy came back to Los Angeles, and Loretta rehearsed her until she was black and blue. She showed her how to walk, how to speak, everything." She won the role of Nurse Susan Ames and would play her for the next six years.

Georgiana recalled this time when Loretta's children were gone and her show cancelled, "I felt sorry for Loretta. She was so alone: sewing, watching television, doing nothing. Nobody called her; nobody invited her.

"It wasn't just Loretta. That happens to all actresses. They're too wrapped up in their careers; they lose their husbands, and they lose their grandbabies, everything. One night we had had a spat, and I was so angry that I went out of her house slamming those big double doors. I got halfway home, and I thought how lonely she was, and I went back. I went in, and we both cried."

Loretta decided to give romance with Tom one more try. It had been agreed that Tom would have the use of the Ojai home, and Loretta recalled inviting herself up to have dinner with Tom and Chris. "I got into my Rolls Royce, and as I was driving up, I was thinking how I was going to seduce this man if necessary. The three of us had dinner at the Inn and finally, at one in the morning, I said, 'Chris, haven't you got someplace you'd like to go?' He kind of laughed, and he went to bed. Tom and I sat around for about half an hour. I don't remember how I approached it, but the answer was negative once again. So, I said, 'See you in the morning', and I went to bed in our bedroom and slipped into my side of my bed, halfway hoping, but he never came in.

"The next morning Chris and I were having breakfast when Tom came in and said, 'I can't tell you how pleasant this visit has been. If there's anything ever I can do for you, Loretta, please don't hesitate to ask.' I looked at him, and I said, 'I did, and you said no!' He went right on, 'It doesn't make any difference where you are, anyplace in the world, always call me.' I think Tom's performance was for Christopher. He wanted Chris always to think that he was the generous one, and I was the one that was pulling away. But the message to me had finally sunk in. I never again tried to entice him back.

"Tom put on an act for our social friends. I avoided going with Tom anyplace where there was high visibility, but one particular evening there was a tribute to Father Peyton, whom we both loved. Tom was sitting next to Rosemary Thomas (Mrs. Danny Thomas) during dinner. She called me the next day and said, 'You've got to take this man out of his misery. He's so wildly in love with you; he doesn't talk about anything else.' I said, 'Rosemary, don't be too upset because it's just not true. I have accepted too many of his invitations to reconcile, that then turned to rejection, not to know exactly how he feels about me. '"

Tom would concoct a plan a few years later that suggested very different roles for him and Loretta. He decided that he wanted to become a Catholic priest. The only way he could get around the obstacle that he was married was if Loretta would agree to enter a convent. Loretta recalled, "He sent me papers to sign two or three times. Of course I didn't. As much as I love my many nun friends, I had no vocation (as a religious) and suspected neither did he."

Gladys suggested another plan for Loretta. She recalled her mother saying, "'Gretch, you think the whole world is a soundstage at a studio. It isn't! There are all sorts of fascinating things to see and do out there. Go out and enjoy it, and in the process maybe you'll learn something about yourself.'"

Josie was ripe to share the adventure, and in the fall of 1966, they set off on their free-spirited journey. The first stop was the familiar stomping ground of Honolulu where they visited old friends. A week in Tokyo followed during which they were invited to speak to a group of eight hundred students at Sophia University, a Jesuit school. Loretta recalled, "The priest introduced us, stating, 'Mrs. Lewis is Loretta Young and Mrs. Wayne is Mrs. John Wayne.' Josie looked at me and I whispered, 'If they don't know that you're divorced, don't volunteer anything. Don't spoil their fun. Anyway, I'll probably get most of the questions.' Not so, they couldn't wait to get rid of me and get to Mrs. John Wayne. Josie was bombarded with questions: 'Is he

as nice as he looks?' 'Does he really walk that way?' She said that
he was just as nice as he looks, 'etc."

Loretta and Josie settled into the Grand Hotel, owned by
Madame Chiang Kai-shek, for their six-week stay in Taipei.
Loretta recalled, "At each hotel, Josie and I made arrangements
that a personal maid would be available for us when we arrived.
I'm embarrassed to say that I was with 24 suitcases, and Josie
was with 23. The maid's job was to unpack both of us, hang our
clothes in each of our rooms, what needed pressing, press, so
that everything was ready to wear at a moment's notice. And, a
day or two before we'd leave, we'd say, 'Well, we'll be leaving on
Friday, so have us both packed by such and such a time.'"

Loretta had had lunch with Bishop Sheen before leaving the
United States. She recalled him saying, "'When you get to Taiwan,
do me a favor. Get yourself all dressed up in your best dress. Put
on your good jewelry and a lot of perfume and go to a
leprosarium and let the residents see something pretty.' So one
day we drove about two hours out of Taipei to the leprosarium.
The first bungalow we went into housed ten young men, and
since it was a hot day, they just had on shorts. There was a
television in the corner and it was on. A priest accompanied us,
and the minute they saw him, they stood up. And when they saw
us women coming in behind him, every single one of them

simply turned their face to the wall. Some of them did have sores on their hands, and face, and neck. Father kept urging them, but they wouldn't turn around. One kept hitting his hands on the wall and shaking his head. Finally, Father just looked at me.

"I put my hand on the boy's shoulder; he didn't know it was me, and I just gently patted him. He didn't pull away. So I said, 'We really don't want to upset you; we don't want to bother you,' and I put my other hand on the other shoulder, and he still didn't pull away, and he calmed down a little. I kept patting him and touching him; it took about five minutes of just talking. He didn't know what I was saying, of course; it was just the tone. Then, all of a sudden, he kind of pulled his hand away from his face, and he turned around and looked at me, and I've never seen such a sweet look on anyone's face in my entire life. It wasn't a smile, but just a sweet face. I turned him around and put my arms around him. There were tears in his eyes, and he put his head on my shoulder. I would guess that he was a boy of 19. Father said, 'I think we've made it.'

"The boy and I sat down on the floor together for about 10 minutes. I kept talking, with Father interpreting, and the boy kept nodding, but he never looked up again. By the time we left, I would say half of the other boys had sneaked a look, but they didn't come near us. We visited additional bungalows with equally moving encounters. As we were leaving, there must have been thirty who came to the top of the hill to wave good-bye. A lot of them were the children."

Loretta and Josie then shopped for three weeks in Hong Kong after which they were invited guests of the Thai government in Bangkok. The flight to Bangkok proved eventful. Loretta explained, "Quite often the captain has invited me up to the cockpit and it happened again on this flight. The pilot said, 'Let Miss Young sit there.' He chatted through the rest of the flight. Then, as he started to make the landing, I started to get up, but he said with a smile 'Stay where you are.' We glided into the airport, and we got down on the ground, and I saw this man on the ground, signaling with his arms, to stop. All of a sudden, I felt a bump. The pilot slammed on the brake, and said to me, 'Leave! Now!'

"Prince Panu and his entourage were there to greet us when we got off the plane. After a few minutes, I saw the captain and the whole crew, and they were all marching like little soldiers. The Captain saw me but pretended not to recognize me. I asked the prince, 'Did anything happen on this ship?' He said, 'I'll tell you when we get into the car.' He explained that a little Volkswagen was out on the runway. It wasn't supposed to be there, and that the pilot hadn't seen it and ran over it. Two people were killed. That was the jar I felt."

India was next to be followed by Iran. Before leaving India, Josie saw an unfamiliar side of Loretta when Pan Am attempted to charge them for extra baggage. They had been photographed upon every leg of their journey wearing Pan Am shoulder bags. This led Loretta to exclaim to Pan Am, "You couldn't buy the publicity, and I'm not going to pay overweight. And when I get to Teheran, if this luggage is not on the plane, I'll sue Pan Am for everything it has ..... and I'll get it!" Loretta recalled, "Josie just looked at me. I only talk that way to producers, not anyone else, and Josie was shocked." Pan Am dropped the charges.

Josie recalled, 'The Shah and the Empress were on a vacation, but his Uncle and Aunt entertained us royally. They insisted, 'You've got to stay until they come back in two weeks.' But then I got word that two of my grandchildren, Bridget and Mark, had been hurt in an automobile accident, and that they were okay. But, of course, I didn't believe it and decided that I had to go home. When I left, it was with the understanding that I catch up with Loretta. Probably in Italy, I knew she was planning on going there. And, of course, I never got back. Once I got home, I got right back into everything. Fortunately, the children recovered.

That trip was marvelous. I have been on many, many trips with lots of people, but that was the best time I ever had in my life."

Loretta spent the next four months in Iran, much of it with the royal court. Her television show was still airing in syndication there.

Europe was next, and Ruth Roberts joined Loretta in Paris. They received an invitation from Ingrid Bergman to spend Easter at her country home outside Paris. The three ladies were good friends. Loretta recalled, "Ingrid's husband, Lars Schmidt, and her son, Roberto, were home for the holiday. Lars said to us, 'You know, it's amazing. My wife can face two thousand people in a theater and not show one iota of nervousness. But let two lady friends come to dinner and she falls apart. She's been cooking for two days, fretting if it will be good enough.'

"I couldn't get over how striking Ingrid's son was. I said, 'Oh, my Lord, Ingrid. He's the best-looking thing.' He was about seventeen at the time. She said to me, 'Yes, he is good looking. Unfortunately, I just can't say no to anything this boy wants. The other day I got a bill for a suit for $350.00. I said to him, 'Now, this is ridiculous. After all, a seventeen-year-old boy! $350.00!' Do you know what he said to me? 'Well, you must admit it looks marvelous on me.' That was his only attitude toward it.' Oh, but he was wonderful looking."

Roberto had been the love child of Ingrid and Italian neorealist film director, Roberto Rossellini. It created quite a scandal because Ingrid was still married to her physician husband Peter Lindstrom when the affair ignited. The Lewises had divergent opinions of Dr. Lindstrom. Loretta remembered, "Tom thought Peter Lindstrom was a wonderful man. I didn't. I remember at the time thinking, 'If he weren't married to Ingrid Bergman you wouldn't think that. I thought he was a bore. He used to pick people up and twirl them around at parties. Now, that's embarrassing! Never Ingrid. She wouldn't let him! I think Tom identified with him, the frustrations of being married to a well-known woman. "

Loretta returned to the United States to fulfill a speaking engagement at Xavier University, a commitment she had made a year earlier. Loretta hadn't been in Los Angeles for almost a year, and she certainly didn't appear to be in any hurry to check in at home. Josie Wayne reflected on that time, "The funny thing was that Loretta never went any place before, would never go. All of a sudden, she was this independent person from her mother and everybody. We all kept saying, 'What's come over Gretch?' "

Loretta had stayed with Jo Anderson, a decorator friend of Gladys's, on previous New York trips. Mrs. Anderson lived in an apartment building at 40 Central Park South, right behind the Plaza Hotel. A three bedroom apartment became available in that building and Loretta decided to take it. Loretta reflected, "I had been traveling the world, and I don't think I knew what to do next. I was searching for something.

"Mama came out to decorate, and I remember Betty Bacall came over one afternoon; she was crazy about Mama. Betty said to me, 'I don't understand. If you have a choice of living in California or in New York, why would you live in New York?' I said, 'Oh, my house is still in California.' 'Oh,' she said, 'then this is just a playground for you.' I said, 'Yes, I guess.'"

Gladys did some serious decorating. The three bedroom apartment became a lavish one-bedroom apartment, huge extended bath, huge dressing room, etc. Loretta's world travels were still incomplete, so when Jo Anderson was planning to sail to Italy for a European buying trip, Loretta decided she would sail with her. Loretta recalled the final preparations, "In those days, if I travelled by ship, I used big cardboard stand-up boxes that I got from Bekins. In one box, I packed six fur coats. There was a sable coat, a bleached nutria jacket that was a creamy color, a black wool coat that was fur lined, and three others, two of them designed for me by Jean Louis. So I finished packing this box and then, for efficiency sake, I wrote 'Furs' on the outside of the box.

"It took five days to cross before we landed in Naples. As we were disembarking, I said, 'The fur box missing.' I went with the assistant purser into the hull, and we couldn't find it anyplace. Well, of course, it never got near the boat, and I still think the driver was in on it. But it's just dumb things that people do, writing in big letters on the outside of the box. But, still, God was really good to me. Just as I was leaving, a delivery man from Beigelisen, Jean Louis' furrier in New York, brought over a lynx coat, just finished, that Jean had designed. I had already put the top on the Bekins' box and put paper around it and strapped it together. My driver asked: 'Do you want me to put this in?' I said, 'No, I don't want to open that thing again. I'll carry that one; don't worry about it.' Thank God I didn't because it was the only coat I had to wear, and I was in Europe for about nine months that time. Anyway, it was gorgeous and it was my newest one."

Peter continued pursuing his music and had also married a high school girlfriend. He reflected on that marriage, "Her background was not really like mine. It was less benevolent, but I identified with her nevertheless. I don't know what she thought of me now that I look back on it, but I guess I was a means of escape for her. We had our son, Evan, and then I fell in love with her. That's just what happened to me. But I guess it was too late for her. She was jealous of the Rock and Roll thing, and she wanted to get at me, so she went out with these people and lost herself in the process."

Peter's luck was about to improve. He recalled, "I was part of a new group and the first night we jammed together, we knew we had this really good band. It all happened very quickly, two months later, we were getting booked into the Fillmore and Avalon Ballrooms in San Francisco. After that, we were approached by a bunch of record companies, and we signed with Columbia who gave us a really huge deal. That's how 'The Moby Grape" happened."

For Peter, it was the biggest thing that had ever happened. He reflected, "Once you've been a mental patient, the whole family treats you like you're not able to make it. When "The Moby Grape" came along, it was my only chance. Bob Dylan and "The Byrds" didn't give a shit about *Loretta Young*, and it was a world dominated by *Loretta Young* in which I felt trapped. This was my big chance."

The "Moby Grape" debut album, "Omaha" became a huge hit. Peter reflected on the excitement surrounding it. "A rock history book recognizes that album as the most definitive album of the Sixties. Columbia Records gave it the biggest promotion they had ever given a rock album. I was to find out later that it influenced other musicians on their way up, such as Steven Stills and "Lead Zeppelin". The title song, 'Omaha' I think went #1, but it wouldn't be fair to look at that song in terms of a big hit because it was really the album that was important."

Loretta had had very little contact with Peter since she returned from Italy. She knew that "The Moby Grape" had had a hit album but it wasn't music she understood. She was staying at her Central Park South apartment and was unaware that Peter and the rest of "The Moby Grape" had arrived in Manhattan to record their second album. She recalled, "It was about 3:00 in the morning. I was reading in bed, and the doorman called, 'Mrs. Lewis, there's a young man down here who says he's your son Peter, and he wants to come up.' I said, 'Send him up.' I opened the door, so he'd know which way to go. Suddenly this young fellah got out of the elevator and started to walk toward me. He looked like most of these Rock and Roll kids with their long hair and dirty blue jeans. He got about ten feet from me, and he started to cry and so did I. He put his arms around me, 'Oh, Ma'. He's 6'4' and big, and we both went down.

"We got inside, and I asked him what he was doing in New York. He explained that they were making an album, and then he said, 'I just can't take it anymore. I just walked out of the studio and came up here.' I said, 'How did you know where I was?' He said, 'I've walked by this apartment building every day since I've been here.' He went on to say, 'One of the guys is on heroin, so it's been real unpredictable; we're just all over the place all the time. CBS won't put up with us in the daytime in that building, so we work at night when nobody's around.' I said, 'All right, you work at nighttime, and then you come home, and you sleep and eat here,' and he did.

"Peter started to drift away from that crowd but it took a couple of years. It was hard because music was the only thing he knew, and really, it's still his passion. But "The Moby Grape"' was the familiar story of too much too soon. They had only been together two months when Columbia put this big promotional push behind them. What did they know about sustaining success when they had all these drugs and groupies? They may have been out to change the world through peace and love, but they didn't know anything about discipline, and without discipline, no success lasts."

Loretta would keep her New York apartment for another year, but she was seldom there.

The Lewises had been separated for thirteen years and had not lived as husband and wife for fifteen. Still, Loretta had made no effort to shed him as her husband, even after all the legal entanglements, until she received a pivotal phone call. She recalled, "Cardinal McIntyre called me to his office and said, 'Loretta, I think you're going to have to get a divorce because Tom's non-ending string of lawsuits continues to cause scandal.'

"I would not go into court with him; consequently he had won seven lawsuits against me, all settled in a lawyer's office and all requiring a financial settlement. And it was all because of that *one little piece of paper*, agreeing to split everything I had ever owned. That meant that he was claiming half from investments that I had made even after I stopped working. It made no difference that I made no claim on any of his investments or from the salary that he made while he was in New York. I think Tom was vindictive. He could never get over his resentment that, in the eyes of the world, I was the one who was famous, not he. But, I understand it to some degree. It must be almost impossible for any man, unless he's a multi-millionaire himself, or very successful, to be married to any actress, and particularly, an aggressive one, and I realize that I am. I'm not a milquetoast."

Loretta reflected on her reluctance to end a marriage troubled for most of its years and conceded, "I realize that, from the world's point of view, some of my decisions look pretty dumb." Father Regis Barwig, Loretta's spiritual confessor, theorized, "Loretta resisted the divorce for so long because her faith encompasses more than a set of beliefs; it's a serious commitment to a way of life. Marriage is a social sacrament. It's not just something between two people but it is something that affects society. We can't be just jumping from one person to another. We made a solemn promise and this is it. It takes faith to accept this. Key to understanding the life of Loretta Young is to understand that she has that kind of faith."

Loretta's sisters had serious misgivings about Tom even before the marriage. Sally recalled, "Norman and I went over to the Sunset house the day before the wedding. We picked up Mom and we walked and walked, and we said, 'Mom, it's not too late!' We were concerned about Tom Lewis because we knew how he had treated Glenda Farrell. She had worked at Warner Brothers and Norman knew her and so did I. We knew he had dumped Glenda after two years and was going to marry Loretta because she was a bigger *somebody*. He was determined to marry somebody big."

Gladys regretted that she hadn't listened to Sally and Norman's words of caution. She regretted even more so writing Loretta the extensive letter from Mexico in which she had suggested Loretta think twice about breaking her engagement to Tom. Loretta recalled, "It was only a couple of years after we were married, and I didn't think anybody knew that we weren't just divinely happy. One day Mama said to me, 'Gretch, I'm just sick. Every time I think about it, it makes me sicker. I should never have butted into your decision about putting your engagement Tom on hold."

Polly Ann and Carter had also joined their voices in opposition to the marriage of Tom and Loretta and had gone to Gladys. Interestingly, neither Polly Ann nor Sally felt that they could have gone to Loretta directly with their concerns. In fact they never acknowledged to Loretta their efforts to thwart her marriage. It's as if the girls and Jack were spokes to a wheel, and Gladys was at the center, the center hub that appeared so unobtrusive but wielded so much control over everyone else's movements.

Brother-in-law, Ricardo Montalban, expressed changing feelings about Tom over the years, "I really, in my mind, would like to have a sense of fair play, and I could see that Loretta, whom I really respect very much, and I love very much, has a very strong character. She had to have, to be the actress that she is and to take hold of her career and make very important decisions. So she was very strong. And at times, I felt a little bit sorry for Tom because marriage is not easy even under the most ideal conditions and this presented, I'm sure, an obstacle in their relationship.

"But, all said and done, when the marriage was over, I expect a man to withdraw gracefully from the marriage. When I saw a man wanting to take advantage of an economic situation, built on the hard work of an actress which is a very difficult profession, it was at that time I really lost total respect for the man. I would have respected him very much had he said, 'Goodbye, Loretta, it didn't work out; I'm terribly sorry ... ' and then make his own way back in the world. Then I would have had a totally different impression of the man. But when he kept suing her and chipping away at her security that she had earned over a lifetime of accumulated work, I totally parted company with the man."

Tom and Loretta were divorced in August, 1969. The charge was desertion and mental cruelty. According to the August 20, 1969, edition of *The Los Angeles Times*, the complaint alleged that Tom had deserted Loretta on April 30, 1956. Loretta sought support of $1.00. An agreement on the couple's property had been worked out before they had come into court. *The Los Angeles Herald Examiner* noted that "Mrs. Josephine Wayne testified on Mrs. Lewis's behalf."

Shortly after the divorce, Josie recalled seeing Tom at a dinner at the Beverly Wilshire, "The hostess, sensitive to my friendship with Loretta, called me earlier that day and said, 'Another one of my guests called me today to say that Tom Lewis was going to be her escort. I hope that won't be a problem for you.' So I said, 'That's all right, but something has come up, and I'll be a bit late.' Everyone was seated when I arrived, and I was just going to sit down when Tom jumped up and said, 'Come on and have the first dance with me.' I said, 'Well, Tom, I haven't even sat down or even spoken to my hostess.' He said, 'Come on, I want to talk to you.'

"We got onto the floor and he said, 'I was shocked to find out that you appeared in court with Loretta. All my friends were shocked, too.' I just pushed him away. I said, 'Why would they be shocked? They evidently don't know me very well or know you very well, Tom. I have known Loretta all my life. Why wouldn't I be there?' He said, 'Well, after we've been such good friends and all, I was just shocked.' I didn't even get his point. I asked, 'What did you think? That I would go to court on your behalf?' I couldn't imagine that he was saying these things to me. It certainly spoiled my evening."

Chapter 25. EXPLORING

The final death rattle to their marriage had been their sparring over the financial settlement. Loretta had opted for the thirty unit apartment complex next door to their home, in large part, to spite Tom. She really didn't want it and unloaded it as soon as she could. Tom claimed the Flores house and then refused to sell it back to Loretta. She recalled, "Instead, he sold it to Craig Stevens and Alexis Smith for $310,000, an amount which was little or nothing for that property even back then.
I had only four months to get out.

"A major reason I was looking for a smaller house was because I was having a problem with servants. They'd stay for two weeks and steal me blind, and then I'd have to give them two week's severance pay. That happened to me three times in a row. I told the real estate agents, 'I want the smallest house in Beverly Hills,' and I walked into this one (what was then Loretta's current Beverly Hills home), and it had nice tall ceilings and a wide stairway. I asked, 'How many bedrooms has it got?' 'Three.' I didn't even look upstairs. I asked, 'How much is it?' They told me and I said, 'Fine, I'll take it.'

"I called Mama and said, 'I bought a little house. You had better go and look at it.' She did and called me back. 'You know there's no basement, there's no attic, there's no maid's room. There's a two-car garage, they claim, but you'll never get more than one car in it. There's no front yard, there's no backyard. You bought a *set*.' And when Mama used a movie-word like *set*, it was her way of saying phony."

The house already had a connection with the movie business. Loretta explained, "Sydney Guilaroff, the head of the hairdressing department at Metro Goldwyn-Mayer, had built it. All the lady stars out there were wild about him. After he had bought this lot, he went to Paris and spotted a bronze baluster. When they pull a house down over there, they keep everything and resell it. The baluster was a rather peculiar shape with a curve at the bottom and a curve at the top. Anyway, he kept talking to Greer Garson and Debbie Reynolds about this gorgeous stairway he had seen. They located it and had it shipped to the States as a surprise birthday present for him.

"When I initially showed Mama the house, I said, 'Of course, this baluster is the first thing that has to go.' She looked at me and she said, 'Are you out of your head? That's the only thing that's any good in this whole house.' That's how much I knew about decorating. Now, of course, I've grown to love it." Gladys installed a chandelier which hung from the second story ceiling down through the curve of the stairway. She also pushed the front of the house out by eight feet and added large window gardens in the back. Extending the west side of the house allowed the master bedroom suite to triple in size. Downstairs, new furniture had to be designed to conform to a smaller space than the previous residence.

It would take Gladys a year and a half to decorate the new home. Jean and Maggie had been Loretta's closest friends for fifteen years, and in the interim, she and Mary Coney joined them at their Malibu beach house.

Maggie was a woman of accomplishment. She had been a model for Hattie Carnegie in New York, and in her post-modeling career, she was one of the first women to produce, direct and write for radio and television. Maggie was a perfect girlfriend for Loretta in that she was both spiritual and worldly. On a bookshelf in the Louis den, a book about the Blessed Mother appeared right next to a "how-to" book on investing in Swiss banks. Maggie also loved to play dress-up. Loretta recalled, "The two of us would get completely dressed, and then Jean would look us over and tell us what to add, or, more often, what to take off. Sometimes Jean would tell us switch dresses with each other, and we would. We both knew that his taste was impeccable."

The wake of Tom and Loretta's divorce was still being felt. Polly Ann had a curious encounter with Rosalind Russell when both just happened to be in an electrical repair shop in Beverly Hills. Rosalind Russell related a recent conversation she had had with Tom in which he told her, "'You know, Roz, going through these divorce proceedings, Loretta took me for everything I have.'" Polly Ann responded, "Roz, everything he had, his wife made for him."

Loretta had spent decades projecting a certain image to the public, and anyone who tampered with it would be at their peril. Loretta recalled such an incident, "A lawyer friend called and suggested I see MYRA BRECKINRIDGE (the film adaptation of Gore Vidal's hugely successful novel). I said, 'Why would I see that?' He said, 'Well I think you should; you're in it.' I couldn't believe it! There was this disgusting scene where Raquel Welch attaches a dildo and looms over a struggling actor who is strapped to a table. He is struggling, protesting, trying to get free as she continues to prepare to rape him. Suddenly, they cut to a big, head close up of me from THE STORY OF ALEXANDER GRAHAM BELL. It's from the marriage proposal scene, and, in the most sensitive, loving voice, I'm saying, 'Don't move; don't even breathe; I want to remember this moment for the rest of my life.' Then they cut back to the two actors and they're all in a frenzy. The music is even more violent than their actions, if that's possible. Raquel Welch looks like she's riding a bucking horse and laughing hysterically.

"MYRA BRECKINRIDGE had been in distribution for several weeks with six hundred prints released here and in the United Kingdom. The first thing I did was to contact my lawyers and tell them that I wanted my image removed from the film, and that they should try to accomplish that before the issue would ever be argued in a courtroom. My lawyers were able to get a Federal Judge in Cleveland to mandate 20th Century-Fox to put up one million dollars that very day, and if they did not remove the clip of me out of those six hundred prints, here and in England, within ten days, that million dollars went to my bank account immediately, before any kind of appeal or anything else. So, indeed, they did remove the clips. A million dollars is a lot of pressure."

The basis for Loretta's suit was the morals clause that had been inclusive in her contracts with 20th Century-Fox back in the Thirties. The clause read, "Any act or thing that would tend to bring the undersigned (Loretta) into public hatred, contempt, scorn or ridicule, tend to shock, insult or offend the community....." Loretta's lawyers contended that the contract worked both ways, and thus, the studio was prevented from using Loretta's image in any way that tended to shock or offend, or subject her to scorn or ridicule.

Loretta had stayed in touch with the nuns from St. John's Hospital in Oxnard. She continued to be particularly fond of Sister Mary Rose Christy, who, as head of the nursing staff, had been so solicitous to her needs when she had been a patient. Loretta described Sister Mary Rose as, "Probably ten years younger than I, a fireball, attractive, bright, funny, very political, very conscious of social justice; I think that's the main thing with her." It was in the spring of 1970 Loretta flew back with Sister Mary Rose to Phoenix, an impromptu trip that would change the focus of Loretta's life for the next six years. She recalled, "Sister Mary Rose was well known in Phoenix. The press loved her, and someone alerted them that she was coming home. There were lots of photographers and in the papers the next day, we were dubbed, 'The Nun and the Movie Star'.

"Sister Mary Rose took me all around Phoenix to show me what her social work interests were, and the reporters seemed to be with us all the time. I was perfectly willing to be interviewed and so was Sister. Finally, Sister took me to St. Thomas parish on Washington Street, a poor area, and introduced me to a Father Hurtado. He was a charming man of about forty whose parents had been migrant workers. Sister said, 'Tell Loretta about the poverty and the children down here.' I listened, and thinking aloud, said, 'I wish that there was something that I could do to help.' Sister said, 'A Loretta Young Youth Project would be marvelous. You can get it going, and then you can just turn it over to Father Hurtado.' I said, 'Good idea. '"

Loretta had gotten off of the sound stages. She went out to see the world and then had her fling at New York. In Los Angeles, she rebuilt a social network filled with parties and charity balls. She was now age fifty- seven and ripe for something new. She was ready to use her name and image to help someone besides herself.

Loretta lived alternating life styles between Los Angeles and Phoenix between the early and mid-seventies. One time she remembered, "Sister Mary Rose and I cruised down the desolate desert highway in the Rolls at a hundred miles per hour. It felt wonderful, like sailing."

"The Loretta Young Youth Project" was really an umbrella of several activities. Loretta recalled, "Volunteer teachers would conduct dancing classes, cooking classes, sewing classes, and health classes, anything to get these kids involved and keep them busy. A darling young man and his wife ran this program for a long time. The kids were mostly Hispanic but there were some Blacks and Anglos as well."

The most ambitious arm of "The Loretta Young Youth Project" was the effort to establish a halfway house for teenage boys getting out of reform school. Loretta explained, "If these boys were forced to go back into their original situations, they would more than likely graduate into the penitentiary. We intended to provide an environment where they had a chance. I bought an eight bedroom home on a two acre lot, and then spent another $100,000 renovating it, adding more bedrooms and bathrooms. It was a fine house and it was in a very good part of town. I built an apartment for myself over the garage where I could live while I was in Phoenix. Of course, Mama came to decorate, not just my apartment, but the whole house. She made five or six trips, and she used her good furniture, fine linen, and everything to her usual top standards. I have some of that furniture in my house today."

Loretta found satisfaction in her efforts helping poor youth but she continued to struggle with the relationships she had with her own sons. The many years of separation while Christopher was in New York had created a gulf between him and his Mother that had yet to close. She felt she hardly knew him. She had attempted not to let her anger toward Tom interfere with the boys' relationship with their father, but shortly after returning to Los Angeles, Christopher managed to steer a conversation with his mother into dangerous terrain.

Loretta recalled, "I think he was just trying to put the pieces together in his own mind. He said to me, 'Dad explained, and I understood, Mom, why you preferred being at the studio rather than at home taking care of us.' I said, 'That's just not true, Chris. I was working because that's what I was, an actress. It was not that I had a choice. I was the breadwinner. How do you think we lived in that house? How do you think we had the automobiles, the clothes, the food, everything?' Chris was unprepared to hear this. He said, 'But Mom, Dad said that that's where you wanted to be because it was a lot more fun and a lot more exciting. I'm just saying I understand and it's all right.' I blurted, 'That's a damned lie and, if you believed your father, you're a jerk. Someone had to provide for us, and your father wasn't doing it.'

"Well, how dare I say that about his father and he slammed out of the house. Ten minutes later, he was back to apologize. Then we sort of talked for a while but didn't really get any deeper. This whole issue was very sensitive for me. I said, 'Honey, I've lived all of this. I don't want to have to explain my way out of it with you or anybody else. At least we now know what not to talk about, and that's your father. I am still very, very angry at him and very, very hurt. And you're not. So there's no sense in my loading you down with what he did to me. Let's just start now from where we are. You start to like me as I am and I already love you. '"

After Chris graduated from USC, finding success in the entertainment business where his parents had both managed to make their mark was daunting. Peter, too, was struggling. He recalled, "I had become disillusioned with the whole Rock and Roll thing for a hundred different reasons. I started hitchhiking all over the country, searching for this transformation thing that wasn't going to happen socially. I saw it slipping away, and I didn't want to become resigned to the way things were before. In my travels I ran across these Jesus communes where people, who had been disenchanted, were still searching for some kind of alternative life to the treadmill that Western civilization puts everybody on. These communes had usually some leader that was a teacher who could show people some truth in scripture.

"At that point, my ex-wife and I were together again. We were hitchhiking with our young son. I didn't like this one commune and had this altercation in front of the guy that was their leader. I took Evan and left, and the wife followed me to Mobile, Alabama, where I got a job playing in this country band. One night while I was playing, she took the kid and went back to this commune.

"When I came back to California, I had this real feeling of not measuring-up. In my own eyes I had failed. I felt I had not been able to ante up when opportunities were given to me, and the opportunity with 'Moby Grape' had been considerable. Blowing that opportunity was not really an asset to me in terms of my position in this family that is real success oriented. But I don't think my grandmother really cared about people being a success or not.

"She gave me a shot. She said, 'I have a job for you, but you have to go to work every day'. I really couldn't have gotten a chance like this from anyone else in the family without feeling like it was some kind of penance. For her, it wasn't like that at all. She could exercise her influence in your life in a way that was sobering without being judgmental. I will always be eternally grateful to her. I don't think I could have handled very much at that time, and without saying anything, she gave me this low stress stuff to do, loading and unloading the truck, hauling furniture. At that point I wasn't using any drugs; she gave me a chance for sobriety to come back into my life. In a sense, I felt that that was my only chance to come home."

Josie Wayne and Loretta began their multi-month travel in the fall of 1966.

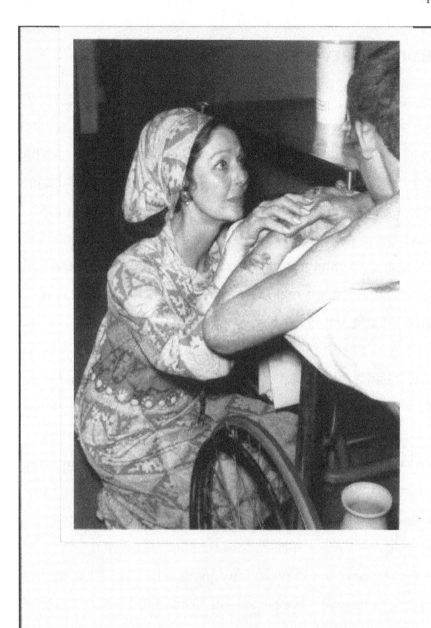

Loretta visits patients at the VA in her retirement years.

Chapter 26. REVELATIONS

Peter would stay with his father from time to time. Their reunion would lead to Tom opening a surprising new door in his own life. Peter explained, "I started talking to Dad about the Bible and the things I had learned on the road. He became interested in the Jesus people, so he decided he wanted to produce a documentary on Katherine Kuhlman, who was a popular evangelist at the time. She was conducting a major service at the Shrine Auditorium and he went down to see her.

"He just had a rebirth. All of a sudden, I think that he found the continuity that he felt was missing in his life. He was able to look back and understand what happened to him, why his marriage didn't work, and other things in a way that allowed him to accept it as if it was all right after all. There wasn't a need to bear guilt for what didn't work out. What he found at the Katherine Kuhlman service was forgiveness, that people needed forgiveness and that they got it by giving it to others. I think he was able to forgive Mom because he needed forgiveness, even if he didn't perceive the problem between him and my mother as something that was caused by him.

He caught on to the idea that it's all right to be human. Tom became active in the Kuhlman ministry, giving inspirational talks and even healing the afflicted.

Loretta also experienced forgiveness – toward John Wayne. The premiere of John Wayne's picture, THE COWBOYS, was a fundraising event, and Loretta recalled the evening, "There was a big dinner afterwards, and I was placed at a table right next to Duke. It was the first time we had been together since he left Josie. Duke asked me to dance and as we were dancing, I still wasn't feeling all that comfortable. Then he said, 'Gretch, did you, in your whole lifetime, think that this would ever happen to me?' I said, 'No, Duke, I never would have believed it.' None of us would. We thought that he was a nice cowboy kid from Glendale. Anyway, that kind of broke the ice and I started to laugh, and he started to laugh, and that's all there was to it. He was limping a little bit, and I asked, 'Is something wrong with your foot?' He said, 'No, I got into an argument with Pilar just before I came out on the stage, and she gave me a kick in the shins.' It wasn't too long after that they separated."

Michael Wayne shared some thoughts about his parents, "When my father left my mother, I suppose that it ruined her life in a way. Oh, she's had an awful lot of fun, and she's got an awful lot of kids and grandkids, but one part of her life was over. Yet she was always supportive of my father. I never heard anything about my father except, 'Pray for him; he's a wonderful man; he's your father.' I can remember situations where Dad would want us to come over, and I wanted to go to a friend's house, and she'd say, 'No, you've got to go to your father's'; that was it. I'm sure she had her own personal feelings, but she never, ever, ever, let that affect any of us. They always stayed in communication, and he provided for her. She's the only one of his three wives that was provided for in the will. To Pilar (they had been separated for years and had reached a financial settlement), he said in his will, 'Hello, Pilar, you are to get nothing.' He did that so that her lawyers wouldn't be able to say, 'He didn't mention Pilar; there must be a mistake.'

"My father said that the biggest mistake that he ever made was leaving my mother, the biggest mistake in his whole life. He not only told me when he was near death, he told me every time he had more than three drinks. Finally, I said, 'Why are you telling me. Don't tell me because I'm not a mailman. I'm not getting into that situation.' But he never would tell her that because he wouldn't have ever assumed that she would take him back. He was very smart and was not presumptuous. He knew that wasn't in the cards."

Loretta continued her participation in The Loretta Young Youth Project. One way she attempted to raise money for the youth project was to auction off a diamond bracelet. Prior to that, she had considered auctioning off some emerald earrings that she had once promised to Judy. Loretta remembered Judy's reaction over the possible departure of the earrings, "Judy called and said, 'What would your granddaughter have to be? Black and poor before you'd pay any attention to her?' She always claimed that I never paid enough attention to Maria. I wasn't around her that much, and when I was, she was a darling little girl, but I always preferred talking to Judy. I'm not the doting grandmother type. I wish I were, for the children's sake, because I think that it's pleasant for them. But, to pretend otherwise would be acting, and I don't want to act for my family."

There was another discouraging development for The Loretta Young Youth Project. Loretta recalled, "We had hired a young social worker and his wife to operate the halfway house for the boys. It was only in operation for three months when this young man called me one night at my home in Beverly Hills. He said, 'Loretta, I'm moving out tomorrow, and I'm taking these ten kids with me. These neighbors are going to send these kids right back into trauma, threatening them with the police for the least little thing!' For instance, one of the boys had left his bicycle on the lawn; the handlebars overlapped onto this lady's driveway by about two inches, so she called the police.

"I was to find out later, that while this neighbor was watching me pour $100,000 over a year and a half's time to redo that house, she had been telling everyone, 'Loretta Young will never move those boys in unless it's over my dead body.' So she and others were out to make it impossible for the halfway house to operate in their neighborhood. They let me finish it all, and Mama move all the furniture from Los Angeles, and then they began the campaign to dislodge us. I called Sister and said, 'I can't work against these odds.' She agreed and the house went on the market; a doctor with six children bought it. Someone had donated a trailer so it was moved down into Father Hurtado's area, and they operated from down there."

The quick demise of the halfway house did not bring The Loretta Young Youth Project to an end. The various classes continued for several years. But eventually, it would come to an ignominious conclusion. The young husband and wife who ran the program had moved on to another opportunity, and Sister Mary Rose hired another young man. Loretta recalled, "Oh, she was thrilled to death with him. Not only was he very likable, but he started running a bingo game that was bringing in $2000 a week. It was our first really good fund raising vehicle, and we were both encouraging to him. Then one day Sister called, 'Well, hold your breath.' I said, 'What?' She said, 'A $10,000 check is missing.' I said 'Oh no.' Then I said, 'I thought it was too good to be true. 'As it turned out, things were even bleaker than we thought. The young man was Mafioso, and he was running a lot more than bingo out of that church basement, all under the pure white skirts of Loretta Young's Youth Project. Sister said, 'We're going to have to pull out of this whole thing because this is too dangerous.'

"Then she said, 'Loretta, why don't you go home? We need a program that the community sustains, and if it needs you here to keep it running, then it's no good.' I said, 'Maybe you're right.' I had been going back and forth to Los Angeles for six years, and I was ready to go home.

"I'm not sorry I did it at all. I think it did a lot for a lot of people, and just for the experience that I got out of it alone, it was worth it. At that period in my life, I needed those kids more than they needed me. It added a great deal to my life. I learned about a lot of realities that I would never have been exposed to otherwise. When you see that others have so much on one hand, and others have so little on the other, I can well understand why people become furious and there are revolutions. "

This enlightenment didn't mean that Loretta stopped enjoying the perks of her celebrity. She joined Jean and Maggie Louis on a trip to Morocco for King Hassan II's golf tournament in Rabat. They stopped in Paris on their way home and attended a dinner party at which Ingrid Bergman was also a guest. Loretta recalled, "Ingrid called me the next day and said, 'We never get a chance to talk. Can you come out to my house tomorrow for tea?'

"So the next day, we were sitting in her perfectly beautiful garden having tea. Out of the blue, Ingrid said, 'Loretta, I want to ask you something. Do you really believe that there is a life hereafter?' It was a surprise to me because in all the years I'd known her, I'd never heard her even mention religion, ever, unless she was studying for a part. I said, 'Oh, yes. Yes! That's why everything that I do is so important because I believe making the right choices will get me a little closer to heaven.' She said, 'That's interesting. Because I don't think there is a hereafter, and that's why I think every moment of every day is so important. I have to make every moment count because that's it.' It was interesting that we came to the same conclusion for entirely different reasons. I think now, as I look back on it, she probably knew then that she had cancer. That's all that she said; we didn't pursue it and went onto something else."

Tay Garnett was another old friend. He had directed Loretta in LOVE IS NEWS, her biggest hit of the Thirties, as well as in ETERNALLY YOURS and CAUSE FOR ALARM. He also directed Lana Turner and John Garfield in the iconic film noir THE POSTMAN ALWAYS RINGS TWICE. Loretta reflected, "Tay called one day, long after he stopped directing, and said, 'I'm in a new line of business.' I said, 'Oh, how marvelous. What?' He said, 'Well, I'm selling Tupperware.' My heart just jumped. He said, 'Gretch, it is wonderful, absolutely wonderful stuff. I'm all set up, and I'd like to come out and show it to you. You buy what you want, or don't buy if you don't want to.' For some stupid reason, I made some excuse; I think I was embarrassed for him. But think how embarrassing it was for him to be calling me. This was one of those moments in my life I wish I could relive. It would have been so easy for me to say, 'Oh, come on out,' and I could have bought his whole line, and he would have felt good about it, and I would have felt good about it. I really would give my eyetooth to live that moment over again."

Loretta's children were making new choices. Judy and Joe Tinney divorced in 1973, and Judy and Maria moved to Los Angeles. By the mid-Seventies, Christopher landed the position of an entertainment newscaster for a Tulsa television station and kept that position for the next eight years. He married Linda Corkran in 1976.

Three years later, Peter met Corinne Scarpelli who had attended a "Moby Grape" reunion concert. They married, and Peter went back to school at the University of California, Santa Barbara. He studied art and English literature.

Meanwhile, Gladys continued working, tackling some of the biggest projects of her career. There was a role reversal going on between Loretta and her mother. When Loretta's career was going strong, her needs were the center of focus. Now it was Gladys's career that events were planned around. When Gladys traveled out of town, Loretta would often go with her just to be with her and to take care of her. Fifty years had rolled by since they had had that kind of time together.

Sally, too, would be in service to her mother's career a few years later. She recalled,

"Mama was still working; she was probably 92 at the time. She couldn't get some money out of this one woman, and I told her, 'I'll get it.' She said, 'Don't be rude.' I said, 'I won't be rude, but I'll get it,' and I did. Mama had ridden over in the car with me, and when I came out, I started driving home. Mama said, 'I hope you weren't rude; you know what a bad disposition you've always had.'

"I pulled the car over to the side and stopped. I said, 'Mom, I don't have a bad disposition, but you put that moniker on me, and that was an excuse for the other kids to do whatever they wanted to me, and everything that was an argument was my fault because I had a 'bad disposition.' Like the time that Pol swept the dirt into the kitchen (back in their childhood boarding house days) after I sparkled it. That was wrong of you not to have said something to Pol. You should have scolded me for swearing, but you should have said, 'Polly Ann, that was very unkind,' but you didn't, and that was the trouble. Mom's reaction was typical. She was just silent. Mama would never allow confrontation. She could say the most cruel things to you, and then she'd say, 'Now, we'll forget all about this.' I'd say, 'Well you might. I won't ever in my whole life, ever, Mama!'"

Georgiana shared some of Sally's frustration. She discussed the two camps in the family, the confronters versus the non-confronters, and reflected, "I've never seen Loretta angry and really mad. I've seen her get upset, and when she gets upset, she just walks out of the room. You want her to turn around and start fighting. She won't. Mom wouldn't fight. Polly Ann would never fight. Bet and I will. Ricardo and I fight a lot. We still do."

Chapter 27. LIVING LEGEND

In February, 1980, *Life* magazine ran a full page picture of Loretta standing at her front door. The caption read, "Loretta Young has no challengers as the last and the most beautiful star from the golden age of Hollywood."

The Eighties would be full of tributes to Loretta, some more significant than others. The 1981 FILMEX tribute would fall into the significant category. Dick Sheppard of the *Los Angeles Herald-Examiner* reported, "After a marathon four hours (consisting) of one feature, THE FARMER'S DAUGHTER, and innumerable film and TV clips, Loretta Young swept down the aisle of the Academy's Samuel Goldwyn Theater, and the capacity crowd came roaring to its feet to salute her rare public appearance. She said, 'That was a lot of work over a lot of years', and then with a laugh, continued, 'no wonder I slept the first year I retired. There were ninety eight movies and over 300 television shows .... and you think this was a long afternoon!' Charles Champlin, critic from *The Los Angeles Times*, fielded questions and later observed in his column, "Young responded with abundant charm and the steely control that was her great strength as a star, and, until late in her career, her great weakness as an actress."

Loretta was surrounded by her family, including Evan Segilman, Peter's oldest son by his first marriage. Loretta recalled, "He must have been eleven, and Peter was just reconnecting with him for the first time since he was a baby. I was thrilled that Peter brought him along. Here's this kid suddenly thrown into Hollywood at its most glamorous, and everyone saying, 'Miss Young this, and Miss Young that ... ' and he's standing around, watching all of this with his mouth half open. Finally, the family got back to the house, and he was sitting beside me on the couch. I said, 'Honey, did you know that your grandmother was Loretta Young?' He said, 'Yes, I did. But I didn't know who Loretta Young was.' Everybody laughed, and I asked, 'Well, do you now?' He said, 'Yes! You're a big actress, Grandma, a BIG actress!' I said, 'Well, I'm glad that's your opinion. Hang onto it.'

"Pete's first wife had remarried a very nice man, Bobby Segilman. He was a carpenter and lived up the coast. She had more children with him. Peter said to me one time, 'I thank God for Bobby; I'll never be able to thank him enough for what he's done for Evan.' Evan's mother had fallen in love with someone else and left Bobby. He told her, 'Fine, but you can't have any of the children.' That included Evan who he raised as his own son."

Loretta appraised her own movie career, the hoopla of her FILMEX tribute notwithstanding, by stating, "I don't think it was too extraordinary of a career. I think I probably could have done a lot better if I had better opportunities, but then again, that's blaming somebody else for not giving me better parts. I have to look at what my priorities have been. Bette Davis wanted to be an actress. She became a movie star because she was such a great actress. I wanted to be a movie star. I never became a great actress, ever, because I always set limitations on myself. I think I was good, at times very good, but I never got near anything like Bette did in some of her work such as OF HUMAN BONDAGE which came very early in her career. You always felt with Bette Davis, no matter how much she gave, there was still a great big thing that she had in reserve, and if she wanted to use it, she could."

Michael Wayne discussed Loretta as an entertainment figure, "First and foremost, she is a *movie star*. Always and 100% a *movie star*. Most competent actresses never get to that plateau. And it's not that she was a *movie star*, she is a *movie star*. Even if someone didn't recognize her, they know when she walks into a room, somebody has just walked in. It's her carriage, it's her whole persona; it's some sort of something that she has, that other people don't have, that makes you turn your head. She demands and gets all kinds of attention wherever she goes. When she comes out, the paparazzi are there."

Friend Robert Mitchum reflected, "Loretta's one of the fundamentals, in the same category with Bette or Joan. She didn't get as much attention as they did because she was never as flamboyant. For instance, Bette Davis and her general attitude and Joan Crawford and her general attitude were going to call a lot more attention to themselves. And, of course, Joan Crawford played all those scandalous ladies, as did Bette. I think that probably Loretta was more selective in the jobs she took because she didn't do anything that she would ever be ashamed of or embarrassed about. She has a certain ethics in her profession. Her own personal ethics, really."

Loretta confirmed Mitchum's observation when she reflected, "My work never did come first. Me, I came first. I never wanted to do anything that might make me less of a person."

Gladys was in the midst of doing three decorating jobs when she had a stroke at age ninety-three, after which she went to live with Polly Ann. Loretta commented, "Polly Ann took very good care of her, but we all took turns. One evening, when it was my turn, we were having dinner in Polly Ann's library watching some award's show. Mama said, 'I don't understand why you're not invited to appear on some of these things.' I said, 'Well, Mama, I am, but there are so many films produced these days I literally hate. I don't want to make a fool out of myself by presenting an award to a picture that I find repugnant.' I could tell that she didn't believe one word I said. In truth, Howard Koch (producer who often produced the Academy Awards Presentation) was kind enough to call me each year to see if I'd go on. I'd say, 'No, I don't think so, not this year.' He had already called for that year, 1982, and I'd given him my usual answer.

"A few nights before the Academy Awards, Howard Koch called back and said, 'Oh, Loretta, we need you so badly. It's for the 'The Best Picture Award' presentation.' In the back of my mind, I heard my mother say, 'I wonder why you're not invited to do some of these things?' So, I said 'Yes.' Frankly, I didn't want Mama, who never liked the picture business, to think that I was being ignored.

"Monday night arrived and it was time for the last award, The Best Picture Award. During rehearsal there had been a ramp to descend, which was bad enough, but now that had disappeared and was replaced by some very narrow and very steep, glass stairs. As I was descending, wearing three inch heels, in my mind, I could hear Howard Koch saying to me, 'Just imagine, Loretta, there are millions of people watching this show tonight.' I reached the podium, and upon opening the envelope, I discovered that the winner's name was upside down. I turned it over, and to my delight, it was CHARIOTS OF FIRE."

Loretta, and Jean and Maggie Louis cruised on the Queen Elizabeth II to Hong Kong the following year. A Hong Kong reporter interviewed Loretta and titled her article, "The Twenty Lost Years of Loretta Young". Loretta reacted, "It really did upset me. I thought, 'How could she be a reporter and not see anything else?' Maybe she couldn't fathom that an actress could ever say good-bye to her career. As far as I'm concerned, those were twenty of the most important years of my life. Like Mama said, I needed to get out and see that the world is, indeed, not a soundstage. If I hadn't time to separate everything and then reintegrate everything, I would be a very miserable old lady."

Gladys experienced two more strokes. Polly Ann recalled her mother's last days. "We shared the same bedroom and sometimes Mom would get up two or three times during the night. I remember her getting up and, I don't know why, but that night, her getting up and down was irritating me. Later on, I thought back and realized that was the only time that that had ever bothered me. Anyway, I heard her get up again, and the next thing I knew, I heard her fall to the floor. I got up and went over to her and pulled her up. It was a cool night and her nightgown was soaking wet with perspiration. I managed to change her but she fought me all the way. I was afraid to leave her alone for as long as it would take me to go to buzz the maid because I was afraid she'd try to get up again and would fall again. I got her under the blankets and then I got into bed with her and held her, so that I could warm her up. Then, finally, I guess through sheer exhaustion, she was quiet.

"By this time it was morning so I got dressed and the nurse soon arrived. I told her what had happened, and she went over and looked at Mom, and I don't know how she knew, but she said, 'Oh, Mrs. Hermann, you'd better call the doctor.' It was a Sunday morning, and he came over and said, 'Mrs. Hermann, the care she needs right now, you can't do for her. I'll call an ambulance and have her taken to St. John's.' I asked the nurse to call my sisters while I watched Mom. I remember that Gretch came over and rode in the ambulance with her. Mom died the following Wednesday without ever regaining full consciousness."

Some months later, Loretta recalled a conversation she had with Georgiana. "I said, 'Mama was never too interested in what I did; she just expected me to work.' Georgi replied, 'Don't kid yourself. In Mama's way, she was so proud of you. When Mama was decorating apartments in New York, and I went with her, she always carried a picture of you in a frame. Now she carried pictures of Pol and Bet and me, but they weren't in a frame. And she'd set it up in the bedroom of the suite we were in, just a picture of you. And if the maid, within two or three days, didn't say something about Loretta Young, she'd say, 'Well, don't you know who that is?' They'd say, 'Well, yes' or 'no', and she'd say, 'She's my daughter.' "

On September 23, 1986, Brandon Tartikoff, President of NBC Entertainment, released an announcement that Loretta Young would be returning to NBC in the holiday movie CHRISTMAS EVE. Loretta had turned down scripts for several TV movies, but Tartikoff was convinced that central character of CHRISTMAS EVE was a part tailor-made for her. The storyline revolved around Amanda Kingsley, an eccentric millionaire, who, upon learning that she has an incurable brain illness, becomes determined to reunite her grandchildren with their estranged father. Amanda was sophisticated, strong, and moral, yet caught in a vulnerable situation. It was the kind of role Loretta had longed for throughout her career. Only one catch, she needed to look like a grandmother. A silver wig borrowed from Jane Sharpe softened Loretta's striking features, and to Jane's amusement, the producers paid her a rental fee.

Loretta was concerned about learning dialogue after twenty-three years. She recalled, "I worked in my bedroom for two months, going over each scene individually. I closed the door and turned off the phone and concentrated."

She described how she was treated on the set, "Most of these young people only knew that I was an old-time movie star, and they were amazed that I could still walk into the room. The protocol had definitely changed. I remember this eighteen-year-old girl knocking on my dressing room door and saying, 'Loretta, we're ready for you on the set.' I couldn't' believe it. I almost said, 'Honey, I'm Miss Young.' But I thought that would hurt her feelings. Still, I think I've earned that much, just my age alone should have demanded a little more respect."

Loretta didn't relish the interviews she was asked to give when she returned to work. She described the process, "Usually, I'm editing everything that I say, and he or she is trying to find out as much as they can, and are digging hard and fast. You assume the interviewer is smarter and quicker and faster than you are, and usually they are if they're good writers or good interviewers. It's like putting little pins in you all over. It's wearing, and it's scary."

Watching CHRISTMAS EVE for the first time was more gratifying. Loretta recalled, "There were about thirty or forty people in the projection room at NBC. The lights went out and the music came up, and the first thing that came on the screen in great big letters, L O R E T T A Y O U N G. Nothing else was on the screen; I really got goose bumps. I remember leaning over to the producer. Michael Filerman, and I said, 'Oh, thank-you.'"

In a *New York Daily News* review written on December 21, 1986, Kay Gabriella wrote, "She doesn't sweep through a doorway tomorrow night with her skirts twirling about, but Loretta Young, star of CHRISTMAS EVE is as stunning at 73 as she was when she hosted her own dramatic series for eight seasons on television. The famous film star is a walking ad for how to grow old gracefully. Eternally beautiful, she appears to have conquered time. As in her earlier Sunday night series, which always had an uplifting message, the NBC drama speaks to us of peace in this holiday season. It is a slim script with little holding it together other than the presence of the elegant star. But, for her many fans, that will be sufficient."

Sufficient it was. CHRISTMAS EVE ranked seventh out of sixty prime time programs measured, helping NBC win the week. *Variety* noted that it had the highest rating of any other holiday programming for the season.

Chapters 28. RHYTHMS

Judy first heard about the rumors of Loretta being her biological mother and Clark Gable her father, from her then fiancé, Joe Tinney. She was age twenty-two. It took another nine years for Judy to find the courage to confront her mother. Loretta responded, "Would you like for it to be true?" Judy said, "Yes." Loretta said, "Well, it is."

However, Judy must have been disappointed if she had hoped that this would open the floodgates, and Loretta would find relief sharing the details of her relationship with Gable, and the particulars surrounding her birth. Judy was left with the unsatisfying task of trying to piece the story together on her own.

Twenty years later, in1986, Judy and Peter joined Loretta for a Mother's Day gathering. It was a fragile time for Peter; he was temporarily separated from his wife and was struggling with depression. He recalled, "Mom couldn't deal with my problem; she didn't understand it. But Judy was there for me, and I had been staying with her for a couple of weeks. In general, the vibes were not good that day. I wasn't in very good shape, and Judy was struggling, working a secretary job.

"I don't recall what happened at the table except that Mom said something to Judy, and Judy said something back to Mom. I was busy eating, so I didn't realize what was going on until there was this pregnant pause. Then it was like lightning went back and forth, and Mom left the table. It wasn't a big deal. It was just one sentence and then a response. At that point, Mom just put her napkin down and stormed out. I really didn't know what it was about then, and I don't think they knew either. But a rule had been broken. Not so much in the last couple of years, but it used to be the rule in Mom's house that you had to decide to keep everything under control. At this point, Judy didn't do it; she didn't play the game.

"My Mom had gone upstairs. I went up after her, and I went into her bathroom and put my arms around her. She felt stiff. She has a way of internalizing her anger which is really scary; it always scared me because you don't know what she's going to do. For me to go up the stairs and go into her bathroom was really stepping out of character for me because I was walking into the lion's mouth. But at that point, I was so wiped out, I figured I might as well go in there and get the whole fucking load. I wanted her to know that I wanted to be a good soul. My thing at that point was to forgive and be forgiven. I was stepping out of my usual mold, so that I could somehow survive this tragedy that was going down in my life. It was weird because I realized that it threw her a little because she was used to being the strong one, not the other way around.

"Mom was crying. She doesn't blubber; she gets frustrated with herself and she's always trying to get the control back. Pretty soon, I heard my sister come up the stairs and then she was right behind me. Judy was scary that night. Judy can be scary, too. Maybe that comes from her dad, now that we know who her dad is. Anyway, my mom walked past me, and they were out in the hall. I remember looking out from the bathroom, seeing them both framed by the doorway, nose-to-nose, and it was the first time I've seen my mom defensive. It wasn't the kind of encounter I've ever had with her. You can't go after her like an equal; it's not what she did with her mother, and that's not what you do with her. But Judy did it.

"Mom was trying to defend herself; I remember her saying, 'Well, your father didn't want you.' Judy said something like, 'I'm not your mortal sin.' There was a lot of dialogue like that, but I don't remember the exact words. I never heard the name Clark Gable, but I think my mom assumed that I just knew that was the deal. My mother told Judy, 'I was always there for you,' and Judy started railing against her. I said, "No, that's true, Judy. Don't bend that into anything other than what it is. If somebody is there for you, then they are, and Mom has been there for all of us.'

"The only thing that stopped me from seeing Judy as the bad guy was realizing I had no idea what it would have been like for me to have been Clark Gable's son, and then have somebody come in and marry my mom, and then have two kids of his own, and then sort of shuffle-me-off-to-Buffalo. That's Judy's interpretation of what happened with my dad. If it did happen that way, it happens a lot. That same scenario happens whether somebody was a movie star or not. But Judy wasn't the only one trying to get my Mom's attention. My mom was busy all the time. My dad was trying to get my mom's attention, too, and I think that vying for my mom's attention was at the root of what was going on between my sister and my father. But Mom was a movie star before they all came into the scene, and she's a movie star when they're all gone. That was the reality, and I think my brother and I, more or less, accepted that.

"Everything said was in such a flurry of temper and feeling that it was like the floodgates had opened. My mom is into damage control and she wanted to get Judy out of there. I don't remember my mother saying that Judy should leave; I don't think Mom did. I think that that was a soap opera thing that would be Judy's impression that Mom said that. The whole scene was a very sad thing. When we left, Judy drove home, and then we just sat in her car, and Judy was banging her head against the steering wheel. I had to stop her from doing that, and then we went in. I was trying to convince her to get into the *forgive and forget* mode, and I said, 'Now, look Judy, in the end you have to forgive the people that hurt you if you ever want out of the loop.'

"A week or two later, I stopped by Mom's. She was up in her bedroom with a headache. She sort of does that when she gets stuck. She'll get a headache and go to bed, put the eye mask on and block it all out. I was sitting by the bed and was looking at her, and she noticed that I was there. She got up and sat on the side of the bed, and the first thing she started talking about was that night with Judy, like she had been thinking about it ever since then. Her hair was down, literally and figuratively. It was just regret; she admitted the deal about Judy and Clark Gable, and it wasn't like she was talking to her son. She was reminiscing about it; it had all been a sad thing."

Loretta's public stance regarding Judy and Clark Gable had been, "It was a rumor then, it's a rumor now; it will always be a rumor." She dealt with it much the same in her private life. She never explained to Tom Lewis who Judy's father was. Loretta was under the impression that Tom thought Spencer Tracy was Judy's father, and she never corrected that impression. Decades had gone by since the topic came up between her, Polly Ann, and Sally.

Why had Loretta felt the need for such obfuscation? Why have a baby, hide her, and then adopt her? Sally commented, "What the hell choice did she have? If she were my child, I would have wanted her, too. But it's been very hard on Loretta, very hard, all the way through: working so hard supporting everyone, and putting up with Tom, and trying to smooth the way for Judy. Who would believe that it would be the daughter, the child who Loretta was protecting, that would drag the scandal into the public?"

Sally was referring to Judy's book, "Uncommon Knowledge", published eight years after the Mother's Day confrontation. Ironically, and or, cruelly, it was released on Mother's Day weekend. At the time, Loretta was unwilling to address issues raised in Judy's book but discussed how the book affected her relationship with her daughter. She reflected, "It was first suggested to Judy that she write a book in the early seventies. I was in Phoenix working with the youth project, and one day Judy called me. She said, 'I've just been offered $100,000 to write my story.' I asked, 'What story?' She said, 'My story with you and *you know,* and it could be so wonderful, so romantic.' I said, 'If you're asking my permission, you don't have it.' We discussed it a little while and I said, 'This was my mistake. We all do things that we're not proud of, some of us do worse things than others. Now there's no reason why it should become a public scandal, a public disgrace for everyone connected with it.' At the time, Judy seemed to understand and was sensitive to my feelings on the matter. My position has never changed. As far as the world is concerned, it's none of their business."

After publication of Judy's book, Loretta related, "I'm having a hard time reading Judy's book because it breaks my heart. I can't believe the misinterpretations, the misrepresentations, the phony psychology I hear in all the stories that she makes up and then assigns motives to people for what they're doing. She couldn't possibly know what was in other people's minds, particularly when she was five years old. I mean complete fabrication of stories that just never happened. Never happened!

"I don't know why I'm reading this book. I think it's because you have to look at the dead body and see that it's all bloody. And, the point is, it's not the book. The book really can't hurt me. But Judy, she can and she has. She has destroyed my trust in her, and that's what I'm grieving about more than anything."

Polly Ann theorized why Judy wrote the book, "My own personal opinion is that something has been working on Judy for a number of years. Judy had not been a successful actress; her marriage did not work out, she was not a prominent person. I think she wanted all of that, and I think that's one reason why she decided to write the book. It was one way of getting the notoriety. You could tell by watching the television screen when she was running around, from show to show, promoting her book. When I watched her I was curious to know how she would behave. She loved every minute of it. She was very sure of herself, smiling as though she was thinking, 'Now all the people are noticing me and who I am.' I was shocked when she was asked on THE LARRY KING SHOW, 'Did your mother ever try reconciliation?' She said, 'No, never.' Well, I know that wasn't true because I saw the note she had written Gretch in response to Loretta's message, 'Let's have lunch, honey, and talk.' Judy responded that she 'didn't feel the time was right but that she'd let her know.'"

Throughout the years of estrangement, Loretta continued to contribute to Judy's mortgage payments. Sally mused, "I really felt that if Judy was finding fault with her mother, then she shouldn't have been taking her money."

Curiously, Gladys had a foreshadowing just a couple of months before she died. Sally explained, "Judy had been over to Polly Ann's house. Just by the way that Judy was talking and laughing,

Mom sensed that something wasn't right. Later, she said to me, 'You know, dear, I think that Judy's going to cause trouble. Oh yes, I really think that she's going to create a big scandal. She's just too insensitive. Thank heavens I won't be alive. '"

Greg Fischer, among more substantial interests, worked for Loretta as a jack of all trades for decades and offered this upbeat assessment of Judy, "She is positively wonderful. She has a very calm manner about her. She looks very much like her mother, only blonde. She has a very beautiful voice. I would say that she is very informal. She's a lot of fun. Like her mother, she has a very good sense of humor. Only, at times, Judy's humor can be sarcastic, and I think that's one of her problems with her mother. Her mother, I think, grew up with the Gladys Belzer version that sarcasm had no place in a fine home. I would describe Judy as being sophisticated. She has an appreciation of style that Mrs. Belzer had given to her girls, and it has gone down to another generation.

"I always thought that Judy and her mother got along, but Judy has a strong, a very strong personality, and her mother has a very strong personality. The acorn falls not far from the tree. And when two strong personalities of the same sex are present at the same time, two different generations, you are not always going to have harmony. I don't think that Judy is a make peace person like her Aunt Polly Ann. More like her Aunt Sally."

Loretta had seen little of Tom Lewis since their divorce in 1979. Once during a restless night, she turned on the television and saw Tom preaching. It was his voice that caught her attention; she didn't recognize him at first, and when she did, she was shocked by how old he looked. She would see him only a few more times in person. She recalled one of those times, "Peter was in town and staying with me. I had some bug, so I was in bed, and it was about 3:00 in the afternoon. Then I heard Pete say, 'Mom, can we come in?' I said, 'Oh, sure, Honey, come on.' In walks Tom. I said, 'Well, Hello!' He said, 'Oh, Loretta, don't worry, you're going to be okay. I'm going to give you a blessing right now, and you're going to get well. I'll say a little prayer over you.' And Pete was standing there, just looking at me and looking at him. Finally Tom said, 'Good-bye, I have to go now,' and he backed out of the room and left."

Tom was diagnosed with prostate cancer and after unsuccessful surgery, died on May 20, 1988. He would have been pleased with the obituary in *The Los Angeles Times*, "Tom Lewis, 86; Founder of Armed Forces Radio." It wasn't until the second column that the name of Loretta Young was mentioned.

Loretta reflected on her life with Tom Lewis, "The main problem at the core of the relationship between Tom and Loretta Lewis was he didn't like me as I was, and I didn't like him. Oh, we were crazy about each other; we were in love with each other, even fascinated with each other for a time, but if you don't like each other, it cannot ever grow into a true love relationship."

Christopher reflected on his father, "Deep down, I think he was terribly disappointed in his relationship with Mom, but, in my opinion, he didn't have the slightest idea of how to remedy that. It was a no win situation going in. Here was someone who didn't have the job skills to compete on the level in which she competed so successfully. And, businesswise, he had absolutely no business sense or timing. Poor guy. If someone would call him Mr. Young, he'd take it personally. His reaction was, 'Well, they're going to know who I am .... '

"Oh, on the surface he was happy, but deep down I don't think he was happy with himself. I don't even know if it was his motivation to be happy. To him, being respected was everything. Dad's bottom line motivation was for people to see that the things that he did were good. But underneath it, he was afraid of not being right.
I have to say that he was a good father to me. He provided a good shelter and guidance."

Peter reflected, "I don't know that Dad knew how to be a good father, but innately, I always got the feeling that he loved me."

Susie Tracy, Spencer's daughter, called Loretta in the mid-eighties and asked if she could come and visit. Loretta recalled her explanation after she arrived, "'In the process of making a move, I've recently found some letters among my father's things. There were four of them with a rubber band around them. Two were from Johnny, one from me, and this one.'"

Loretta reflected, "As she put the letter down, I could see written, 'Mr. Spencer Tracy' on the envelope and that it was my handwriting. Susie said, 'I've thought about burning it two or three times, but I just couldn't.' I opened it and glanced at it, and it started out, 'My Darling,' and was signed, 'me'. I asked, 'Susie, how did you know this letter belonged to me?' She said, 'Because there have only been three women in my father's life: my mother, Katharine Hepburn, and you. And you were the only one who would have written this kind of a letter. I think that nobody but you should have it.'

I read the letter.

"My darling, first of all, I want to tell you again that you haven't been out of my thoughts for a moment since you left me last Tuesday night. The few hours that I haven't been thinking, wondering, and worrying about you, I've been dreaming about you. As I've already told you, I'm writing this to you because, when I'm with you or listening to your voice, I seem to have little or no logic for common sense and most certainly no resistance. I felt the most difficult thing I would have to face, as far as my heart is concerned, happened five years ago (Loretta didn't remember what or whom this was in reference to). Up until last night, that was true. Now, if possible, my darling, I love you even more and, therefore, I'm frightened even more. Because it seems the struggle of the past few years has taught me absolutely nothing unless I am able at this time to see you and still live up to the same promise I made five years ago. That promise, my darling, is simply this. If God would see me through our breakup without any serious trouble for either of us, if He would let me go to sleep just two nights a week, maybe, without crying myself to sleep and a thousand other gifts which I will not bore you with now, that I will never again, under any circumstances, allow you, if I could prevent it, or myself, to forget Him to the extent of committing a sin. That's why, my darling, it is impossible for us to see each other unless we can be, truthfully and honestly, a good boy and a good girl. I've already told you, but it is important enough to repeat it here. It's enough for me just to be able to look at you and talk with you, and although this may sound stupid to say at this time, I know I could do it if I knew I had even a tiny bit of help from you, Spence.

I've prayed that you'll think this out with your whole heart and soul because it means so terribly much to me. Be honest with yourself, my angel, and if you decide that it's an impossibility for you, I'll understand. I'll just go on loving you. In my deepest heart, I've loved you for a very long time now already. I've already said a prayer that whatever you decide will be the right way. I would love to be able to close this note without saying what I've had to say, but I can't. I've also said a prayer that you will call me tomorrow night. I love you. Me. '" (He didn't call)."

Loretta recalled her feelings upon reading the letter, "I thought, 'Oh, that poor girl, poor little thing. I felt so sorry for her because she was in an impossible situation and knew it. But now, sixty years later, it all seemed so far away."

Susie Tracy commented on that visit, "I had heard from sources outside of the family that my father and Miss Young had been involved. That's why I contacted her. I thought to myself, 'If I'm wrong, it's going to be terribly embarrassing.' But it seemed like the right thing to do, and if I was right, I thought that she would like to have the letter and to know that he had kept it all of these years. When I met her, I liked her immediately. As she read the letter, I could tell that she was quite moved. I remember telling her that I thought it was a timeless letter; it could have been written by anyone who had to say good-bye to someone they loved."

About that same time, Loretta attended a party in Malibu with Jean and Maggie Louis. Walter Mathau was also there and he approached Jean. Jean recalled, "He knew that I was close with Loretta. He told me something that Spencer Tracy had supposedly confided to Garson Kanin late in his life: that even after all the years that had passed, he still considered Loretta as the love of his life."

Loretta responded, "That was just because in his mind, he remembered all those wonderful feelings when you first fall in love. He was probably the big love of my life, and he probably always will be, and for the same reason because our relationship never came to its culmination. We never got beyond the infatuation stage. You can call it 'lost love', but it never really got to that point. You can't really love someone until you've been through a lot more than we had been through together."

The friendship between Loretta and Josie Wayne withstood the test of time. Loretta commented, "Both of our lives have been full, almost more than either one of us can handle. So we did not have to lean on each other for excitement. We were there to support each other." On a lighter note, Loretta added, "Josie tells the dirtiest stories in the entire world." Josie didn't deny that claim, stating, "I think that's true. Bob Hope says, 'Josie tells these dirty stories like she's reading the Bible.' But my point is, I just tell them, we laugh and then forget about them. I don't think anybody dwells on any of it."

Maggie Louis died November, 1989. Loretta had lost one of her best friends.

The following month, the television film LADY IN A CORNER aired. It proved an unsatisfying experience for Loretta. She had specified certain changes to the storyline before she signed. From Loretta's perspective, they filmed it that way, then edited it back to the original storyline of a bitch fight between an older and a younger woman.

Chapter 29: FAREWELLS

In 1993, Loretta grabbed some fresh headlines when she married Jean Louis. Loretta was eighty and John Louis, eighty-five.

Jean grew up in Paris and started work as a sketch artist for the House of Agnes Drecoll Place Verdome. He sailed to New York in 1935. An intended two week pleasure trip turned into an opportunity to become one of Hattie Carnegie's top designers. Seven years later, Harry Cohn coaxed Jean to Hollywood to become the head courtier for Columbia Studios. Jean would be nominated fourteen times over the next twenty-five-years for an Academy Award. He won for 1956's SOLID GOLD CADILLAC starring Judy Holliday. Jean also had many famous designs not seen in the movies such as: the black negligee Rita Hayworth wore in her famous World War II pin-up, the gowns Marlene Dietrich wore in her late live concert career, and the sequined dress now hanging in the Smithsonian Institution worn by Marilyn Monroe the night she sang "Happy Birthday" to President John Kennedy.

Over a period of thirty-five years, Loretta, Jean, and Maggie travelled the world together and shared homes in California, Palm Beach, New York and Paris. So, it wasn't surprising, when

Maggie knew she was dying, that she turned to Loretta for a big favor. Jean had always been the creative one, Maggie the business person in their marriage. She worried that if Jean's mind started to fade, he would fall prey to opportunists. Maggie asked Loretta to sign an agreement making her Jean's financial conservator.

Jean spent weekends with Loretta for several months after Maggie died, and then Loretta began to see less of him. That status changed in December of 1992 when she received a letter from a lawyer asking her to sign a form releasing her from the conservatorship of Jean's finances. Jean's mind had started to slip, and two of his female neighbors in Montecito started keeping an eye on him. They tired of the responsibility after a few months and decided that Jean would be best served by moving into a supervised care facility. They also thought that his will should be changed to benefit their favorite charities. It was one of their lawyers who had contacted Loretta.

Loretta, along with her lawyer, travelled to Montecito and confronted Jean's well-intentioned neighbors. Jean was not going into a facility. That was precisely the kind of predicament Maggie had hoped to avoid for Jean, and that's why she had solicited Loretta's help. Loretta returned to Beverly Hills with a much relieved Jean in tow.

Loretta had just assumed responsibility for a forgetful eighty-five-year old man. Now what? They went to Palm Springs after Christmas and stayed at Chris and Linda's for several weeks. Jean seemed so comfortable in the desert that they decided to buy a home there. They married the following September.

It was not the traditional love story, but one of convenience. Loretta came to the realization that instead of financially managing his books, her books, and their books, it would be much simpler to manage just their books. Jean was thinking clear enough to realize that he could no longer care for himself and was grateful for the new security in his life. Loretta knew that the course of her life was altered, and she accepted it as God's will.

She and daughter Judy had not spoken in eight years. Now seven months after the "Uncommon Knowledge" publication, she found the courage to attempt to break the impasse. She sent Judy the following note from her home in Palm Springs:

"Dear Judy. I have decided that there can be no peace until I can forgive and be forgiven. So if you feel the same way, I'd like to see you on the 23rd (November). I'll be in town at two o'clock at the house. But you must come in peace. No recriminations, no who did what to whom. If you don't feel this way, take your time because you'll come to it. Love, Mom

Judy quickly wrote back, replying that she would be there.

The doorbell rang promptly at two o'clock the following Wednesday. Loretta's hair had gone from salt and pepper to decidedly gray in the eight years since Judy had seen her mother. Judy appeared unchanged. They exchanged pleasantries at the door but did not hug. They went into the living room and sat down, and a silence fell as if they were strangers. Finally, Loretta confessed that she didn't know what to say. She said that she couldn't bring herself to talk about the book; that had been too painful, but that she did want to start a fresh relationship. Judy smiled in a sweet way and suggested that Loretta tell her about her recent trip to Medjugorje (a Marian apparition site located in Bosnia). That filled in the next two hours.

That day marked a new beginning for both of them, but as Loretta noted the following day, "Neither of us was able to fall into each other's arms. It will take time; I think the hurt goes too deep for both of us. It's not like the plot for CHRISTMAS EVE. That was a movie; this is real life. The family, I must say, is overjoyed. Today I told Sally and she burst out crying. She said, "Oh Gretch, this is an answer to prayers." Peter, also. He called

446

last night and I said, 'I saw Judy today.' He said, 'What!' I said, 'She stopped here, and she's fine,' and he burst out crying."

A few years after Jean and Loretta married, she realized how little they were using the Beverly Hills house, and she put it on the market. Packing was a daunting task in which Loretta supervised every detail. As she emptied the safe that was hidden in her bedroom, besides jewelry and financial papers, were mementos of her children: a lock of Judy's baby hair, letters from Christopher when he was living in New York, and Peter's doodlings after returning to Los Angeles to live with her.

Six months after Loretta's move from Beverly Hills, Polly Ann died from complications of emphysema. She was eighty-eight. Polly Ann was a huge loss to Loretta; it was like losing Gladys all over again.

 Fortunately, she had her marriage to Jean as a focus. It was the most honest of her three marriages. The two of them entered knowing that Loretta would be in charge, and that Jean needed care. During those years, Jean was able to give Loretta a wonderful example of someone who lived in the present. One day, Loretta approached Jean in their garden and asked him what he was thinking. He replied, "'I'm just thinking how beautiful this flower is.'"

She, in turn, kept a social life humming, hosting small dinner parties. The key qualification of faces invited back again and again: you had to be fun.

Loretta confided to Sally at the time of their third wedding anniversary that she had never been happier. She expressed the same sentiment to Jean in a birthday note in October, 1995.

"My dearest and beloved Jean, What a real gift you are to me! Your kindness, your downright lovableness, has truly turned my life into joy. Who would have believed it all those years ago when you walked into Harry Cohn's office, and we were introduced, that at our ages, we'd be married to each other and happy! Happy birthday my darling husband, Lovingly, Loretta"

On a quiet Sunday in April, 1997, everything would change in an instant. Jean died of a stroke sitting by the pool, doing what he loved most, watching the afternoon shadows drift over the San Jacinto Mountains, allowing him to discern the subtle hues in the diffused light.

Loretta's family and close friends were taken aback by the depth of Loretta's grief. They understood Loretta's love for Jean, but no one had ever seen her so vulnerable. Loretta married Jean in the role of a rescuer. She hadn't counted on how much she'd receive in return. The essence of Jean, in spite of his senility, had remained intact. His gentleness, his consideration, his ability to live in the moment brought a new peace to Loretta. Jean's soft, heavily accented voice combined with Loretta's hearing loss limited their conversation. Yet, they knew each other so well they read each other's minds. If Loretta was feeling overwhelmed, Jean would simply take her hand and hold it. No words necessary.

That spring, a dentist assessed eighty-six-year-old Sally and said, "You take such good care of yourself, you'll probably live to be 114." He then suggested she proceed with costly dental work. By fall she was dead of brain cancer. Loretta's brother Jack passed away in December after an even briefer illness.

The meeting between Judy and her mother resulted in more of a truce than a healing. It was Sally's funeral that offered a new opportunity. Loretta knew that Judy would be somewhere in the church and asked her brother Jack to find her and bring her to sit with the family. The two women rode to the cemetery together and were amazed at the ease they felt in being together. Still, neither quite knew what to do about it. Then, just a few months later, they were together at Jack's funeral. This time Loretta invited Judy to come to Palm Springs for a weekend. There were no dramatic resolutions with the unspoken finally spoken, or tears of joy shed. It was a quiet visit and, amidst the quiet, peace emerged.

Loretta was diagnosed with ovarian cancer in 2000. She spent her last months with her children. Toward the end, she was a patient at St. John's Hospital in Santa Monica , and right before she died, requested to be discharged to her sister Georgiana's home. In her last hours, it was her son Christopher holding her hand. The date was August, 12, 2000. Loretta was eighty-seven.

Loretta's funeral was held at St. Louis Catholic Church in Cathedral City, California. It was open to the public as was the luncheon at the Rancho Mirage Country Club. Loretta, the movie star, had not always welcomed the attention of fans, but she was generous in the end. Old friend Josie Wayne, now blind, came to say goodbye.

A few days later, Loretta was buried at Holy Cross Cemetery in Culver City, California. She had requested that her body be cremated and the remains placed in her mother's grave. Gladys had always been the most significant person in her life.

Loretta had unequivocally been a movie star even if many people today are unaware of her. Perhaps that's because she chose, with the exception of two made–for-television movies in the

Eighties, to walk away from her career in 1963 at age fifty. That was a long time ago. It's more likely that people who do remember her, remember her from her television show.

Loretta own assessment was that her movie career, "Didn't amount to much." She had a point. Few of her ninety-eight films are memorable. However, one could take that same observation and stand it on its head by noting that it had to be Loretta's own star power that drew audiences into the theaters. Producers only finance films they think will make money, and over a twenty-five year period, Loretta's films made money. Very few misfires. She never hit a dry stretch during which she was dubbed "box office poison."

One could argue that it was really Loretta's leading men who carried many of her successful films but again, producers wouldn't have hired her if she didn't demonstrate her own ability to draw an audience. Loretta worked with more top-tier male stars than any actress of her era, and a construct of that observation could be that she had the versatility to do so. She was vulnerable enough to appeal to the strength of Clark Gable and Gary Cooper. She was sophisticated enough to work with Cary Grant and David Niven. She was beautiful enough to share the screen with Tyrone Power and Robert Taylor. She was forceful enough to stand up to James Cagney and Robert

Mitchum. She was intelligent enough to demonstrate parity with Spencer Tracy and Orson Welles. And, overarching all these facets, she was amorous enough to be romantically convincing with all her leading men. The list goes on: William Holden, Charles Boyer, Alan Ladd, Edward G. Robinson, John Wayne, Van Johnson, John Barrymore, Douglas Fairbanks, Jr., Fredric March, plus second-tier leading men such as Jeff Chandler, George Brent, Ray Milland, Robert Cummings, Brian Aherne, Franchot Tone, Melvyn Douglas, Richard Greene, Don Ameche, etc.

The genres Loretta crossed also demonstrated her versatility: depression era grit, historical dramas, suspense, film noir, westerns, soapy dramas, and romantic comedies. She also worked at more studios than most stars of her time. Loretta's contract years began at First National Studios which, after the advent of sound, was absorbed by Warner Brothers. She then signed with Twentieth Century which, after merging with Fox, became Twentieth Century Fox. While still under big studio contracts, she was loaned to Fox, Columbia, Metro Goldwyn-Mayer and Paramount. Later, she worked at Samuel Goldwyn Studios, RKO, International Pictures, and Universal. At all these studios, she took on producers and studio heads whenever she felt her career compromised.

Loretta appeared on the cover of 489 magazines, including eleven covers of *TV Guide*. The *TV Guide* statistic confirms Loretta's popularity with television audiences of the time. Loretta must have been pleased as she felt she did her best work on her television show. There were 256 episodes over the eight-year period of THE LORETTA YOUNG SHOW in which she starred in 162 of them. It was during her television years, and the decade of syndication that followed, in which she became best known in this country and abroad.

There were only two exceptions quite early in her career, ROAD TO PARADISE and BORN TO BE BAD, in which Loretta played 'bad" girls. Joan Crawford, Bette Davis and Barbara Stanwyck films are more memorable today because, in part, they played edgier characters. Loretta wasn't willing to earn the antipathy of the audience as a trade-off for better scripts. She was afraid they may think she was like that in real life. Her dad's walking out the door when she was age four fueled a rejection that she was unwilling to consciously repeat. She played the good girl and as her career progressed, the strong, good girl.

Loretta never appeared in any film in which she did not receive top female billing since the ensemble casting of LADIES IN LOVE in 1936. THE LORETTA YOUNG SHOW was the longest-lasting, star-driven anthology television series in the '50s into the '60s.

She won a Best Actress Oscar, three Emmys (her show won an additional eight Emmys), and a Golden Globe. Altogether, she was bestowed sixty-six awards. She set out to be a movie star. She succeeded: both in a competitive sense but also in the way that the biggest of the stars uniquely do.

From silent films through the glory days of Hollywood, and then smoothly walking through "her door" onto television, she managed a unique and flourishing career. She did it, not by continuously reinventing herself, but by successfully marketing an image that resonated with successive generations.

Her greatest triumph may have been transcending that image in her personal life. Peter's view is that the stability in his mother's life came from her faith. He observed, "The expectations of *Loretta Young* were relentless and her faith provided her a plan to follow, a way of knowing the difference between *Loretta Young* and who she really was. The lives of other famous people have become like leaves in the wind, no real substance to them, unable to live outside of an image and blown from here to there by the whims of other people's expectations."

###

Acknowledgements:

This project had been long dormant until Linda Lewis, Loretta Young's daughter-in-law, called me in 2012, urging me to bring this book into new life. Loretta's family also allowed permission to use family photos. Most of all, I thank Loretta Young, a guarded woman by nature, who finally decided to tell a very personal story. In doing so, she enlisted the help of her three sisters, Polly Ann Hermann, Sally Foster and Georgiana Montalban. Loretta's brother, Jack Lindley also cooperated as did Georgiana's husband, Ricardo Montalban. Loretta's life-long friends, Josie Wayne and Jane Mullen Sharpe, offered interesting perspectives. Robert Mitchum agreed to an interview. Murray Bolen, who had a career in advertising and early television, offered observations about both Loretta and her husband, Tom Lewis. These people have all passed on but, for me, their voices are very present in the writing of this book.

Loretta's two sons, Christopher Lewis and Peter Lewis, also contributed with extensive interviews. Greg Fischer, who worked for Loretta in various capacities, saw a side of her and the family that broadened my understanding. Salvador Iglesias, Loretta's largest collector, not only provided pictures for the book, but invaluable information of Loretta's career that was used in the summation. Over ninety-five percent of the material in this book comes from direct interviews, most lengthy but some brief. Actor Stuart Whitman's comment regarding Loretta came while standing next to him at a party hosted by Robert Mitchum.

Theresa Schoen and Malcolm Woodhouse edited the book as did my niece, Kate Funk. Her sister Rosie Funk employed her techy expertise to guide me through the world of social media for marketing purposes. My sister Mary Margaret Funk, author of seven books, pushed and pulled me to complete all the tedious details of copy work.

About the Author:

Edward J. Funk had been a ghost writer for business moguls who wanted to write their life stories to help promote their enterprises. The opportunity to work with Miss Young was quite different. It escorted him inside the golden age of film and the early days of television, both eras that had long held his fascination. More importantly, Miss Young invited him into the last ten years of her life with access to her family and friends. With each passing year, the personal story overtook the gloss of her professional life.

Mr. Funk's relationship with Miss Young has produced a trilogy of books about her; this is the first. The other two are "Loretta and Me" and "Eavesdropping: Loretta Young Talks about her Movie Years". Mr. Funk now lives in Indianapolis, Indiana.

Photo by Paul Robinson

Cover photo: Permission to use from the Loretta Young Estate.

Cover design by The National Group

CPSIA information can be obtained
at www.ICGtesting.com
Printed in the USA
BVHW030803170220
572558BV00001B/3